Aversive Democracy

The twenty-first century has brought a renewed interest in democratic theory and practices, creating a complicated relationship between time-honoured democratic traditions and new forms of political participation. Reflecting on this interplay between tradition and innovation, Aletta J. Norval offers fresh insights into the global complexities of the formation of democratic subjectivity, the difficult emergence and articulation of political claims, the constitution of democratic relations between citizens and the deepening of our democratic imagination. *Aversive Democracy* draws inspiration from a critical engagement with deliberative and post-structuralist models of democracy, while offering a distinctive reading inspired by contemporary work on the later Wittgenstein. This is a creative and insightful work which reorients democratic theory, elucidating the character of the commitments we engage in when we participate in democratic life together.

Aletta J. Norval is Reader in Political Theory in the Department of Government at the University of Essex. She is the author of *Deconstructing Apartheid Discourse* (1996).

Aversive Democracy

Inheritance and Originality in the Democratic Tradition

ALETTA J. NORVAL

CAMBRIDGE UNIVERSITY PRESS
Cambridge, New York, Melbourne, Madrid, Cape Town, Singapore, São Paulo, Delhi

Cambridge University Press
The Edinburgh Building, Cambridge CB2 8RU, UK

Published in the United States of America by Cambridge University Press, New York

www.cambridge.org
Information on this title: www.cambridge.org/9780521878425

© Aletta J. Norval 2007

First published 2007

Printed in the United Kingdom at the University Press, Cambridge

A catalogue record for this publication is available from the British Library

ISBN 978-0-521-87842-5 hardback
ISBN 978-0-521-70268-3 paperback

For David and James

It is when Emerson thinks of thinking, or conversion, as oppositional, or critical, that he calls it aversion.

Cavell, *Conditions Handsome and Unhandsome* (1990, 36)

The alternative to speaking for myself representatively (for *someone else's* consent) is not: speaking for myself privately. The alternative is having nothing to say, being voiceless, not even mute.

Cavell, *The Claim of Reason* (1982, 28)

Hence the calculation of units, that is, what are called *voices* or *votes* [*voix*] in democracy…What is a voice or a vote?

Derrida, *Rogues* (2005, 30)

Contents

Acknowledgements

This book has been long in the making. I would like to acknowledge the assistance of many friends and colleagues over the years that I have been working on this project in one form or another. I have been very fortunate to have been in a Department in which there is no lack of intellectual challenge and inspiration. The initial ideas for this book were formed in the context of the PhD seminars in Ideology and Discourse Analysis at the University of Essex, when I first taught a course on Wittgenstein to a cohort of graduate students and visiting post-doctoral fellows. Then, and more recently, the students on this programme proved to be both insightful commentators and critical readers of my arguments. I cannot mention these seminars without also immediately acknowledging my enormous debt to Ernesto Laclau, whose acute and perceptive style of political analysis inspired me to take up the challenge of developing a distinctively Wittgensteinian approach to thinking about democratic politics. But beyond this, I am deeply appreciative of his efforts to create and foster an institutional context and community in which intellectual debate and engagement with a wide variety of perspectives became possible. Several colleagues at the University of Essex also read and commented repeatedly on early drafts and chapters. I wish to thank, in particular, the members of the University of Essex Political Theory group for their encouragement and engagement with this project. I am particularly grateful to Albert Weale and Sheldon Leader, as well as to Jason Glynos and David Howarth for patient reading and engagement with early drafts of chapters. I also am deeply appreciative of the time and attention David Howarth and Jason Glynos devoted to reading and commenting on the final version of the manuscript. James Tully and David Owen read the manuscript for

Cambridge University Press and gave me enormously helpful comments both on the content of arguments and the structuring of the text. Special thanks also to David Owen, who met up with me to discuss the manuscript in detail. It is not often that one finds such an erudite reader. Many other colleagues and friends also commented on various occasions when I presented sections of this book in seminars. Michael Freeden kindly invited me to give a paper in the Centre for Political Ideologies, Oxford and I have benefited from his contributions, as well as from those of his students. I presented a version of Chapter 3 to the Political Theory Colloquium at Northwestern University, where Bonnie Honig and Linda Zerilli both commented in some detail on my arguments. Linda Zerilli subsequently provided me with an extremely thoughtful commentary and thought-provoking questions. I also presented sections of the argument at conferences in Copenhagen, where Eva Sørenson and Jacob Torfing of the Centre for Democratic Network Governance at the University of Roskilde provided me with encouragement and always engaged generously with my arguments. Lasse Thomassen at Limerick University most recently also probed my arguments in his usual gentle style. Finally, Andy Schaap, Samuel Chambers, Alex Thomson and Emilios Christodoulidis all provoked me to rethink and defend my arguments at a stimulating workshop held in Edinburgh.

I also would like to thank the Leverhulme Trust, from whom I obtained a year's research leave at the start of this project. The Department of Government, University of Essex also provided me with generous study leave at crucial points in the project. I would like to thank David Sanders in particular for his support. I am also grateful to colleagues who took over some of my supervision during my research leave. Here David Howarth and Jason Glynos, who took on most of the additional burden of supervision and teaching, deserve a special thanks, as do Sarah Birch and Hugh Ward. I have been very fortunate also to have had the help of Noreen Harburt, who kindly agreed at a late stage to help with the final preparation of the bibliography and the production of the text. In this regard, I would also like to thank John Haslam, Carrie Cheek, Joanna Breeze and Sue Dickinson, for their help and careful advice in steering my manuscript through the production process.

Finally, I also have debts of a more personal nature. I am grateful beyond words for the love and support of my family: James, whose cheerful disposition kept the writing process in perspective, David Howarth, who remains one of my most critical readers, as well as my sister, Betsy Stoltz and my mother, Nanda Norval, whose encouragement sustained me throughout this project.

Chapter 1 was published in S. Critchley and O. Marchart (eds.), *Laclau. A Critical Reader* (Abingdon, Oxon.: Routledge, 2004). Chapter 3 was published in *Political Theory* 34, no. 2 (2006), 229–55.

Introduction: towards an aversive account of democracy

We don't start from certain words, but from certain occasions or activities.[1]

The democratic elections in South Africa and the subsequent experience of the Truth and Reconciliation Commission, both of which exemplify the so-called Third Wave of democratization, raise vital questions for democratic theory. For example, how do democratic practices become embedded in a society; and what is the relationship between these processes and the assumption of democratic subjectivity? How do we account for the articulation of political demands and its relation to the constitution of political identity and community? While these issues appear rather stark in the context of societies undergoing democratic transitions, they are not irrelevant to the workings of more established democracies. Even in societies with long traditions of democracy, the question of political community, the forging and expression of political demands, and the fostering of democratic forms of citizenship, remain extremely important. In the latter contexts, these issues arise in a slightly different form. They are not principally concerned with the initial establishment of democratic forms of subjectivity and community, but with their maintenance and reactivation. However, it would be mistaken to regard these two sorts of questions as they arise in the different contexts as entirely different in character, for this would assume too large a gap between processes of innovation and the reactivation of tradition. The argument developed in this book arises from this central concern and seeks to elaborate an account of democratic practice that takes account of

---

[1] L. Wittgenstein, *Lectures and Conversations on Aesthetics, Psychology and Religious Belief*, ed. C. Barrett (Oxford: Basil Blackwell, 1989), p. 3.

well-established traditions at the same time as it thinks about innovation and renewal. One may expect, in reflecting on these issues, that democratic theory will be able to provide deep insight and critical tools for the analysis of these processes. The matter, however, is more complicated than that. It is characteristic of much political theory, and democratic theory in particular, to distance itself from the ordinary practices, commitments and concerns of democratic life. While most would accept that this is necessary for theorizing and thinking about democratic life, such distancing can take different forms and fulfil different practical and theoretical functions.[2] At best, it may provide us with the requisite imagination to sustain and deepen democratic life. At worst, it can prevent us from engaging

---

[2] There is a wide range of possible positions on the question of abstraction. As O'Neill argues, abstraction is necessary and unobjectionable in that it only abstracts or brackets predicates that are true of a given object. (See O. O'Neill, 'Political liberalism and public reason: A critical notice of John Rawls, *Political Liberalism*', *The Philosophical Review* 106, no. 3 (1997), 419.) However, O'Neill suggests that abstraction has to be contrasted with idealization, which substitutes false predicates for true ones. (O'Neill takes both Rawls's and Habermas' conceptions of rational agency to commit the error of idealization.) While acknowledging that idealizations may be of great help in theory-building, she contends that it is particularly problematic in the case of practical reasoning, 'whose aspiration it is to fit the world (to some degree) to certain conceptions or principles'. (O'Neill, 'Political liberalism and public reason', 419.) Laclau holds a broadly similar position on the necessity of abstraction, though his deconstructive reading clearly takes distance from O'Neill. With regard to the question of 'transcendentality' Laclau argues (like O'Neill) that 'the transcendental dimension is unavoidable' since there is 'no object without conditions of possibility transcending it'. Yet (contra O'Neill), he argues that 'transcendentality, in the full sense of the term, is impossible (that is why we can speak of quasi-transcendentals)' because it is not possible to draw a neat frontier with the empirical. (See E. Laclau, 'Identity and hegemony: The role of universality in the constitution of political logics', in J. Butler, E. Laclau and S. Žižek, *Contingency, Hegemony, Universality. Contemporary Dialogues on the Left*, Phronesis (London: Verso, 2000), p. 76.) Habermas' account of a 'reconstructive sociology' is relevant in this regard and the issue is captured in the title of *Between Facts and Norms*. He suggests that the idealizations of proceduralism can be linked to empirical investigations through the identification of 'particles and fragments of an "existing reason" already incorporated in political practices'. Yet, for him, this leads into a set of idealizations that would be regarded as illegitimate for both O'Neill and Laclau. (See J. Habermas, *Between Facts and Norms. Contributions to a Discourse Theory of Law and Democracy*, trans. W. Rehg (Cambridge: Polity Press, 1997), p. 287.)

with democratic theory in a way that addresses practical needs.³ In what follows I hope to reorient democratic theory around the axis of our 'real need', as Wittgenstein puts it, by elucidating what we are doing and committing ourselves to when we participate in democratic life together.⁴ In this context, I will argue, it is particularly important to understand the process of making claims on each other, and of contesting or defending established norms and practices, as well as to investigate how our identities as democratic citizens are sustained in and through democratic practices. The key questions informing my account can thus be formulated in the following terms. How do we become democratic citizens, and what role does the articulation of political claims play in this respect? How are we to understand the constitution and eruption of new claims, and how do we make sense of the terms in which such claims are expressed? Once expressed, how do such claims become generalized and what do such claims and demands tell us about the relations between democratic citizens? Perhaps more broadly, how are we to account for the interplay of tradition and innovation in democratic life, and what light can existing democratic theory shed on these issues arising in democratic politics? While much democratic theory rightly occupies itself with what we ought to do when we engage in democratic practices, I aim in this book to shift away from these concerns to a different set of questions and engagements. Rather than starting out from an

---

³ O'Neill suggests that this focus addresses the needs of 'spectators who are looking for ways of assessing or appraising what has been done'. O. O'Neill, *Bounds of Justice* (Cambridge: Cambridge University Press, 2000), p. 7. Though the activity of assessing is clearly perfectly legitimate, everything depends on how the theorist is situated with respect to it.

⁴ 'The preconceived idea of crystalline purity can only be removed by turning our whole examination around. (One might say: the axis of reference of our examination must be rotated, but about the fixed point of our real need.)' L. Wittgenstein, *Philosophical Investigations*, trans. G. E. M. Anscombe (Oxford: Basil Blackwell, 1992), § 108. Cavell suggests that real need here can be understood in contrast to the invocation of 'false' needs in philosophizing that demands, for instance, that there 'must be something common' in the words we use. These sorts of demands often lead to a deprivation of the human voice. See S. Cavell, *Philosophy the Day after Tomorrow* (Cambridge, Mass.: The Belknap Press of Harvard University Press, 2005), p. 199.

articulation of what in the best of all possible worlds we ought to do, this investigation sets out from what I will argue is an inevitable sense of 'restiveness', which is often expressed in terms of disappointment with the ongoing practices associated with contemporary democratic life, driven as it is by a sense that things could be better.

DEMOCRACY, DISAPPOINTMENT AND PERFECTIONISM

Following a well-established line of contemporary thought, a recent commentator on what is perceived to be a deep-seated malaise in contemporary democracy suggests that the growing discontent with formal politics is best explained by a number of misunderstandings about the nature of democracy.[5] As Gerry Stoker puts it, 'citizens fail to fully appreciate that politics in the end involves the collective imposition of decisions, demands a complex communication process and generally produces messy compromise'.[6] In short, according to these perspectives, politics is designed to disappoint. Nevertheless, Stoker insists that it is crucial to take on board the fact that it is always possible in a proper functioning democracy to re-open discussion of any particular issue. Hence, what initially looks like a deflationary thesis is thus used to emphasize the open-endedness of democratic interactions. And this involves 'that hardest of human skills: listening carefully to the opinions of others and their expression of their interests'.[7] These 'hardest of human skills' can in many respects be taken as the subject matter of this book, as they serve to invoke the question of what Cavell calls 'the conversation of justice', though it is important to stress that conversation in this regard is not just about talk, but an entire 'way of life together', one which is opaque and non-transparent, where the virtues most in

---

[5] See, for instance, M. Warren, 'What can democratic participation mean today?', *Political Theory* 30, no. 5 (2002), 677–701, and R. D. Putnam, *Bowling Alone. The Collapse and Revival of American Community* (New York: Simon and Schuster, 2000).

[6] G. Stoker, *Why Politics Matters. Making Democracy Work* (Basingstoke: Palgrave Macmillan, 2006), p. 10.

[7] Stoker, *Why Politics Matters*, pp. 10–11.

demand are those of listening, responsiveness to difference, and an openness to change.[8]

Disappointment is not only empirically relevant for our discussion of democracy. Disappointment, restiveness, even a sense of crisis, is equally important in outlining a theoretical account of democracy. It is unquestionably the case today that democratic theorists, from Habermas, Rawls and Iris Marion Young to Connolly, Mouffe and Laclau start with a sense of disappointment in current arrangements and the accompanying urge to provide something better in its place. For example, Habermas begins *Between Facts and Norms* with an account of the loss of orientation and self-confidence faced by those citizens in contemporary Western societies who are governed by the rule of law, but are faced with the challenges of ecological limits to growth, global inequality and immigration from impoverished regions.[9] However, it is noticeable that this account is followed almost immediately by a rejection of defeatism and an invocation of the promise held out by radical democracy. Habermas suggests in this respect that the rule of law cannot be enjoyed or maintained without radical democracy: 'private legal subjects cannot come to enjoy equal individual liberties if they do not *themselves*, in the common exercise of their political autonomy, achieve clarity about justified interests and standards. They themselves must agree on the relevant aspects under which equals should be treated equally and unequals unequally.'[10] The specific assertions made here will be treated in some detail in the forthcoming chapters. Of particular importance for us at this point is Habermas' emphasis on both the need to claim liberties as ours, and to do so under conditions in which equality itself is in question and cannot be given or assumed.

These are the issues at stake in this text. In what follows, I develop and defend a perfectionist account of democracy which

---

[8] S. Cavell, *Cities of Words. Pedagogical Letters on a Register of the Moral Life* (Cambridge, Mass.: The Belknap Press of Harvard University Press, 2004), pp. 172–4.
[9] Habermas, *Between Facts and Norms*, p. xlii.   [10] Ibid.

attends to the emergence of claims arising out of the ordinary activities of democratic citizens but which nevertheless runs against the grain of the dominant norms of recognition of legitimate claims and traditional ways of dealing with them.[11] There are several features of this account that are worth drawing attention to at this stage. It is important that it starts from and attends to the emergence of claims that arise from the ordinary activities of democratic citizens. The emphasis on the ordinary in this regard not only suggests a concern with the specificity of our democratic practices, language and communication but also tells us something about the grammar of our democratic practices, in short, with our responsiveness to each other. It is, moreover, important that my concern is with the emergence of claims, and the relation between such claims and existing practices and traditions. Perfectionism, which is the province 'not of those who oppose justice and benevolent calculation, but of those who feel left out of their sway, who feel indeed that most people have been left, or leave themselves out, of their sway',[12] provides us with some guidance here. Characterized in this way, perfectionism returns us to the current malaise in democratic theory and practice, which I described as a certain restiveness or dissatisfaction with the present and with the self. Cavell puts it in the following terms. Perfectionism, he argues,

> provides a position from which the present state of human existence can be judged and a future state achieved, or else the present to be better than the cost of changing it. The very conception of a divided self and a doubled world, providing a perspective of judgment upon the world as it is, measured against the world as it may be, tends to express disappointment with the world as it is, as the scene of human activity and prospects, and perhaps to lodge the demand or desire for a reform or transfiguration of the world.[13]

---

[11] In this respect, my work clearly follows in the footsteps of James Tully and Stanley Cavell.

[12] Cavell, *Cities of Words*, p. 25.   [13] Cavell, *Cities of Words*, p. 2.

In other words, it suggests a close relation between our disappointments with existing political practices and the desire for something better.

However, as I will argue more fully later, my defence of perfectionism is resolutely non-teleological, denying us the ability to provide a list of features or characteristics that if achieved and instituted would give us the ability to claim that we (and our institutions) are 'above reproach'.[14] It does not furnish us with an end state to be achieved, precisely because these demands (for a set of delineable features and a clearly defined end state) run the risk of complacency, both theoretically and practically. Were we to have such a set of features, the risk is that we concentrate on those elements only or to the exclusion of other, often unforeseen and unforeseeable events, concerns and demands that may arise. To furnish an account of perfectionism that is compatible with the demands of democracy requires a break with the idea that there is one path or one mode of being in the world that could act as a model for all to follow.[15] To put it differently, the perfectionism I wish to defend here acknowledges the excess of being over thought. Hence, it calls for attentiveness, not only to the emergence of demands, but also to the contouring of the space in and against which demands are articulated and the relations it implies between ourselves and others, as well as to ourselves. What Cavell calls 'aversion to conformism' acts as the guiding thread of my argument in this respect, helping to inform my critical engagement with contemporary democratic theory. Conformism, Cavell suggests, makes slaves of us. Aversion to conformism, that is, aversion to the

[14] See Cavell's incisive treatment of Rawls's discussion of the conditions under which we may claim to be 'above reproach', in Cavell, *Cities of Words*, pp. 164–89.
[15] Cavell notes that 'the path from the *Republic*'s picture of the soul's journey (perfectible to the pitch of philosophy by only a few, forming an aristocratic class) to the democratic need for perfection, is a path from the idea of there being one (call him Socrates) who represents for each of us the height of the journey, to the idea of each of us being representative for each of us ... Emerson's study is of this (democratic, universal) representativeness ... under the heading of "standing for" ... as a relation we bear at once to others and to ourselves'. Cavell, *Conditions Handsome and Unhandsome. The Constitution of Emersonian Perfectionism*, The Carus Lectures, 1988 (Chicago: University of Chicago Press, 1990), p. 9.

demand for conformity, politically draws attention to those aspects of a democratic grammar that highlight our democratic responsibilities, to the need to give attention to the exercise of our political voice and to the claims to community that it inevitably invokes and/or contests.

The concerns addressed in this book arise against the backdrop of a fast-changing social and political world. Much attention in recent years has been given to the local and global challenges to traditional arenas of democratic participation, and to their purported effects upon national democratic institutions. However, this renewal of democratic challenges also takes place in surroundings where serious concerns about the lack of interest and apathy displayed by citizens of countries with long-established democratic traditions are expressed. In a similar vein, the international milieu has undergone significant changes, ranging from the 'velvet revolutions' of the late 1980s and 1990s to the 'colour revolutions' of the first decade of the twenty-first century. In all these cases, there has been a complicated interplay between time-honoured democratic traditions and the challenges offered by new forms of transition to democracy. This interplay between innovation and renewal, on the one hand, and tradition on the other, raises important questions for reflecting on the grammar of democracy, understood as delimiting a horizon of what is sayable and doable at any given point in time, as well as what we may expect from others and what others may expect from us in the articulation of claims upon one another. It also allows us to reconsider the processes through which democratic renewal erupts onto the scene and gets instituted. These processes are, moreover, suggestive in thinking about the extension and projection of democratic imaginaries, the reach of democratic horizons, and the claims made in its name. Unfortunately, writing during the first decade of the twenty-first century, these reflections cannot be overwhelmingly optimistic. The project of a forceful imposition of democracy in Iraq, and the shallowness of its uptake elsewhere, cast a shadow over any sense of possibility that accompanied the fall of the Berlin wall and the wave of democratizations following in its wake. The disclosing of new arenas of struggle, in which nothing is guaranteed, should alert us to just how much is at stake in the current theoretical and practical debates about democracy. Having witnessed the transition to democracy in South Africa, these questions have personal resonance and hold particular theoretical interest for me.[16]

DEMOCRATIC THEORY REORIENTED

The arguments I develop in this book have emerged in part from a long-standing interest, but also certain unhappiness, with the political insights that can be gleaned from a post-structuralist approach to political theory. And the turn to deliberative democratic theory in an attempt to resolve what I perceive to be perplexing and deep-seated problems in both mainstream normative theory and post-structuralism has been an enriching experience. I thus critically engage in this text with both these traditions in order to cast light on what I find problematic in our contemporary accounts of democracy. In addition, I draw much inspiration from the writings of the late Wittgenstein, and have sought to work through and extend his theoretical and ethical insights in order to analyse contemporary politics in general, and democratic theory in particular. Both his method and the substance of his philosophical insights have proved constant companions in this process. His picture of leading words home to their ordinary use, together with the peculiarly uncanny sense of the ordinary, has alerted me to some of the excesses of abstractionism and the consequent demand for rules and standards of democracy drawn from realms other than our ordinary engagements and commitments. I have found similar inspiration in the work of Derrida, particularly his careful attention to textual detail and nuance, but also his continual breaches with

---

[16] As Grassi puts it, 'Every problem that concerns us may not and cannot be conceived in an abstract and purely formal way. If the question that presents itself to us has a basis, then it must bear upon us in a way that oversteps subjective limits.' E. Grassi, *Rhetoric as Philosophy*, trans. J. M. Krois and A. Azodi (Carbondale and Edwardsville: Southern Illinois University Press, 2001), p. 1.

context that provide a sometimes dizzying perspective on the issues under discussion. My reading of both thinkers works from the postulate that their works cannot be treated as a mere propaedeutic to political analysis, which can therefore be separated from normative insights. Like other commentators, I suggest that Wittgenstein's and Derrida's engagement with the philosophical tradition is deeply infused with an ethic that has significant consequences for the usages we may make of their works in political analysis.[17] In the case of Derrida, this approach is vindicated in the latter's own writings and forays into the domain of political theory. In the case of Wittgenstein, the recent resurgence of interest among political theorists in his work has smoothed the road for me, and I follow the exemplary investigations of Wittgenstein's reflections for political theory advanced by Cavell, Tully and Zerilli whose engagements with the ordinary has been pivotal for enabling me to articulate what I mean by aversive democracy.

The challenges to traditional forms of democratic participation in established democracies, as well as the more recent transitions to democracy, raise issues not addressed adequately in contemporary democratic theory. Two key areas are singled out in this respect. The first concerns the character of democratic argumentation. My attention to different aspects of argumentation allows me to better understand the mechanisms involved in the formation and articulation of new demands; the respective roles of reason and rhetoric in this

---

[17] I deal in some detail with readings of Wittgenstein, and his relation to ethics and politics in Chapter 4. There has been extensive debate on the relation between deconstruction, and politics and ethics. See, for instance, D. Wood, 'The experience of the ethical', in R. Kearney and M. Dooley (eds.), *Questioning Ethics. Contemporary Debates in Philosophy* (London: Routledge, 1999), pp. 105–19; S. Critchley, *The Ethics of Deconstruction. Derrida and Levinas* (Oxford: Blackwell, 1992); J. Dronsfield and N. Midgley (eds.), *Responsibilities of Deconstruction* (PLI, *Warwick Journal of Philosophy* 6, University of Warwick, Summer 1997); E. Laclau, 'Deconstruction, Pragmatism, Hegemony', in S. Critchley, J. Derrida, E. Laclau and R. Rorty, *Deconstruction and Pragmatism*, ed. C. Mouffe (London: Routledge, 1996), pp. 47–68, and A. Norval, 'Hegemony after deconstruction: The consequences of undecidability', *Journal of Political Ideologies* 9, no. 2 (2004), 139–57.

process; and the importance of imagination in the construction and projection of new political horizons, as well as the extension of particular democratic demands in specific contexts. The second relates to the treatment of democratic subjectivity. Here it is crucial to understand the processes involved in the formation and maintenance of democratic forms of subjectivity; the role of practices, passions and the visceral dimensions of identification in their formation and sustenance; and the characterization of the relations between democratic citizens. Without a focus on these processes, our understanding of the institution and maintenance of a democratic ethos will remain severely hampered, a situation limited further by the excessively abstract character of much contemporary democratic theory, in which theorists are reluctant to engage with aspects of the ordinary in thinking about the grammar of democracy. These two key areas of concern are either under-theorized or not addressed at all in the two main theoretical traditions on which I focus: the deliberative conception of democracy as developed by Jürgen Habermas and his followers and post-structuralist accounts of radical democracy as found in the works of Ernesto Laclau, Chantal Mouffe and Jacques Rancière. While developing my own arguments from within a post-analytical Wittgensteinian perspective, I aim to establish a dialogue between these approaches, while also developing a critique of the risk of overly decontextual forms of argumentation that are present in different forms in both deliberative and post-structuralist approaches.

Throughout the development of my argument, I attend to the demands of different aspects of democratic grammar, ranging from the conditions in which democracy is first established to situations where it has become sclerotic. However, I seek to avoid the simplistic dichotomization that informs both post-structuralist and deliberative accounts in this respect. Post-structuralists tend to work with too sharp a distinction between the moment of the political, which is usually understood in terms of the institution of regimes, and the ordinary ongoing business of politics, in which they denigrate the latter in favour of the former. As I show in the book, this tendency has important negative consequences for their accounts of democratic theory, including a bracketing of normative questions and an over-emphasis on the political as dislocation and disruption. As a consequence, the grammar of ongoing democratic politics has remained largely unanalysed and under-theorized. By contrast, deliberative accounts fail to engage with the institution and actual formation of democratic subjectivity, neglecting this in favour of a too abstract account of democratic deliberation and procedures in existing democracies. *Aversive Democracy* puts forward an account of democratic grammar that gives attention to the interplay between tradition and novelty in democratic politics, but seeks to avoid the tendency to treat all forms of novelty as radical breaks, and all tradition as a mere repetition of the same.

Drawing on a Wittgenstein-inspired account of the ordinary, I analyse the grammar of democracy with specific reference to the nature and character of democratic argumentation and the question of democratic subject formation. This critical analysis highlights the extent to which each of the approaches under discussion is held captive by a 'picture' of argumentation and subject formation that potentially leads to an impoverishment of democratic debate and debate about democracy. I seek to make visible the contours of these pictures and to put them into question. Finally, by pulling together the arguments developed in the encounter with deliberative and post-structuralist approaches I set out an alternative account of democracy that draws deeply on, but also moves beyond, some of the strictures of the post-structuralist model. In so doing, I develop insights gleaned from my reading of Wittgenstein in order to offer a nuanced account of the character of democratic argumentation and subject formation. Cavell's reading of Emerson provides me with a starting-point from which to develop an account of the character of democratic identification that is commensurate with broader post-structuralist insights, but which is not reluctant to address issues of a normative character. The title *Aversive Democracy*, which is drawn from Cavell's adumbration of Emersonian perfectionism and which emphasizes the idea of an aversion to conformism as a key feature of democratic subjectivity, captures the core elements of this account. This reading also facilitates an engagement with the processes through which democratic horizons are imagined and expanded, so picking up the thread of argumentation with which this book is introduced, namely the question of the universalization of norms and demands.

THE ARGUMENT

The analysis offered here takes the form of a reciprocal critical elucidation of deliberative and post-structural democratic theory. In so doing, I aim to establish the respective strengths and weaknesses of each perspective, as well as the different ways in which they may supplement each other by focusing on a number of key areas. As suggested, the first concerns the difficulties that attend deliberative theory in its movement from ideal to non-ideal theory, as well as the different ways in which post-structuralists can provide ways of avoiding these problems. The second concerns the problems faced by post-structuralists in theorizing the character of democratic institutions, and the way in which the conceptual resources of deliberative democracy can be helpful in this task. I also elucidate their common limitations in addressing the sources and resources of democratic identification – the ways in which we become and sustain ourselves as democratic subjects – and the normativity of our manifold democratic practices. In response to these concerns, I develop a Wittgensteinian approach that provides the means for overcoming the problems posed for democratic theory.

In order to set the scene for the analysis of these issues, I start by outlining and exploring a set of key concerns, through which I contrast and compare deliberative and post-structuralist accounts of radical democracy. This is an important place to start, not least because there is little serious discussion of their differences and similarities in the existing literature. I seek to remedy this deficiency in Chapter 1, while also providing an overview of the basic theoretical assumptions that structure these two approaches. The vital question analysed in this regard concerns the nature and structure of the arguments deployed in the process of making universalizable claims. The respective positions put forward in deliberative and post-structuralist accounts of this process are discussed in relation to the status of such claims and their motivational premises. Are they universal claims based upon generalizable norms, agreed upon through reason, or are they universalized claims forged through a process of hegemonic articulation? How in each of these accounts is democratic argumentation understood? Is the aim of democracy to reach agreement of a universal character, or to maintain dissensus, even as we universalize claims? In addressing these questions, the first chapter serves as a background to the rest of the text, thus setting the scene for the analysis of two of the key issues to be explored in more depth: those of democratic argumentation and the formation of democratic subjectivities.

Chapter 2 concentrates on an analysis of the force of argumentation in democratic theory. It explores the different accounts offered of this force in deliberative and post-structuralist approaches, with their contrasting treatments of the respective roles of reason and rhetoric. I claim that it is important to consider actual forms of democratic argumentation in order to deepen our understanding of democracy. And to do this I argue that one needs an account of language that takes ordinary language seriously, not in order to affirm its potentially conservative tendencies, but so as to be able to explore the specificity of democratic forms of interaction. Taking my lead from Wittgenstein, and drawing on contemporary developments in rhetorical theory, as well as a hegemonic understanding of the structure of politico-linguistic interactions, I develop an account of democratic argumentation that highlights the need to break with the constraints of a rationalistic model of language and engage with the intricacies of democratic argumentation and the role of rhetoric in its constitution and elaboration. In so doing, I attend to a much-neglected dimension of democratic argumentation, namely, the role of imagination in the formation and extension of the horizons of our democratic grammar.

In general, then, contemporary political theory reflects on the conditions under which democratic activity may flourish in principle, where ample attention is paid to the various sociological changes in our contemporary democratic landscape. However, little consideration is given to those crucial moments that turn the subject into a democratic subject and the practices that may be required to sustain those forms of identification over time. The failure in deliberative and post-structuralist conceptions of democracy to account for these moments in which we assume democratic subjectivity leaves us unable to think through how it is that we become democrats, and make democratic subjectivity ours. This failure arises for different reasons in each case. For deliberative theorists it is related to the rarified character of discourse that informs their account of democracy, which when combined with their proceduralist ethics tends to foreclose an investigation into the critical junctures in which individuals take up democratic subjectivity. On the other hand, while post-structuralists account for the formation of the subject, the construction of democratic subject positions is often relegated to the domain of mere contextual political articulation. In short, the absence of reflection on these issues leaves us unable to appreciate the specificity of democratic identification, including how we become democratic subjects. In Chapter 3, I draw on Wittgenstein's account of aspect change, combining this account with Laclau's powerful theorization of the place of identification in subject formation, in order to conceptualize two distinct facets of the formation of democratic identities. The first consists of the initial 'take up' of a democratic subjectivity while the second emphasizes subsequent iterations of that 'take up', the repeated processes through which we reassert our identities as democratic subjects. I also emphasize the importance of what might be termed the visceral dimensions of identification, as well as practices other than those of argumentation in the development of subjectivity. In so doing, I aim to open up, and then give an initial account of, the specificity of democratic identification, casting it in Wittgensteinian terms as 'identification as'. It is in this context also that I reconnect my argument with the interplay between inheritance and originality, tradition and novelty, in democratic grammars.

Chapter 4 extends this analysis by investigating the constitution of a common democratic space and the role of the articulation of claims in that process, as well as the relations between democratic subjects that are instituted as a result of claim making. It starts with a critical reading of Rancière in order to think through what is involved in the constitution of a shared space of argumentation, an aspect ignored by most deliberative theorists. The emphasis then shifts to consider the role of articulating claims in politics in general and in democracies in particular. The former is elucidated by drawing on Laclau's seminal work on the role of demands in politics, while I address the latter by appropriating aspects of Cavell's work on claim making and the responsibilities it invokes between democratic subjects. In developing this account, I argue that a Cavellian account of perfectionism, as well as Derrida's theorization of 'democracy-to-come', allows us to attend to the normative dimensions of democratic grammar within a post-structuralist approach.

In the concluding chapter, where I outline my account of aversive democracy in a more explicit fashion, I seek to supplement agonistic conceptions of democracy, such as that developed by Mouffe, by giving due consideration to the areas of democratic practice neglected in contemporary democratic theory. Here I engage with the grammar of democracy in its fullest manifestations, where I draw upon a wide array of factors, including visceral, non-verbal, reasonable and passionate elements, which enter into the development of democratic argument and identification. In so doing, I return to the key questions raised in opening the account of democracy in this book. More particularly, I attend to the role of exemplars in the development, expansion and universalization of democratic imaginaries, as well as to the cultivation of a democratic ethos. The main aim in addressing these issues is to reflect on what it may mean democratically to follow an example and to 'manifest for an other' another way, to act as an exemplar for another. Finally, I return to the question of democracy and passion, extending my earlier account of 'identification as' so as to take full cognizance of the role of rhetoric and passion in a domain of argumentation not already ruled by convention.

I Democracy, universalization and (dis)agreement

> Democratic theorists now take deliberation to be the exemplary practice or activity for democrats, and they gear their arguments toward its realization.[1]

> A picture held us captive. And we could not get outside of it.[2]

An explosion onto the scene of new claims and demands mark contemporary politics. Sometimes they become sedimented into a specific or wider programme of action. At other times, the demands remain isolated, unable to appeal to a wider audience or even to sustain themselves in their particularity. The reasons for the seeming frequency of emergence of new demands are multiple, ranging from the speed of contemporary life,[3] and the dislocations and disruptions associated with it, to the ability of issues to transcend borders at a pace previously unknown. A key task of democratic theory today is to address, account for and analyse the formation and character of these demands. This involves giving attention to a number of different issues. We need to be able to understand the structure of such demands, including the varied elements – verbal and non-verbal, rational, emotional and imaginative – that go into their formation. In addition, consideration has to be given to how demands become universalized and to the nature of such universalization. A plethora of further questions arise in this respect. Does universalization depend upon the reaching of democratic agreement? If this is the case,

---

[1] L. M. Sanders, 'Against deliberation', *Political Theory* 25, no. 3 (1997), 347.

[2] L. Wittgenstein, *Philosophical Investigations*, trans. G. E. M. Anscombe (Oxford: Basil Blackwell, 1984), § 115.

[3] For a consideration of speed in contemporary life, see W. E. Connolly, 'Speed, concentric cultures, and cosmopolitanism', *Political Theory* 28, no. 5 (2000), 596–618.

what role does disagreement play in democratic discourse? How is democratic discourse related to rhetoric, imagination and the more visceral dimensions of politics? These and many other questions form the backdrop to contemporary treatments of the nature and character of democratic decision-making, and the forging of common interests and identities in democratic theory today. In this chapter, I start out with a discussion of the questions raised by universalization as they are treated in contemporary democratic theory. It may be argued that consideration should logically first be given to the processes involved in the formation of demands. However, the debate between deliberative and post-structural theorists of democracy focused initially on the question of universalization and ignored that of the formation of demands themselves. Hence, I return to this issue at a later stage in the argument.

In contemporary theoretical debates on democracy, conceptions of universalization are conceived of either as based upon the generalization of norms, or as resulting from the hegemonization of demands. This divide is accompanied by an emphasis on either the reaching of agreement or the maintenance of the possibility of disagreement as a core feature of democratic discourse. These features are present in two approaches that have dominated the debate, namely, the Habermas-inspired model of deliberative democracy and the post-structuralist model of the decision in the theory of radical democracy as articulated in the works of Ernesto Laclau and Chantal Mouffe.[4] I offer a critical reading of these approaches, examining the central assumptions underpinning them, in order to clear the ground for the articulation of a modified version of radical democratic politics, which aims to do justice to what I will call the agonistic spirit of

---

[4] I will not here focus on a third prominent approach, namely, a social choice approach. See D. Miller, 'Deliberative democracy and social choice', in D. Held (ed.), *Prospects for Democracy. North, South, East, West* (Cambridge: Polity Press, 1993), pp. 74–92. However, even here the issue of identification – which I discuss later in some detail – arises since democratic self-restraint, as Miller points out, relies on people thinking that 'it is more important that the decision reached should be a genuinely democratic one than that it is the decision that they themselves favour' (p. 66).

democracy[5] and seeks to address some of its shortcomings.[6] The Habermas-inspired deliberative approach, I will argue, fails to offer a workable account of the relation between ideal conditions of deliberation and actual processes of democratic decision-making. As a result, its final characterization of the construction of generalizable interests is problematic in that it draws on suppositions excluded from the original normative model. The approach exemplified in the works of Laclau and Mouffe, on the other hand, concentrates on the construction of hegemonic outcomes. While it provides a plausible account of the universalization of demands, it does not give sufficient consideration to the extent to which this process can in fact be described as democratic. In this case, the root of the problem could be located in the overemphasis on an ontological analysis of decisions specifically, and hegemonic politics more generally. To overcome these problems, one needs to reconsider the nature of democratic argumentation and decision-making while also giving greater attention to the forms of subjectivity commensurate with it.

DELIBERATIVE DEMOCRACY AND ITS CRITICS

Over the years persistent questions have been raised concerning deliberation, its presuppositions, and its relation to actual democratic practice.[7] Habermas and his defenders have sought to develop responses to these queries and criticisms.[8] Given this it may be

---

[5] For a discussion of an agonistic model of politics, see W. E. Connolly, *Identity\ Difference: Democratic Negotiations of Political Paradox* (Ithaca, N.Y.: Cornell University Press, 1991). For a somewhat broader interpretation of agonism, see S. Benhabib, 'The democratic moment and the problem of difference', in S. Benhabib (ed.), *Democracy and Difference. Contesting the Boundaries of the Political* (Princeton, N.J.: Princeton University Press, 1996), pp. 7–9.

[6] Benhabib recently noted that this is the theoretical task that is at hand for democratic theorists. Benhabib, 'The democratic moment', p. 9.

[7] See, for instance, S. Lukes, 'Of gods and demons. Habermas and practical reason', in J. B. Thompson and D. Held (eds.), *Habermas. Critical Debates* (Cambridge, Mass.: MIT Press, 1982), pp. 134–48; and M. Walzer, 'A critique of philosophical conversation', *The Philosophical Forum* 21, no. 1–2 (1989–90), 182–96.

[8] See J. Habermas, 'A reply to my critics', in Thompson and Held (eds.), *Habermas. Critical Debates*, pp. 219–83; J. Habermas, *Between Facts and Norms. Contributions*

appropriate to start with a brief outline of the general parameters of the deliberative model of democracy.[9] The Habermas-inspired conception of deliberative democracy has been and remains particularly influential in the development of democratic institutions and mechanisms, such as deliberative forums, citizens' juries, and deliberative polling.[10] It is not difficult to see why it offers an attractive model for democratic practice.[11] In contrast to adversarial conceptions of democracy, it places a great deal of emphasis on the reaching of consensual agreements. In contrast to aggregative models of democracy, it focuses on the formation of opinions, interests, and democratic wills. Consequently it seeks to avoid the pitfalls of assuming that opinions and interests are already in existence *before* the making of democratic decisions. Agreements reached under conditions specified, it is argued, have the power to legitimate institutions and political principles in a way that the simple aggregation of votes does not, since it places citizens under a publicity requirement: they must offer reasons for their positions and claims,

---

to a *Discourse Theory of Law and Democracy* (Cambridge: Polity Press, 1996); and S. Chambers, *Reasonable Democracy. Jürgen Habermas and the Politics of Discourse* (London: Cornell University Press, 1996).

[9] There is no singular model of deliberative democracy. Recent works have drawn, for instance, both on Habermas and on Rawls. I concentrate in the main on those works taking their inspiration from the former. For volumes including a broad discussion of deliberative democracy, see S. Macedo (ed.), *Deliberative Politics* (Oxford: Oxford University Press, 1999); M. Passerin D'Entrèves (ed.), *Democracy as Public Deliberation* (Manchester: Manchester University Press, 2002); and J. S. Fishkin and P. Laslett (eds.), *Debating Deliberative Democracy* (Oxford: Basil Blackwell, 2003).

[10] See, for instance, the contributions in O. Renn, T. Webler and P. Wiedemann (eds.), *Fairness and Competence in Citizen Participation. Evaluating Models for Environmental Discourse* (Dordrecht: Kluwer Academic Publishers, 1995); as well as J. S. Dryzek, 'Political and ecological communication', *Environmental Politics* 4 (1995), 10–30.

[11] Commentators differ widely on the role of the ideal speech situation and its relation to democratic practice. Walzer, for instance, points out that while it may be worthwhile to strive for more open debate and a more egalitarian politics, the reasons for doing so precede ideal speech rather than emerge from it. Thus, the picture of ideal speech cannot serve as a test of the processes through which these ideas are generated (see Walzer, 'Philosophical conversation', 194). In contrast to this, Chambers argues that idealizations must be presupposed 'in order to criticize the distorting effects of power and domination'. Chambers, *Reasonable Democracy*, p. 9.

and must defend those reasons publicly. In turn, this emphasis has shifted the focus of theorizing to reflection on the conditions under which processes of decision-making may be deemed democratic. In this respect, the stipulation of discourse rules is taken to provide clear guidance on such conditions. For instance, it allows theorists and practitioners of democracy to argue that a decision will be democratic if and only if no one with the competency to speak and act is excluded from the process; if everyone is allowed to question or introduce any assertion they wish, while also expressing their attitudes, desires and needs; and if no one is prevented, by internal or external coercion, from exercising these rights.[12] These rules make explicit that under conditions of democratic deliberation we must treat each other as equal partners; that individuals must be given the space to speak; and that we must listen to each other, and justify our positions to one another.

Moreover, it seems possible to ascertain in practice whether these guidelines are being followed, and thus whether any particular process in fact measures up to the standards of democratic practice specified in the model. For instance, in her book *Reasonable Democracy* Chambers fleshes out these conditions in the following fashion. First, approximating the condition of universality means that there should be an absence of barriers excluding people or groups from debate.[13] As many voices as possible should be heard, which means that there is a requirement for a high level of participation (including reading, weighing opinions, and having discussions with friends and so forth).[14] Practically, one has to ask the following questions: Have any groups been excluded? Are there organizations and movements through which the public can voice its opinion? Is there a high level of

---

[12] Chambers, *Reasonable Democracy*, p. 100.

[13] She emphasizes 'approximation', for she holds that the idealizations of the speech situation cannot simply be realized in the real world (Chambers, *Reasonable Democracy*, p. 9). They need to be translated into practice. This process, I would argue, weakens them considerably.

[14] Chambers suggests that Habermas underestimates and downplays the dependence of his conception of discourse on an ethos of citizen participation.

interest and involvement on the part of all those affected?[15] Second, approximating the conditions of rationality (being persuaded by the force of the better argument) and non-coercion means that agreement must be autonomous.[16] Conditions under which deliberation takes place must exclude both internal and external coercion and should emphasize the need for critical reflection and evaluation.[17] Finally, approximating reciprocity means that we must ask how close we come to maintaining respect and impartiality.[18] To what extent do participants approach disputes discursively as opposed to strategically? Indicators of 'sincere acting' by participants include consistency in speech, consistency in speech and action, and coherence. Indicators of respect and impartiality include acknowledgement of the moral status of opposing views, a cultivation of openness, and starting from the point of view of reaching possible agreement.[19]

Even though deliberative models of democracy are commonly celebrated for their clear practical implications, a spate of critical

---

[15] This raises the question as to whether this model is simply too demanding. Chambers overcomes this problem by arguing that it is not if it is seen in terms of long-term discussion, rather than as a decision rule. Participation is not a good in itself (as for republicans). It is important insofar as it has the power to shape politics.

[16] Who decides whether consent is autonomous? Chambers argues that a theory of deliberative democracy cannot be combined with false consciousness, since it holds that generalizable interests do not exist prior to our entry into discourse. However, deliberative models assume 'a theory of mistaken consciousness'. That is, people can come to see that they were mistaken to believe such and such to be in their interest (Chambers, *Reasonable Democracy*, p. 205). This cannot be determined from an observer's point of view. Participants themselves must question their motives, look at the genealogy of their beliefs, and ask what interests their arguments serve. Chambers does not address the conditions under which such self-reflexive questioning becomes a possibility. I argue later that it is only once disagreement, rather than agreement, becomes an essential part of a democratic ethos that such questioning becomes a realistic possibility.

[17] External coercion includes threats and bribes, while internal coercion involves psychological pressure, rhetorical manipulation, and deception. Both ideas of coercion stand in need of further discussion, especially with respect to the conception of subjectivity they presuppose.

[18] Chambers, *Reasonable Democracy*, pp. 208–9.

[19] For an excellent discussion of these conditions in cases where sensitive issues are under discussion, see M. E. Warren, 'What should and should not be said: Deliberating sensitive issues', *Journal of Social Philosophy* 37, no. 2 (2006), 163–81.

writings have recently begun to challenge this consensus. David Miller, Lynn M. Sanders and Iris Marion Young, among others, have added their voices to the criticisms made by commentators such as James Tully almost a decade ago.[20] These arguments may be categorized into three broad groups. The first group includes those such as Sanders, who are initially located within deliberative democratic theory, but who end up problematizing the idea of deliberative democracy. The second includes those loyal critics who, starting from positions internal to the conception of democracy defended, wish to bolster and strengthen it through their criticism.[21] Here I would locate the work of Chambers, Dryzek and Bohman. Finally, there are those who criticize deliberative democracy from the 'outside', and aim to develop a conception of democracy starting from very different, if not conflicting, premises. All of these criticisms, in their different ways, can be related to the claims to universality made in the name of deliberative democracy. Here I focus initially on the work of the first two groups, and then turn to the third when I discuss post-structuralist critiques of deliberative democracy. However, it should be noted that these divisions return in subsequent chapters with respect to the discussion of different features of democracy.

Sanders' work exemplifies the approach taken by the first group. Contrary to received opinion, she suggests that where there are tensions between deliberation and democracy they are likely to be resolved in favour of deliberation. If one of the main aims of deliberative theorists is to deepen democracy, it fails since it in fact displays anti-democratic tendencies. These tendencies can be ascribed to

---

[20] D. Miller, 'Is deliberative democracy unfair to disadvantaged groups', in D' Entrèves (ed.), *Democracy as Public Deliberation*, pp. 201–25; Sanders, 'Against deliberation'; I. M. Young, 'Difference as resource for democratic communication', in J. Bohman and W. Rehg (eds.), *Deliberative Democracy. Essays on Reason and Politics* (Cambridge, Mass.: MIT Press, 1997), pp. 383–406; J. Tully, 'Wittgenstein and political philosophy: Understanding practices of critical reflection', *Political Theory* 17, no. 2 (1989), 172–204.

[21] Chambers, *Reasonable Democracy*; Benhabib, 'Liberal dialogue versus a critical theory of discursive legitimation', in N. L. Rosenblum (ed.), *Liberalism and the Moral Life* (Cambridge, Mass.: Harvard University Press, 1998).

a variety of factors. To begin with, Sanders draws attention to the fact
that deliberation is not typically justified by arguments that deliberative democracy is what 'ordinary citizens would themselves
recommend'.[22] While this may not in itself make deliberation undemocratic, it does open up the possibility of investigating the arguments as to why deliberation may not appeal to ordinary citizens.
These may be divided into arguments attaching to the conception of
deliberation advanced by theorists of deliberative democracy, and
those that relate to issues not addressed or ignored by this conception
of democracy, thus seemingly falling outside its scope. Arguments
relating to the conception of deliberation utilized include the connotations of 'rationality, reserve, … community, selflessness, and
universalism'. These features, Sanders suggests, undermine the
democratic claims made in the name of deliberation since citizens do
not all have the same capacity for articulating their arguments in
'rational' terms. In other words, while proclaiming its universality
deliberative democracy in fact favours one particular argumentative
style over another. This criticism by Sanders is bolstered by arguments relating to issues not receiving sufficient attention by deliberative democratic theorists. The latter pertain to questions of voice,
especially where they overlap with an uneven distribution of the
material prerequisites for deliberation.[23] In this respect Sanders
argues that deliberation requires 'not only equality in resources and
the guarantee of equal opportunity to articulate persuasive arguments
but also equality in "epistemological authority", in the capacity
to evoke acknowledgement of one's arguments'.[24] Young raises

---

[22] Sanders, 'Against deliberation', 348.

[23] Fraser argues that Habermas needs to take account of the economic requirements
of deliberative democracy. See N. Fraser, 'Rethinking the public sphere: a
contribution to a critique of actually existing democracy', in C. Calhoun (ed.),
Habermas and the Public Sphere (Cambridge, Mass.: MIT Press), pp. 109–42. See
also W. E. Scheuerman's discussion of her relation to Habermas in 'Between
radicalism and resignation: Democratic theory in Habermas in Between Facts and
Norms', in P. Dews (ed.), Habermas. A Critical Reader (Oxford: Blackwell, 1999),
pp. 153–77.

[24] Sanders, 'Against deliberation', 349.

related problems, contending that as a consequence of the emphasis
deliberative democracy places upon universality and the exclusion of
particular perspectives it is, at best, blind to the resource of difference
for enriching democratic discussion and, at worst, undemocratic in
its overemphasis of apparently universalistic 'public-spiritedness'.[25]
Rather than seeing a stark opposition between the impartial and
unitary on the one hand, and the partial and differentiated on the
other,[26] Young argues that democratic dialogue must, of necessity,
include critical dialogue among the plurality of socially differentiated
perspectives present in the social field.[27] In each case, the question of
'universality' in deliberative democracy is at issue. Its favouring of an
idealized form of discussion aiming to resolve normative disputes to
the satisfaction of all, far removed from day-to-day communication,
together with its emphasis on agreement[28] assume that a clash of
opposing forces can move participants forward in a search for a
'common ground'.[29]

DEMOCRATIC AGREEMENT AND GENERALIZABLE INTERESTS

The search for agreement is the motivational premise of deliberative
democracy.[30] Habermas takes 'the type of action aimed at reaching

[25] Young, 'Difference as a resource', pp. 383–406.
[26] This is a common strategy followed by adherents to Habermas' theory of communicative rationality.
[27] Young, 'Difference as a resource', pp. 400–1.
[28] Chambers, *Reasonable Democracy*, p. 98.
[29] Chambers, *Reasonable Democracy*, p. 162. Such a common ground, Chambers argues, may range from 'agreement on substantive generalizable interests' to an agreement to disagree, or an agreement to settle for a compromise. She suggests that even, and especially in cases where there is no common ground, we should keep our disputes within the bounds of fair communication. If we do not try to reason with each other, we are left only with the option of coercion (Chambers, *Reasonable Democracy*, pp. 162–3). This, Wittgenstein would argue, is just playing with words. From the foregoing, it does not seem as if the 'common ground' has any limits; hence, it has no purchasing power either. I return to the issue of the common ground and its constitution in Chapter 4.
[30] Where does an interest in agreement come from? Chambers argues that motivation is tied to the importance of the norm to the participants and the actions they want

understanding to be fundamental'; 'other forms of social action – for example, conflict, competition, strategic action in general – are *derivatives* of action oriented to reaching an understanding'.[31] If agreement is the motivational premise of deliberative democracy, the question immediately arises as to what people can agree upon, and how that agreement comes about. If people simply deliberated on the basis of furthering their own interests, then the possibility of agreement would rest on their sharing an interest. However, Habermas does not treat interests as fixed in advance; they are not understood as 'brute facts'.[32] Rather, part of what discourse is about is judging what is in one's best interest. As Chambers points out,

> deliberation is really about working out interests we share with each other which can furnish a reason for collectively recognizing [*sic*] a norm. According to Habermas, what we search for in practical discourse are generalizable interests.[33]

What then are generalizable interests?[34] Three characteristics of generalizable interests, of which traffic rules and laws against murder are examples, are of particular importance. First, generalizable interests represent overlapping particular, but not necessarily identical interests (i.e. an interest in peace and one in *agape* may lead to agreement on the norm of religious toleration). Second, the conception of interests at work here includes not only material benefits, but also the pursuit of moral ideals. Third, this idea does not presuppose a set of universally true human needs that we attempt to discover through discourse. The idea is that through criticism,

---

to continue. 'If we wish to continue, we must resolve the dispute' (Chambers, *Reasonable Democracy*, p. 191). Hence, agreement is presupposed by the whole approach. If so, an ambiguity is immediately introduced for agreement becomes both what is presupposed and what is to be sought through the process of deliberation.

[31] Habermas, quoted in Chambers, *Reasonable Democracy*, p. 157. Emphasis added.
[32] Chambers, *Reasonable Democracy*, p. 102.
[33] Chambers, *Reasonable Democracy*, p. 102.
[34] Chambers, *Reasonable Democracy*, pp. 102–4.

argument and so on, one can arrive at an interpretation of a collective need. Thus, generalizable interests are open to revision. The central issue with respect to such interests concerns their link to Habermas' universalization principle.[35] For Habermas, justifiable (universalizable) norms are those norms that incorporate generalizable interests.[36] The test for such norms is whether they are acceptable in actual argumentation to all those who are potentially affected by them.[37] The nature and character of the process of rational deliberation through which such norms are established, and generalizable interests are reached, is thus of the utmost importance. Habermas provides an account of this process, *inter alia*, in *Between Facts and Norms*. There he sets out to develop a reconstructive sociology of democracy, which chooses its basic concepts in such a way that it can identify 'particles and fragments of an "existing reason" already incorporated in political practice, however distorted these may be'.[38]

In outlining his process model of democracy, Habermas distinguishes three stages, coinciding with different types of discourse.[39] Stage 1, characterized by *pragmatic* discourse, occurs where experts construct possible programmes and their consequences as, for instance, occur in parliament. Expert knowledge is fallible, not neutral and uncontested. Actors make decisions on the basis of hypothetically presupposed interests and value preferences. 'Ought' is relative to given ends and values. Such pragmatic discourses justify

---

[35] For a discussion of Habermas' universalization principle, see S. K. White, *The Recent Work of Jürgen Habermas. Reason, Justice and Modernity* (Cambridge: Cambridge University Press, 1989), pp. 48–58.

[36] White, *The Recent Work of Jürgen Habermas*, p. 49.

[37] This procedure stands in contrast to the Kantian test of the categorical imperative, which can be tested monologically. McCarthy (quoted in W. Outhwaite, *Habermas. A Critical Introduction* (Cambridge: Polity Press, 1994), p. 54) argues that the emphasis here shifts from 'what each can will without contradiction to be a universal law to what each can will in agreement to be a universal norm'.

[38] Habermas, *Between Facts and Norms*, p. 287.

[39] Habermas, *Between Facts and Norms*, pp. 162–5. In his 'Postscript' Habermas points out that these three aspects should be understood as analytically distinct, but should not be treated as a matter of linear development. See Habermas, *Between Facts and Norms*, p. 565, note 3.

rational choices between alternatives, but preferences and interests remain external to these discourses. In Stage 2, characterized by *ethical-political* discourses, value orientations themselves are up for discussion and call for a form of discourse that goes beyond contested interests. At this stage, the hermeneutic self-understanding of participants develops and they become aware of deeper consonances of common forms of life. Thus, there is an overlap between rules of argumentation and membership of historical community. Examples provided by Habermas include ecological questions, traffic control, and immigration policy. Finally, in Stage 3, characterized by *moral* discourses, contested interests and value orientations are submitted to a universalization test within a constitutional framework of rights. This demands a type of discourse in which there is a stepping back from all contingent existing normative contexts, and a break with everyday taken-for-granted assumptions, so that an 'autonomous will' or rational consensus can be developed.[40]

A SUPPLEMENTARY RELATION:
RATIONAL CONSENSUS, BARGAINING AND
COMPROMISE FORMATIONS

The nature of generalizable interests, generated in the process of the development of a rational consensus, can be further clarified when contrasted with what is involved in bargaining and compromise formations. Habermas acknowledges that often neither ethico-political nor moral discourses are options. It is here that we move towards bargaining producing compromise formations.[41] Compromise formations arise where it is clear that the sort of agreement required by deliberation cannot be reached since interests continue to conflict.

---

[40] Ferrara argues out that these three types of discourse provide different answers to the questions 'What should I do?' and 'What should we do?' See A. Ferrara, 'The communicative paradigm in moral theory', in D. M. Rasmussen (ed.), *Handbook of Critical Theory* (Oxford: Blackwell, 1996), pp. 127–9.

[41] For a discussion by Habermas of Elster on bargaining, see, Habermas, *Between Facts and Norms*, pp. 165–7. See also J. Elster, 'Introduction', in J. Elster (ed.), *Deliberative Democracy* (Cambridge: Cambridge University Press, 1998), pp. 5–7.

Habermas argues in this respect that the 'basic guidelines for compromise construction must themselves be justified in discursive terms'.[42] This, White argues, makes it possible to distinguish between legitimate or fair and illegitimate compromises, where the latter would be mere disguises for power relations. While in the case of rational consensus, the reasons have to convince participants in the same way, in the case of compromise formations parties may accept a compromise for different reasons. In the latter case, there are no generalizable interests, and power relations cannot be neutralized. As a result, we find bargaining between success-oriented parties willing to cooperate. The discourse principle (D) is still brought to bear, but only indirectly so, since parties use threats and promises (all parties are given the chance to intervene so that (particular) interests have an equal chance of prevailing).[43]

Now, it is important to clarify the implications for democratic will formation implied by the movement from rational consensus to compromise formations and vice versa. Habermas contrasts the democratic process and will formation theorized in his discourse theory with liberal and republican models of democracy.[44] He argues that the liberal model takes the form of compromises between interests, and the rules of compromise formations are justified in terms of liberal rights with an emphasis on universal and equal suffrage. In the case of republican politics, democratic will formation is tied much more closely to the ethico-political self-understanding of the community.[45] Consequently, deliberation draws on the substantive support of a culturally established background consensus shared by citizens. While the discourse model draws on aspects of both the foregoing, it is distinguished from them by the fact that it is not grounded in universal human rights, or in the ethical substance of

---

[42] White, *Recent Work of Jürgen Habermas*, p. 76.

[43] For a critical discussion and contextualization of the U (Universalization) and D principles, see Ferrara, 'The communicative paradigm in moral theory', pp. 131–5.

[44] See Habermas, *Between Facts and Norms*, pp. 296–302.

[45] Habermas takes Hannah Arendt to be exemplary of the republican tradition.

the community. Rather, as we have seen, it is grounded in rules of discourse oriented to reaching understanding, which arise, in the final instance, from the structure of linguistic communication. The democratic process is thus invested with stronger normative connotations than in the liberal model, but weaker than in the republican case. The emphasis is on the institutionalization or proceduralization of will formation, and the latter is not dependent upon the presence of an active collective citizenry.

The process of democratic deliberation involves all three aspects of practical reason outlined above: its pragmatic, ethical and moral uses. Democratic deliberation may include and mix together any of these uses of reason. It is thus 'a complex discursive network which includes argumentation of various sorts, bargaining and compromise, and political communication for the purposes of the free expression of opinions'.[46] Bohman argues that this conception of democratic deliberation still sets the standard of consensus – that laws must meet the agreement of all citizens, and that the process of law-making be discursive (structured according to mutual recognition of each other as free and equal) – too high. The introduction of compromise as an alternative democratic outcome by Habermas does not, according to Bohman, solve the problem of diverse and potentially conflicting cultural self-understandings entering into the debate on particular issues.[47] I do not wish here to enter into what is already a long-standing debate on the extent to which discourse theoretic principles could be kept pure and free from contamination by any specific cultural content.[48] What is important here, is a related question, but one which focuses on the status of the relation between rational consensus and compromise formations: is it logically possible both to introduce modifications and extensions to the

[46] J. Bohman, 'Critical theory and democracy', in D. M. Rasmussen (ed.), *Handbook of Critical Theory* (Oxford: Blackwell, 1996), p. 206.

[47] Bohman, 'Critical theory and democracy', p. 206.

[48] See, for instance, M. Walzer, *Thick and Thin. Moral Argument at Home and Abroad* (Notre Dame, Ind.: University of Notre Dame Press, 1994).

conceptualization of consensual will formation, and to retain the absolute primacy of rational consensus over compromise formations? This question can be, and has been formulated variously. At its most abstract it concerns the nature of supplementarity, understood here in the Derridean sense,[49] but it also emerges in the attempts to modify Habermasian discourse theory in the move from ideal to real political discourse. The charge is that in either case a discourse of mere 'addition' will not do.[50] A supplement supplements since it fills a lack, adding something to what was previously considered to be 'full' and complete in itself. Whatever else may be necessary, a relation of supplementarity calls for a reconsideration of the original model. Thus the claim is that no dualistic ideal/real or theoretical/empirical model would overcome the problem, since such models still depend on a thinking of the original as pure and intact, not recognizing the lack present in it.

FROM DECISION RULES TO ONGOING PROCESSES

Numerous commentators on Habermas' discourse theory have recently focused on the question of the movement from the ideal to the real. Indeed, as William Rehg states in his Introduction to *Between Facts and Norms*, this book is conceived of as an attempt to bridge normative and empirical approaches to democracy[51] and

---

[49] Supplementarity here is understood in the Derridean sense. See, J. Derrida, *Of Grammatology* (Baltimore, Md.: The Johns Hopkins University Press, 1974), especially Part II. For a discussion of supplementarity as infrastructure, see R. Gasché, *The Tain of the Mirror. Derrida and the Philosophy of Reflection* (Cambridge, Mass.: Harvard University Press, 1986), pp. 205–12. It is important to note that the deconstruction of a conceptual ordering is thus not simply a matter of inverting the relationship of centre and margin. Rather, 'it is a matter of showing ... that the distinction between center and margin in question can only be made ... via a covert dependence on its marginalised component'. B. Harrison, 'White mythology revisited: Derrida and his critics on reason and rhetoric', *Critical Inquiry* 25 (1999), 514.

[50] Both Habermas and Elster are guilty of this move, and so are countless other commentators. They both assume that the 'original' model of deliberation can be left intact, while 'bargaining', 'argumentation' and so on, are 'added' onto the idea of a pure deliberation.

[51] W. Rehg, 'Translator's introduction', in Habermas, *Between Facts and Norms*, pp. ix–x.

Habermas himself articulates it as a central question, acknowledging that at present 'it is unclear how this procedural concept, so freighted with idealizations, can link up with empirical investigations that conceive politics primarily as an arena of power processes'.[52] Habermas sets about correcting this deficit via a 'reconstructive sociology of democracy' and his process model of democracy referred to above draws on the insights he gains as a result. One of the most sustained attempts within the deliberative democratic tradition to work through the shift from the ideal of undistorted communication to a discussion of 'real' politics is that offered by Chambers in her *Reasonable Democracy*. The main question occupying me in respect of her work is whether the modified account of deliberative democracy she outlines can ultimately be reconciled with the idealized presuppositions of Habermas' work, or whether it necessitates a weakening of that model in crucial respects.

Chambers' treatment of the movement from ideal to real is informed by the acknowledgement that real agreements can only ever be an approximation of the ideals set out in the Habermasian model:

> real agreements can never be perfectly universal, they never settle a
> question once and for all. Through the idea of an ideal
> communication community we can imagine the conditions of a
> perfectly rational consensus, but inasmuch as we can never attain
> the ideal in the real world, the question becomes the degree of
> *approximation*.[53]

Everything here depends on how 'approximation' is understood and how precisely it relates to the ideal of a 'perfectly rational consensus'.[54]

---

[52] Habermas, *Between Facts and Norms*, p. 287.

[53] Chambers, *Reasonable Democracy*, p. 171, emphasis added.

[54] It is clear that the ideal speech situation represents only the formal conditions of discourse. As Chambers argues, 'The philosopher reconstructs the conditions that would have to hold if we wanted to say that an agreement was reasonable and authentic ... As a formal representation, the ideal speech situation is drastically limited. It can tell us what would have to be the case for a political norm to be considered collectively binding, but it cannot, by itself, tell us which norms would

Before proceeding to investigate this question directly, it is useful to note why Chambers finds it necessary to introduce the idea of an approximation at all. She holds, in common with other commentators on deliberative models of democracy, that the idea of an ideal speech situation is too rigid and narrow 'to capture all that is entailed in a collective evaluation of the appropriateness of a norm'. In particular, she argues, it does not capture the idea that practical discourse is primarily intended 'to be an undertaking in the real (less than ideal) world by real (less than ideal) social actors'.[55] Nevertheless, she regards it as a misunderstanding of discourse ethics to think that we should in all spheres of life strive for the achievement of consensus.[56]

Even though achieving consensus is not conceived of as the aim of all social interaction, there is no disputing the fact that the model of deliberative democracy does indeed privilege consensus over dissensus. Chambers, for her part, nevertheless suggests that this privileging of consensus (the reaching of full understanding between actors) does not put into question the role of pluralism, diversity, and difference within discourse ethics.[57] In contrast to liberal pluralists, post-structuralists and rational choice theorists, all of whom have objections in this respect, Chambers argues that discourse ethics offers no guarantee that discourse will always be successful. The problem of otherness, disagreement and so on may be permanent features of our collective life, but we cannot draw the conclusion that all problems are of this nature. On Chambers' reading, deliberative democratic theory argues only that deliberation *may* lead to convergence, and this is premised on the idea that preferences are shaped by culture and communication. This means that certain types of

---

or would not pass the test ... By itself [it] has no content.' (Chambers, *Reasonable Democracy*, p. 166.)

[55] Chambers, *Reasonable Democracy*, p. 155.

[56] We cannot 'make a living, write a book, teach a class, or run a business discursively'. The ideal speech situation provides guidelines, not for all social interaction, but for the process of deliberation. Chambers, *Reasonable Democracy*, p. 156.

[57] Chambers, *Reasonable Democracy*, p. 157.

culture and communication are more likely than others to promote an interest in cooperative dispute resolution.[58]

As noted earlier, this rendering of deliberative democratic theory amounts to a substantially weaker account than Habermas' much stronger claims concerning universalizability. Chambers denies that there is a principled conflict between pluralism and consensual will formation since the search for agreement ignores the fact that 'disagreement, conflict, dispute, argumentation, opposition, in short, nay saying, are *essential aspects* of the discourse process'.[59] This claim stands in sharp contrast to Habermas' argument that conflict, competition, and so forth, are *derivatives* of action oriented to reaching an understanding, and are thus subordinate, if not supplementary to it. Thus, even though Chambers concurs with Habermas' view that pluralism,[60] diversity and difference 'furnish the very conditions that make universalized norms possible' in post-conventional societies, she cannot resolve her breach with the basic status accorded to agreement and disagreement respectively in Habermas' work. Chambers' emphasis on the approximation of the real to the ideal also

---

[58] Chambers, *Reasonable Democracy*, p. 162. This way of dealing with the possibility of convergence is much weaker than in Habermas. For a discussion of the different forms of agreement reached in different sorts of discourse (negotiated compromise, ethico-political and moral discourses) see Habermas, *Between Facts and Norms*, pp. 180–4. See also Habermas' argument that whereas parties 'can agree to a negotiated compromise for different reasons, the consensus brought about through argument must rest on identical reasons able to convince the parties *in the same way*'. Habermas, *Between Facts and Norms*, p. 339.

[59] Chambers, *Reasonable Democracy*, p. 158.

[60] Chambers, *Reasonable Democracy*, pp. 158–9. There are numerous issues here in need of further discussion, in particular, the concept of pluralism deployed by Chambers and Habermas, both of who start from what they call the 'fact of pluralism'. Exactly how weak this is, is reflected in what Habermas regards as examples of disagreement, such as traffic rules and basic institutional rules. Habermas holds that there are enough examples to suggest that 'increasing scope for individual options does not decrease the chances for agreement concerning presumptively common interests' (quoted in Chambers, *Reasonable Democracy*, p. 159). The 'in principle/in practice' dichotomy, the evolutionary view of society underlying the move from 'traditional' to 'post-conventional' societies, and the absence of an account of the subject of 'consensual will formation' all stand in need of further investigation.

leads her to introduce other modifications to Habermas' model. In particular, she argues that Habermas overemphasizes purely procedural requirements. More attention should be given to citizens' willingness to participate, and to practical discourse understood as a process of interconnected discourses, many of which do not take place in formal settings. These considerations lead Chambers to assert that we need more emphasis on processes of argumentation.[61] Nevertheless, this acknowledgement does not lead her to investigate actual processes of political argumentation, or the different kinds of argumentation in which one may engage. I will argue that both of these dimensions need to be explored in full if the full consequences of her modifications are to be pursued.

Chambers limits herself to point out that people are 'swayed by arguments'.[62] This, she points out, happens over time. People often re-evaluate their positions between conversations rather than during them. This gradual, fragmentary process of becoming 'convinced of something' is the product of a web of conversational interaction that includes many exchanges. This emphasis on a 'web of conversations' changes the way in which we think about consensus. Crucially, for Chambers consensus is no longer conceived of as reached at this or that point, but is a product of many conversations. Thus, practical discourse should be understood as a *long-term consensus-forming process* and not as a *decision procedure*. The latter implies a set of rules that govern closure; as a decision rule, discourse stipulates that full, rational agreement under the ideal conditions of discourse of all affected by a norm constitutes the point of closure. The former is to do with the formation of opinion preceding the making of decisions. This means that 'consensual will formation' should not be understood as the outcome of *one* conversation but must be seen as the cumulative product of many criss-crossing conversations over time.

---

[61] Chambers, *Reasonable Democracy*, p. 196.

[62] Chambers, *Reasonable Democracy*, p. 170. I return to the question as to what precisely is meant by 'being swayed by arguments' and the 'force of the better argument' in Chapter 2.

As Chambers' argument shows, the move to actual argumentation entails a considerable weakening of the claims advanced by Habermas (even though Chambers does not focus on these consequences of her argument). In particular, the shift from decision-procedures to a long-term consensus-forming process loosens the grip of the emphasis on the 'reaching of rational agreement under ideal conditions of discourse'. It is not only that we need more emphasis on the 'process of argumentation' as she suggests. This very shift in emphasis also necessitates a re-valuation of the nature of argumentation and its role in democratic politics. In particular, we need to give careful consideration to the variety of additional issues that arise once attention is shifted to practices of reason-giving. I turn to a fuller discussion of these issues in Chapter 2. However, it is worth noting at this point that several commentators have sought to offer reformulations of the Habermasian position on deliberation. Elster, for instance, suggests bargaining as an alternative mode of decision-making to deliberation.[63] Sanders focuses on testimony as an alternative to deliberation in order to overcome the problems associated with 'voice' and epistemic authority she locates in the deliberative model.[64] It is also interesting to note that she explicitly associates this move with the search for a model of democratic engagement that 'allows for the expression of different perspectives rather than seeking what's common'.[65] Hence, here the pursuit of commonality itself is problematized. Others have developed more general positions concerning the role of argumentation in, for instance, policy processes,[66] as well as analysis of styles of argumentation.[67] What these

---

[63] See Elster, 'Introduction'. Several of the contributions to this volume take this further, and develop further conceptual distinctions as, for instance, between deliberation and discussion.

[64] Sanders, 'Against deliberation', 369–73.

[65] Sanders, 'Against deliberation', 371.

[66] See, for instance, G. Majone, *Evidence, Argument, and Persuasion in the Policy Process* (New Haven, Conn.: Yale University Press, 1989).

[67] See I. Hacking, 'Styles of scientific reasoning', in J. Rajchman and C. West (eds.), *Post-Analytic Philosophy* (New York: Columbia University Press: 1985), ch. 9.

writers have in common is their concern with developing finely grained arguments concerning kinds of argumentation, all of which could be taken to problematize the idealized view of 'deliberation' conceived in the Habermasian sense. Nevertheless, these conceptual refinements are, more often than not, simply treated as 'additions' to deliberation. Like Elster, Sanders and Chambers fail to explore the consequences of their insights for the very idea of deliberation. They singularly neglect to inquire, for instance, whether any revision in its status as norm is needed, whether a wider conception of argumentation also necessitates re-engagement with the relation between persuasion and deliberation, and between agreement and deliberation. It is to an alternative model of democracy that one needs to turn in order to find the space in which these and related issues could be thematized explicitly.

POST-STRUCTURALIST CONCEPTIONS OF RADICAL DEMOCRACY: THE PLACE OF DISAGREEMENT

The principal ideas of radical democracy may be related back, on the one hand, to the liberalization of the radical tradition (while holding onto the latter's insights into the inequalities of power) and, on the other hand, to the democratization of the liberal tradition.[68] Contemporary radical democrats reject both the instrumental character of liberalism and the anti-political reductionism of much of the Marxist and socialist traditions. They also share three core ideas. They include, first, the centrality given to the political; second, an emphasis on the construction and articulation, rather than mere aggregation, of interests and identities; and third, the attention given to the process of subject formation in general, and the constitution of democratic identities in particular. However, beyond these broad statements, differences among radical democrats inspired by critical theory and post-structuralist thought respectively start to emerge. There are three key

---

[68] I have discussed this further in A. J. Norval, 'Radical democracy', in J. Foweraker and B. Clarke (eds.), *Dictionary of Democratic Thought* (London: Routledge, 2001).

areas in which radical democratic theorists differ quite markedly from one another. The first concerns the goal of democratic argumentation. As argued above, for deliberative theorists the goal is the reaching of a rational consensus. This stands in sharp contrast to radical democrats in the post-structuralist tradition, who are concerned with the disruptive and dislocatory potential of democracy. Secondly, while deliberative conceptions of democracy proceed from a model of unconstrained dialogue, devoid of power and of 'distortions', post-structuralists argue that power relations are intrinsic to their account of democracy. Finally, in contrast to the Habermasian project, post-structuralists make no attempt to specify normative preconditions and foundations for democratic discourse. Whereas deliberative democratic politics, in its strong procedural form as defended by Habermas, immunizes politics against the forces of cultural and ethical life,[69] theorists of agonistic and antagonistic politics emphasize the need to contest such ethical and cultural questions.

What then, more specifically, do post-structuralist accounts of radical democracy have to offer us? Most centrally, it brings into consideration relations of power, hegemony, argumentation and an emphasis on disagreement[70] rather than consensus as central to an understanding of democratic processes. The centrality given to disagreement in the post-structuralist theorization of democracy arises directly from one of its basic ontological presuppositions, namely, the 'impossibility of closure' of any identity or structure. This is important, for it affects the status of disagreement in the model, making it not simply an empirical feature of political life, but something arising from a constitutive characteristic of modern society. This *ontological* claim finds different forms of expression in different theorists.[71]

---

[69] Benhabib, 'The democratic moment', p. 9

[70] I use the term 'disagreement' here to indicate a plethora of phenomena – including dissensus, conflict and antagonism – conceptualized in very different ways within the post-structuralist tradition.

[71] For Laclau it consists in the thesis of the 'impossibility of society'; for Žižek in the thesis of the lack in the subject; for Lefort, in the non-closure of the gap between being and discourse, and for Mouffe in the centrality of the political understood in

For instance, for Lefort a forgetting of the primary division upon which it is instituted marks the formation of the modern state. While society can relate to itself only on the condition that it forges a representation of its unity, these representations are secondary accretions, covering over the fundamental breach between 'being' and 'discourse'.[72] The moment of the institution of a social order is thus always already that of a particular imaginary regime. Lefort argues that it is here that we find one of Marx's main contributions to our understanding of modern society, for Marx glimpses the illusion that lies at its heart, namely, the idea that the institution of the social can account for itself. But this illusion, Lefort argues, is always subject to failure. Ideology cannot operate 'without disclosing itself, that is, without revealing itself as a discourse, without letting a gap appear between this discourse and that about which it speaks, and hence it entails a development which reflects the impossibility of effacing its traces'.[73] In modern democratic societies, this primary division is not simply effaced, but is marked in a specific manner. Lefort holds that democracy

> is instituted and sustained by the *dissolution of the markers of certainty*. It inaugurates a history in which people experience a fundamental indeterminacy as to the basis of power, law and knowledge, and as to the basis of relations between *self* and *other*, at every level of social life.[74]

While the work of ideology is to cover over this dissolution and to attempt to re-establish certainty, it ultimately is doomed to failure given the constitutive character of social division. Nevertheless, in the case of a democratic regime, the dissolution of the 'markers of

the Schmittian sense. See E. Laclau and C. Mouffe, *Hegemony and Socialist Strategy. Towards a Radical Democratic Politics* (London: Verso, 1985); C. Lefort, *The Political Forms of Modern Society* (Cambridge: Polity Press, 1986); and S. Žižek, *The Sublime Object of Ideology* (London: Verso, 1989).

[72] Lefort, *The Political Forms of Modern Society*, p. 196.

[73] Lefort, *The Political Forms of Modern Society*, p. 204.

[74] C. Lefort, *Democracy and Political Theory* (Minneapolis: University of Minnesota Press, 1988), p. 19.

certainty' opens a privileged place for the role of dissent, disagreement, antagonism, difference, and all those figures that, in the deliberative model, are indicators of a less than perfect consensus. Other radical democrats of a post-structuralist persuasion share these insights. Jacques Rancière articulates an argument not dissimilar to that of Lefort. For Rancière, anti-democratic politics also entails depoliticization, the demand that 'things should go back to normal'.[75] Chantal Mouffe, inspired by Carl Schmitt, similarly argues that the denial of the 'irreducible antagonistic element present in social relations' can have disastrous consequences for the defence of democratic institutions, for to negate the political will not make it disappear. It can only lead 'to bewilderment in the face of its manifestations and to impotence in dealing with them'.[76] For all of these thinkers, indeed, disagreement, conflict and dissensus take their central role from the fact that it arises, and is reflective of, a deeper ontological condition, a condition that is of crucial importance in the formation of democratic regimes.[77]

However, it is significant that, contrary to the manner in which it is often portrayed by deliberative theorists, there is nothing irrational or subjectivist in this emphasis on disagreement. To the contrary, disagreement forms the core of the logic of the political. As with the concept of disagreement itself, 'the political' is characterized variously by different post-structuralist political theorists. As already noted, Mouffe takes her lead from Schmitt in this respect arguing that he makes us 'aware of the dimension of the political that is linked to the existence of an element of hostility among human

---

[75] S. Žižek, *The Ticklish Subject* (London: Verso, 1999), p. 188. The specific manner in which Rancière accounts for this depoliticization is of special importance, for it directly addresses the question of the relation between participants in the process of democratic argumentation. I return to these issues in Chapter 4.

[76] C. Mouffe, *The Return of the Political* (London: Verso, 1993), p. 140.

[77] Not all radical democrats inspired by post-structuralism conceptualize the relation between this ontological condition and democracy in the same fashion. For Rancière, for instance, there is a direct relation between democracy and the ontological conditions that make disagreement central. For Laclau, on the other hand, dislocation may be one of the conditions making possible the emergence of a democratic regime, but it is not internally related to it.

beings'.[78] Politics then becomes an activity aimed at working through
the effects of the political in social life, and democratic politics
requires an introduction of a distinction between the figure of the
enemy and that of the adversary.[79] It is clear that neither in the general
nor in the specific case of democratic politics is disagreement something that escapes a political logic. This is even more clearly articulated in the work of Rancière, for whom politics 'occurs when the
egalitarian contingency disrupts the natural pecking order', and when
this disruption produces a specific mechanism, namely, 'the dividing of
society into parts that are not "true" parts; the setting-up of one part as
equal to the whole in the name of a "property" that is not its own, and
of a "common" that is the community of a dispute'.[80] The disagreement at the heart of the political logic is not one linked to the het-
erogeneity of language games, as it is for Lyotard. Nor is it a case of
participants engaging in an intersubjective relation 'in order to oppose
each other's interests and value systems and to put the validity of these
to the test' as for Habermas.[81] Rather, what is at stake is the problem of

> knowing whether the subjects who count in the interlocution 'are'
> or 'are not', whether they are speaking or just making a noise. It is
> knowing whether there is a case for seeing the object they designate
> as the visible object of the conflict. It is knowing whether the
> common language in which they are exposing the wrong is indeed a
> common language.[82]

One cannot therefore presuppose a mutual understanding as
Habermas does. Indeed, *the very possibility of commonality* and,
hence, of political community is what is in dispute in political
argumentation and disagreement, and what gets constituted through

---

[78] Mouffe, *The Return of the Political*, p. 2.
[79] Mouffe, *The Return of the Political*, p. 4. I return in Chapter 4 to a more detailed treatment of Mouffe's distinction between the 'enemy' and the 'adversary'.
[80] J. Rancière, *Disagreement. Politics and Philosophy* (Minneapolis: University of Minnesota Press, 1999), p. 18.
[81] Rancière, *Disagreement*, p. 44.   [82] Rancière, *Disagreement*, p. 50.

such argumentation. Rancière argues, for instance, that the utterance 'we proletarians' appeals to a community which is not already realized, and which does not already exist:

> a subject of enunciation creates an apparatus where a subject is named precisely to expose a particular wrong, to create a community around a particular dispute. That is to say, there is politics precisely when one reveals as false the evidence that the community exists already and everyone is already included.[83]

The disagreement at the heart of the political logic is thus not simply an empirical feature that can be overcome in favour of consensus. It is, indeed, constitutive of that logic, and a marker of its presence in democratic regimes. It marks the manner in which both argumentation and political subjectivity are understood. These concerns are elaborated upon in the chapters that follow. Suffice it to note at this point that, given this concern with disagreement, the argument on epistemic authority outlined by Sanders in her critique of the tension between deliberation and democracy ought not to be limited to a simple empirical feature of the democratic process. Gaining such authority is not simply a matter of adjusting or rectifying the relation between partners in deliberative discussion for this model presumes equality between participants. As Tully has shown in his analysis of constitutionalism in *Strange Multiplicity*, relations of domination more often than not shape such interactions. In this context he asks: 'How can the proponents of recognition bring forth the claims in a public forum in which their cultures have been excluded or demeaned for centuries?' and suggests two responses that have been typical within the traditions of modern constitutionalism:

> They can accept the authoritative languages and institutions, in which case their claims are rejected by conservatives or

---

[83] J. Rancière, 'Post-democracy, politics and philosophy', interview with J. Sumič and R. Riha, in D. Howarth and A. J. Norval (eds.), *Reconsidering the Political*, special issue of *Angelaki* (1994), 174.

comprehended by progressives within the very languages and institutions whose sovereignty and impartiality they question. Or they can refuse to play the game, in which case they become marginal and reluctant conscripts or they take up arms.[84]

This impasse, which can only be addressed once what Tully calls the 'restricted vision' held in place by modern constitutionalism is questioned, is discussed further in Chapter 4 in relation to the voicing of democratic claims and demands. Tully's point here serves to highlight the insufficiency of the response by defenders of deliberative democracy, namely, that our democratic practices simply have to be made 'more inclusive' and that there is in principle no problem with its conception of democracy. As Rancière's argument shows, what is at stake, what has to be constructed, and what cannot be presupposed is precisely the common space in which an argument may be made and heard and disagreement expressed. From this point of view, attempts finally to overcome disagreement as such are based on a misconception of the nature of the political in general, and demo-cratic politics more specifically. Nevertheless, this does not mean that disagreement is simply 'given'. As Mouffe argues, the fact that it is constitutive does not mean that it is not subject to negotiation. Radical democratic politics precisely aims to encircle and engage with this ontological feature, without attempting ever completely to supersede it. *How* this is done could be accounted for by means of a hegemonic approach to politics, an approach which precisely aims at conceptualizing what is involved in the articulation of commonalties and communities of dispute. In this context, as Tully argues, the 'perspicuous representation' of reasoning deployed to deal with dis-agreements should take place in the very language used to handle actual cases since abstract redescriptions of disputes (for instance in

---

[84] J. Tully, *Strange Multiplicity. Constitutionalism in an Age of Diversity* (Cambridge: Cambridge University Press, 1995), p. 56. See also Honig's important discussion of 'democratic takers' in B. Honig, *Democracy and the Foreigner* (Princeton, N.J.: Princeton University Press, 2001), p. 79.

the language of individual and collective rights) often 'shackles the ability to understand and causes us to dismiss as irrelevant the concrete cases which alone can help to understand how the conciliation is actually achieved'.[85]

A HEGEMONIC ACCOUNT OF UNIVERSALIZATION AND THE POSSIBILITY OF DEMOCRACY

Now, this call for attention to the actual and concrete cases in thinking about the process of constructing generalizable interests must avoid the extreme particularism and the subjectivism of which so-called 'post-modern' accounts of politics and social life stand accused. Laclau and Mouffe's work on radical democracy sets out to avoid precisely these problems.[86] Their conceptualization of radical democracy, and with it their account of the construction of generalizable interests, emanates from a post-Gramscian understanding of hegemony. Following Lefort, Laclau and Mouffe argue that a democratic order is one in which the locus of power becomes an empty place, a place that cannot be occupied. No 'individual and no group can be consubstantial with it'.[87] The break introduced by the democratic invention is one in which democratic society could be 'determined as a society whose institutional structure includes, as part of its "normal", "regular" reproduction, the moment of dissolution of the socio-symbolic bond'. As Žižek points out, for Lefort, at the moment of elections 'the whole hierarchical network of social relations is in a way suspended, put in parentheses; "society" as an organic unity ceases to exist'.[88] It is this suspension that brings to

---

[85] Tully, *Strange Multiplicity*, p. 173. Tully further points out that projecting 'such a general scheme over particular cases is analogous to, Wittgenstein suggests, a pupil in geography bringing a mass of falsely simplified ideas about the course and connections of the routes of rivers and mountain chains'.

[86] See, for instance, Laclau and Mouffe, *Hegemony and Socialist Strategy*, ch. 4; and C. Mouffe (ed.), *Dimensions of Radical Democracy* (London: Verso, 1992).

[87] Lefort, *Democracy and Political Theory*, p. 17. See also Laclau and Mouffe, *Hegemony and Socialist Strategy*, pp. 152–9.

[88] Žižek, *The Sublime Object of Ideology*, pp. 147–8.

the centre stage the struggles to occupy the place of power, and so foregrounds a non-foundationalist conception of hegemony.

Their understanding of radical democracy is reached via an elaboration and critique of the concept of hegemony in Marxist theory. Contrary to the dominant understanding in political science of hegemony as domination, Laclau and Mouffe follow Gramsci in his argument that hegemony involves ethical, moral and political leadership. However, while for Gramsci such leadership ultimately has a class core, Laclau and Mouffe untie the concept of hegemony from its class basis in Marxist theory, and hegemony becomes a form of social relation in which the unity of a political force is constituted through a process of articulation of elements with no necessary class belonging. This unmooring facilitates a two-fold shift in focus. First, it allows the emphasis to shift towards a concern with the construction and deconstruction of political identities and interests in general and, secondly, it opens up a whole realm of theorization of social and political relations based on their contingent articulation.[89] Similar to Rancière's argument outlined above, Laclau and Mouffe thus hold that both interests and identities result from contingent, historical processes of enunciation and articulation.

It is precisely these emphases that have led commentators to argue that an approach that apparently denies the possibility of universalism cannot but be 'subjectivist' and relativist. However, Laclau and Mouffe have persistently avoided the endorsement of subjectivism, relativism and particularism.[90] This is particularly clear in Laclau's account of the relation between particularism and universalism.[91]

---

[89] Articulation, in contradistinction to mediation in the Hegelian sense, involves a process of putting together of elements with no necessary belonging, such that their identity is modified as a result of the articulatory practice. See Laclau and Mouffe, *Hegemony and Socialist Strategy*, p. 105.

[90] They argue that far from such endorsement, making visible the contingency of social relations through a questioning of the logics of necessity dominant in the Marxist tradition leads to a rethinking of both those logics.

[91] See E. Laclau, 'Universalism, particularism and the question of identity', in E. Laclau, *Emancipation(s)* (London: Verso, 1996), pp. 20–35.

Drawing on deconstructive insights, Laclau endeavours to show the mutual imbrication and fundamental interconnectedness of the relation between universalism and particularism, instead of viewing them as mutually exclusive logics.[92] Neither a pure logic of universality, nor one of self-enclosed particularity is a possibility here. The articulation of claims to self-determination clearly demonstrates this point, for any specific and particular claim to the right to self-determination must also, of necessity, invoke the universal right to self-determination any appeal to particularity must, of necessity, always already pass through the universal. Now, in contrast to conceiving of the relation between the two in terms of incarnation, on the one hand, or in terms of a secularized eschatology on the other, an alternative appears. Laclau suggests that we think of the universal as a symbol of missing fullness, while the particular emerges as the always-failed attempt to embody that universal. As he puts it: 'The universal emerges out of the particular not as some principle underlying and explaining the particular, but as an incomplete horizon suturing the dislocated particular identity.'[93] This argument provides the link to their non-foundationalist conception of hegemony and democracy. A hegemonic politics is nothing other than a politics of struggle over the occupation of the position of the universal. And, if democracy is possible, Laclau argues, it is because 'the universal has no necessary body and no necessary content; different groups, instead, compete between themselves to temporarily give to their particularisms a function of universal representation'.[94] Moreover, this struggle, as we have seen, is a never-ending one since the place of power cannot be finally occupied. As a consequence, society generates a whole vocabulary of 'empty signifiers' whose function it is to attempt to fill this place temporarily.[95] Laclau

---

[92] A similar argument is also present in Balibar's writings on universalism. See E. Balibar, 'Ambiguous universality', *Differences: A Journal of Feminist Cultural Studies* 7, no. 1 (1995), 48–74.

[93] Laclau, *Emancipation(s)*, p. 28.   [94] Laclau, *Emancipation(s)*, p. 35.

[95] Griggs and Howarth argues in their analysis of the politics of airport expansion that signifiers such as 'freedom to fly', 'sustainable aviation' or 'demand management' can be regarded as empty signifiers, produced through the logic of linking demands

illustrates this point by reference to the symbols of Solidarity, which moved from being the particular demands of a group of workers in Gdansk, to signify a much wider popular camp against an oppressive regime. Once this has happened, its symbols 'became the symbols of the absent fullness of society'. In this case, the particular 'has transformed its very partiality' into a transcendent universality.[96]

To return to our earlier discussion of 'generalizable interests'. From the viewpoint of a non-foundationalist hegemonic politics, the very idea of generalizable interests would have to be recast in terms of a hegemonization of particular demands and the construction of empty signifiers. That is to say, particular demands, or identities, may become universalized in and through a process of contingent articulation and political struggle. The universality achieved under these circumstances is not 'merely' that reflecting the status quo or existing power relations. While the dimension of power can never be eliminated, and to seek to do so is to seek to live in a fully transparent society, the universalization of demands arising from a struggle for hegemony must transcend the specific demands and interests of a particular group. This conception of universalization also does not lack a set of standards against which political practices may be evaluated. While these standards are generated from drawing upon and developing the Gramscian conception of hegemony, they must, nevertheless, retain an intrasocietal character. In other words, they cannot be specified, as in the case of the conditions of ideal speech, outside any context, even though they are not limited to that context either. To see exactly how this is possible, it is necessary to return to the conceptualization of a Gramscian conception of hegemony.

As noted earlier, hegemony denotes a type of political relation as well as a substantive achievement. In the former case, one is

together into an equivalential chain with which subjects can identify. See S. Griggs and D. Howarth, 'Populism, localism and environmental politics: The logic and rhetoric of the Stop Stansted Expansion Campaign in the United Kingdom', www.essex.ac.uk/centres/TheoStud/onlinepapers.asp

[96] E. Laclau, *On Populist Reason* (London: Verso, 2005), pp. 81 and 226.

concerned with a type of articulatory relation where persuasion predominates over the use of force. In the latter case, one is concerned with whether or not a particular force has managed to achieve supremacy by imposing its will onto the rest of society through the creation of consent and the incorporation of interests of rival forces.[97] In this respect, it is useful to recall Gramsci's important distinction between economic-corporate struggles or 'bastard' forms of hegemony, and hegemony proper. In his early works, Gramsci argues that the working class can only become hegemonic if it takes into account the interests of other social classes and finds ways of combining them with its own interests. It therefore has to go beyond economic-corporate struggles in order to become a national force.[98] It is in and through this process of going beyond the specific interests animating a particular group's interventions in the political arena that the universalization of particularistic demands takes place. Without such universalization, we would not have hegemony, but a mere imposition of those demands on subordinate groups. The very process of constructing hegemony thus has a two-fold character. On the one hand, demands are always specific, even particularistic, in that they arise from the experiences and conditions of particular and limited groups. On the other hand, for those demands to become universalized, to function as a horizon in which more generalized demands may become inscribed, they need to be marked by something transcending their particularity.[99] Thus, there is both a

---

[97] For an in-depth discussion of the concept of hegemony in Laclau and Mouffe's work, see D. Howarth, 'Ideology, hegemony and political subjectivity', in I. Hampsher-Monk and J. Stanyer (eds.), Contemporary Political Studies, vol. II (Oxford: Political Studies Association of the UK, 1996), pp. 944–56.

[98] C. Mouffe, 'Hegemony and ideology in Gramsci', in C. Mouffe (ed.), Gramsci and Marxist Theory (London: Routledge and Kegan Paul, 1979), p. 180.

[99] Laclau introduces the terms 'myth' and 'imaginary' to characterize these different processes. For a discussion of the relation between these terms, and a Gramscian conception of hegemony, see A. J. Norval, 'Future trajectories of research in discourse theory: Political frontiers, myths and imaginaries, hegemony', in D. Howarth, A. J. Norval and Y. Stavrakakis (eds.), Discourse Theory and Political Analysis (Manchester: Manchester University Press, 2000), pp. 219–36.

contextual and a context-transcending dimension in the process of the hegemonization of a field of demands.

With this we have an account of the construction of interests and identities that fulfil some of the core requirements specified earlier, which are necessary to a theory of generalizable interests. That is, this theorization, with its emphasis on hegemonic universalization, offers an escape from the alleged particularism and subjectivism of post-modern narratives on identities and interests. Moreover, it does not shun the demand for context-transcending criteria of valuation. However, it does avoid positing a model of valuation in such a manner as to construct an unbridgeable gap between the ideal and the real. The theorization of the mutual contamination between universality and particularity, between context-transcending and contextual dimensions of interests and identities undermines the strict separation between these poles without collapsing them into one another. It is for this reason that, I would argue, a hegemonic approach is most suitable to account for the ongoing processes through which Chambers argues convergence and agreement may be achieved, which entails that agreement is not here understood as achievable in any final sense. Moreover, there is a clear correspondence between what Habermas characterizes as 'compromise formations' and the sorts of commonalities that may result from hegemonic universalization. However, from the perspective of the latter it has to be emphasized that such commonalities or 'compromise formations' are not second-best alternatives and they do not, as for Habermas, leave the identities and interests of participants unchanged. Rather, since they acknowledge and shun the problematic emphasis on rational consensus in a context devoid of political struggle, they also manage to avoid the potentially depoliticizing effects entailed in the deliberative model insofar as it fully accepts the Habermasian strictures.

What is still needed, however, is a more elaborated conceptualization of the relation between hegemonic universalization and democracy. Whereas the Habermas-inspired model ultimately does not succeed in bridging the gap it posits between the ideal and the real, it does provide us with a theorization of generalizable interests that entails democratic agreement as a core feature. From the point of view of a hegemonic account of universalization, democratic agreement can never be *entailed* in such universalization. There can be no positing of an internal relation between universalization and democratic agreement, however attractive that path may look at the outset. I explore this apparent 'democratic deficit' next.

In his *New Reflections on the Revolution of Our Time* Laclau deepens the discussion of hegemony in a direction that may be useful in addressing the question of the democratic deficit outlined above. This consists of a radicalization of the model of hegemonic relations discussed above.[100] Laclau argues that not only are particular signifiers subject to political struggle and contestation but political projects themselves are also penetrated by contingency. Moreover, this contingency is not simply empirical in character. Rather, it is, as Laclau puts it, inherent in the structure itself.[101] Let us take the example of the signifier 'democracy' that is articulated in two different contexts. From this perspective, 'democracy' means one thing when it is articulated with 'anti-fascism' and something quite different when articulated with 'anti-communism'.[102] For Laclau, the key questions here concern the location and source of the 'ambiguity' expressed in the signifier 'democracy'. It could be located in the specific signifier ('democracy'); or in the political discourse or project in which that signifier is inscribed ('struggle against fascism'), and its source could be (merely) empirical (i.e., arising from the struggle between two projects, both of which vie to give a particular articulation to democracy), or it could be ontological (inscribed in the

---

[100] Each of the degrees of radicalization implies a different articulation of the necessity–contingency relationship. See E. Laclau, *New Reflections on the Revolution of Our Time* (London: Verso, 1990), pp. 27–31.

[101] Laclau, *New Reflections*, p. 29. See also A. J. Norval, 'Hegemony after deconstruction: The consequences of undecidability', *Journal of Political Ideologies* 9, no. 2 (2004), 139–57.

[102] Laclau, *New Reflections*, p. 28.

'structure itself'). A properly hegemonic understanding of politics, for Laclau, must not only take account of the struggles around particular terms or between particular political projects. It must, in addition, acknowledge the ontological contingency to which all terms, projects and identities are exposed. It is only once this is acknowledged that we become aware of the consequences of this account of contingency: there is nothing that is not, in principle, open to rearticulation. In other words, the possibility of final closure obtaining is ruled out in principle, rather than as a result of empirical limitations of actors or projects. Both the possibilities for political struggle and hegemonization of demands and the identities of subjects will be penetrated by contingency in the sense that neither would be determined by the structure. The degree to which contingency is regarded as penetrating political projects, demands and identities should now be related to the question of democracy and democratic agreements.

While Habermas' work on the possibility of democratic agreement is informed by the thesis of a movement towards post-conventional morality, there is nothing in Laclau's analysis that allows for what amounts to a teleological logic. For Laclau, the dislocations characteristic of late capitalism are conceived of as resulting in 'an open structure in which the crisis can be resolved in the most varied of directions'.[103] As a result, any hegemonic rearticulation of the structure will always be eminently political in character. Democracy, whether liberal or radical, cannot be assumed to resolve this crisis in the direction of its own development. This account is thus both more 'pessimistic' than that offered by Habermas, in that it does not presume or entail development to occur in a particular direction, and more 'optimistic' in that it opens up the possibility of a more radical constructionist approach to democracy. Laclau and Mouffe, nevertheless, do not develop their insights into the institution and formation of democratic processes any further. The hegemonic account of politics stands in need of deepening its theorization of the

---

[103] Laclau, *New Reflections*, p. 50.

nature of decisions and argumentation, as well as the character of subjectivity in a democratic context. The emphasis on hegemony and contingency, nevertheless, is a crucial starting-point and precondition for the further reflection that is necessary in this respect.

DEMOCRACY RETHOUGHT

A rethought conception of democracy that will do justice to certain of the central insights of both deliberative and post-structuralist conceptions of democracy will have to give renewed attention to, first, argumentation and persuasion in contradistinction to deliberation; secondly, the relation between agreement and disagreement in the reaching of democratic decisions; and thirdly, to the way both of these are related to underlying conceptions of democratic subjectivity.

In relation to the issue of the respective emphases on agreement and disagreement in the conceptualization of democracy, I have argued that there is, first, an overemphasis on the reaching of rational consensus in the deliberative model, and second, a conceptual difficulty in reconciling such consensus with the need to introduce other modes of reaching decisions – for instance by means of compromises – into the picture. If the picture of rational consensus holding the deliberative model captive cannot account for a wide variety of features of actual democratic decision-making, as is acknowledged by Habermas, then the introduction of supplementary modes will have the consequence of putting into question that very picture. I have argued that the alternative picture provided by post-structuralist accounts of democracy better accounts for the actual processes of decision-making discussed by, for example, Chambers. In addition, it has the advantage of being able to accommodate an enlarged conception of argumentation. That is to say, deliberation in its strict determination in the Habermasian model could be understood as one form of argumentation amongst others. Such a generalized conception of argumentation would also aim to accommodate its rhetorical features, so central to any account of the persuasiveness. It is thus not a matter of replacing deliberation understood in the narrow sense, or of merely adding a set of features to it. Rather, an alternative account will have to come to terms with the permeability of the boundaries between such deliberation and the force of rhetoric and persuasion in argumentation. This, indeed, is the subject matter of the next chapter.

The post-structuralist account that I have set out still suffers from two further shortcomings, which reflect the strengths of the deliberative democratic model. The first concerns the consequences of its ontological emphasis on disagreement as constitutive of social life in general, and of democracy in particular. The second concerns the lack of attention given to the need to institutionalize democratic arrangements. These two concerns are not unrelated. In fact, it is my contention that the second is a direct, although not necessary, consequence of the first. The lack of attention given to the institution of democratic arrangements arises from a carrying over of the emphasis on disagreement from an ontological level to an ontical level. To say this is not to question the ontological status of disagreement. There is today increasing agreement on the importance of the need to take account of the insights for democracy provided by the post-structuralist emphasis on disagreement.[104] This has taken the form of a far greater centrality given to need to think the relation between democracy, difference and radical pluralism in deliberative thinking.[105] Having said this, the ontological emphasis has fostered an overemphasis on disagreement also on the ontic level. While post-structuralist theorists have excelled in critical, deconstructive readings aimed at the ontological assumptions of deliberative theory, they have not given enough attention to the need to develop a deconstructive account of the relation between agreement and disagreement at an ontic level. Instead, they have focused exclusively

---

[104] Waldron, for instance, argues that disagreement is one of the circumstances of politics; nothing, he argues, 'we can say about politics makes much sense if we proceed without taking this ... into account'. J. Waldron, *The Dignity of Legislation* (Cambridge: Cambridge University Press, 1999), p. 153.

[105] This is reflected in the increasing attention given to questions of radical pluralism and difference within the deliberative tradition. See, in this respect, Benhabib, *Democracy and Difference*.

on activities of questioning, disruption and desedimentation in democratic practice. While these are no doubt central, democratic activity cannot be limited to them. As Connolly has argued, democratic politics is a 'site of a tension or productive ambiguity between governance and disturbance of naturalized identities. It thrives only while this tension is kept alive.'[106] Keeping this tension alive means overcoming the false dichotomy between consensus and contestation at the level of actual democratic practice and in our conception of democracy. Only then will it be possible to construct a democratic theory that combines 'a critique of consent and consensus when they are absent *with a critical engagement of both* when they are present'.[107] Since democracy contains the possibility of heightening the experience of contingency, the ethos of democracy is a disruptive and denaturalizing one. However, and this is what needs to be emphasized and developed, an alternative account of democracy must also act as the medium in which general purposes become crystallized and enacted. It is only when democracy maintains the tension between these interdependent antinomies that it can function 'as the perfection of politics'.[108] Crucially this requires attention to the actual practices of the institution and maintenance of democratic forms. And for this to be possible much greater consideration has to be given to the forms of subjectivity appropriate to democracy, both with respect to the latter's institution and its maintenance. This is the subject matter of Chapters 3 and 4, where I flesh out an account of democratic subjectivity that aims to address this most serious of lacunae in post-structuralist democratic theory today.

---

[106] W. E. Connolly, 'Democracy and contingency', in J. H. Carens (ed.), *Democracy and Possessive Individualism. The Intellectual Legacy of C. B. Macpherson* (Albany: State University of New York Press, 1993), p. 208.

[107] Connolly, 'Democracy and contingency', p. 213, emphasis added.

[108] Connolly, 'Democracy and contingency', p. 210.

2   Democratic argumentation: rhetoric and imagination

In extreme cases we run up against the limits of our understanding, and the interpretations which we use in vain to solve difficult problems come to a standstill. But they become fluid again when familiar facts are seen in a different light in a new vocabulary, so that fixated problems can be put in a new and more fruitful way.[1]

Only *ingenium* is able to grasp [*coligere*] the relationship between things in a concrete situation in order to determine their meaning. This capacity has an 'inventive' character, since it attains an insight without merely bringing out what is present in the premises as reason does in a logical derivation. *Ingenium* reveals something 'new' [*ingenio ... ad res novas proclives*], something 'unexpected' and 'astonishing' by uncovering the 'similar in the unsimilar,' i.e., what cannot be deduced rationally.[2]

THE FORCE OF ARGUMENT

If there is one of Habermas' expressions set to solicit the agreement of virtually all theorists of democracy it is probably that of the 'force of the better argument'. There seem to be no plausible grounds upon which one could reasonably disagree with the sentiment that the authority of the better argument should carry the day. Aiming to secure the rational character of motivation,[3] Habermas suggests that 'the unforced force of the better argument' should, under idealized

---

[1] Habermas, quoted in J. Bohman, 'Two versions of the linguistic turn: Habermas and poststructuralism', in M. Passerin D'Entrèves and S. Benhabib (eds.), *Habermas and the Unfinished Project of Modernity* (Cambridge: Polity Press, 1996), p. 208.

[2] E. Grassi, *Rhetoric as Philosophy*, trans. J. M. Krois and A. Azodi (Carbondale and Edwardsville: Southern Illinois University Press, 2001), pp. 91–2.

[3] For him, arguments are 'reasons proffered in a discourse that redeem a validity claim raised with constative or regulative speech acts; thus they rationally motivate those taking part in argumentation to accept the corresponding descriptive or normative statements as valid'. J. Habermas, *Between Facts and Norms. Contributions to a Discourse Theory of Law and Democracy*, trans. W. Rehg (Cambridge: Polity Press, 1997), pp. 225–6.

conditions, determine the position one takes in a debate.[4] However, as Bernstein points out, while abstractly there is something 'enormously attractive' about an appeal to the force of the better argument, how precisely this 'binding force' operates is never clearly specified by Habermas.[5] Other than reiterating the expectations created by the appeal to validity claims in the context of the distinction he draws between two functions of language (that of action coordination on the one hand and world-disclosure on the other[6]), little guidance is offered on how to evaluate different arguments.[7] In the case of communicative action, it seems, the force of reason must be supposed to be carried transparently within the reasons given.[8] If, however, one were to leave this space of idealization and move to the terrain of democratic practices of reason-giving, a range of wider considerations must be taken into account. In particular, the force of reasons could no longer be presupposed to be entirely independent from the context in which it operates and from the terms in which they are expressed. Under these circumstances it is necessary to give greater attention to

---

[4] Habermas, *Between Facts and Norms*, p. 541, n. 58.

[5] Many commentators take for granted Habermas' uptake of Austin's treatment of the illocutionary force of an utterance. White, for instance, points out that for Habermas, it is 'the underlying mutual expectation between actors that they can, if challenged, defend the specific claims they raise that, in turn, creates the 'binding force' for the coordination of action'. S. White, *Political Theory and Postmodernism* (Cambridge: Cambridge University Press, 1991), p. 25. However, several others refer to a lack of further qualification and question the transparency of this mechanism. See R. J. Bernstein, *The New Constellation. The Ethical–Political Horizons of Modernity/Postmodernity* (Cambridge, Mass.: MIT Press, 1992), p. 220; D. Panagia, 'The force of political argument', *Political Theory* 32, no. 6 (2004); and M. Hesse, 'Habermas and the force of dialectical argument', *History of European Ideas* 21, no. 3 (1995), 368.

[6] See White, *Political Theory and Postmodernism*, pp. 23–8; and Bohman, 'Two versions of the linguistic turn', pp. 203–4. White calls the conditions specified by Habermas 'idealized imputations'. White, *Political Theory and Postmodernism*, pp. 24–5.

[7] As Flyvberg points out, Habermas is criticized on this point by a range of commentators, including Heller, Wellmer and Luhman. See B. Flyvberg, 'Ideal theory, real rationality: Habermas versus Foucault and Nietzsche', Paper presented to the Political Studies Association's 50th Annual Conference, 'The Challenges for Democracy in the 21st Century', London School of Economics and Political Science, 10–13 April 2000, 6–7.

[8] I would like to thank David Owen for drawing my attention to this point.

how the force of an argument operates. What precisely is meant by
'force' and how is it related to reasons and to the language and context
in which they are expressed? How do we account for the changing
force of arguments including, for instance, the weighting of particular
reasons within a given space of argumentation, and/or the possibility
of the expansion and transformation of such a space so that new
reasons may enter the fray?

In the opening quote of this chapter Habermas marks what is at
stake here. However, it is not at all clear what the implications might
be of things 'becoming fluid', so that we can see things in a new way.
What precisely happens when things 'become fluid'? How do we
come to see things in a new way? Does this affect the way we see the
practice of reason-giving? These questions inform the argument presented in this and the following chapter. Chapter 3 looks in detail at
the presuppositions of seeing things in a new way by drawing on
Wittgenstein's remarks on aspect dawning, with a view to thinking
through the implications for our understanding of democratic subjectivity. In this chapter the focus is specifically on the character
of argumentation, and the way in which Habermasians and post-
structuralists conceive the relation between reason and rhetoric in
the context of attempting to specify what is involved in the 'force' of
an argument.[9] Both approaches acknowledge that rhetoric could be
regarded as a form of public discourse that is 'able to link reason and
power, knowledge and interests, leaders and people' and that it
could 'generate consent, mobilize support, and thus render law and

---

[9] The opposition between reason and rhetoric is historically based upon a particular –
and contested – understanding of both of the elements constituting the dichotomy.
For a critical discussion of Plato's critique of rhetoric in the *Gorgias*, see B. Vickers,
In Defence of Rhetoric (Oxford: Clarendon Press, 1998), p. 88. In this he follows
commentators such as Dodds, who argues that *Gorgias* is a polemical document,
which presents an extremely biased picture of Athenian politics in its reduction of
all human communication to the reason/rhetoric, educative/corrupting dichoto-
mies, a series of reductive binaries that is but one stage on the road to monism, in
which one pole is accepted and the other cancelled out. See also E. R. Dodds, *Plato,
Gorgias. A Revised Text with Introduction and Commentary* (Oxford: Oxford
University Press, 1959).

government legitimate'.[10] However, rhetoric enters the picture at very different points in the two approaches.

More precisely, I will show that Habermasian deliberative democrats attempt to address situations 'where we run up against the limits of our understanding' by appealing to the persuasive force of rhetoric and to narrative as a mere supplement to the 'unforced force of the better argument'.[11] In contrast to this strategy, which concedes only an instrumental or strategic role to rhetoric and that does not rework the status and functioning of reason, post-structuralists treat rhetoricality as an internal part of all reason-giving. In giving such centrality to a generalized rhetoricality, all reason-giving is argued to involve a dimension of 'showing' in the Wittgensteinian sense. Nevertheless, despite being able to offer a richer account of the relation between reason and rhetoric, post-structuralists do not have much to say about the specificity of democratic reason-giving. In order to begin to address this aporia, I turn to a discussion of analogy in political reasoning, drawing out the implications of non-subsumptive forms of analogical reasoning for democratic argument. I conclude the chapter with some reflections on the role of imagination in the constitution of political argument and the disclosure of new worlds, and in thus extending the political forms and relations we are able to imagine. This discussion leads me to the question of aspect dawning and democratic identification, which is the subject matter of Chapter 3.

THE CHALLENGE OF THE ORDINARY

Before embarking upon a more detailed discussion of the under-standings of democratic discourse as outlined by deliberative and post-structuralist theorists, and so as not to set out with too rarified

---

[10] B. Fontana, C. J. Nederman, and G. Remer, 'Introduction: Deliberative democracy and the rhetorical turn', in B. Fontana, C. J. Nederman and G. Remer (eds.), *Talking Democracy. Historical Perspectives on Rhetoric and Democracy* (University Park: Pennsylvania State University Press, 2004), p. 19.

[11] Habermas himself, of course, refrains from doing so. Panagia notes that Habermas here overlooks the tradition of rhetoric altogether. See Panagia, 'The force of political argument', 833.

and reductive an account, it is useful to remind ourselves of what some contemporary theorists hold to be the key characteristics of actual, rather than idealized, versions of 'liberal and democratic talk'. Walzer in his critique of 'philosophical conversation' sketches out some of its key features in the following way.[12] He argues, first, that liberals and democrats are rather less likely than the subjects of a king or dogmatic followers of a particular ideology or sect to agree on a range of issues. Hence their conversation is best characterized as 'unpredictable and inconclusive', reflecting 'the indeterminacy of any nonideal and unpatrolled (natural) conversation, in which rhetorical skill, or passionate eloquence, or insidious intensity may carry the day (but only the day)'.[13] Secondly, liberalism and democracy also sometimes require freedom from interlocution so that arguments can be made and developed and subsequently tested (in hearings, cross-examinations, press conferences and so on).[14] As Walzer points out, these occasions are not particularly conversational; they are subject to conventional rules and procedures. Third, democratic subjects play an array of different roles on different occasions; they speak, listen, question, and such speech often has an adversarial quality. Fourth, though in democracies we do need to reach agreement, these agreements are the result of a range of processes of which conversation is only one. Others include negotiation, law-making and socialization. Yet, fifth, for a conclusion to be reached, authority, conflict and coercion are often needed. For Walzer, conversation without constraints 'would never produce even those conventional (and temporary) stops which we call decisions or verdicts', and because of these constraints stopping points will appear arbitrary. However, these features are also those that have the potential to re-ignite the conversation. Hence for Walzer real democratic talk is 'unstable and restless', and it 'reaches to reasons and arguments that none of its

---

[12] M. Walzer, 'A critique of philosophical conversation', *The Philosophical Forum* 21, no. 1–2 (1998–90), 182–96.

[13] Walzer, 'Philosophical conversation', 189.

[14] Walzer, 'Philosophical conversation', 90.

participants can anticipate'.[15] Many of these points are echoed in Barber's work on political judgement, which is defined by 'activity in common'. In this picture, democratic debate and politics themselves define the limits of the democratic polity, as struggle is crucial to democracy and 'democracy is the regime within which the struggle for democracy finds legitimacy'.[16] Democratic talk also has clearly distinguishable features, including among other things the articulation of interests, persuasion, agenda setting; exploration of mutuality, affiliation and affection, as well as the maintenance of autonomy, witness and self-expression, reformulation and reconceptualization, and community building.[17]

In this chapter, I explore the work of contemporary political theorists with a view to deepening our understanding of the making of democratic claims and the forging of democratic arguments. However, as suggested, it should be noted that the aim of this exercise, though theoretical in character, is not to produce an account of democratic discourse that is abstracted from the 'stream of life' and removed from each and every context.[18] There is no presupposition here that political grammars in general, and democratic forms of argumentation in particular, could or should be abstracted from ordinary contexts, and from the interests and passions that inspire engagement in democratic politics in the first instance. This desire to separate politics from the

---

[15] Walzer, 'Philosophical conversation', 195.

[16] B. R. Barber, 'Foundationalism and democracy', in S. Benhabib (ed.), *Democracy and Difference. Contesting the Boundaries of the Political* (Princeton, N.J.: Princeton University Press, 1996), p. 357.

[17] B. Barber, *Strong Democracy* (Berkeley: University of California Press, 1984), pp. 178–98.

[18] For Habermas, rational discourse is 'a form of communication that is *removed from contexts of experience* and actions and whose structure assures us: that the bracketed validity claims of assertions, recommendations, or warnings are the exclusive object of discussion; that participants, themes, and contributions are not restricted except with reference to the goal of testing the validity claims in question; that no force except that of the better argument is exercised; and that, as a result, all motives except that of the cooperative search for truth is excluded'. J. Habermas, *Legitimation Crisis*, trans. T. McCarthy (London: Heinemann, 1976), pp. 107–8, emphasis added.

concerns of the ordinary usually stems from a Platonic denigration of rhetoric and an excessive valorization of the claims of reason. Those calling for some grounding to our practices that exceeds the ordinary are like sceptics, who hold that we need something else to assure us – an impersonal metaphysics – in order 'to relieve us of our responsibility for our own words, for making ourselves intelligible'.[19] This demand entails a repudiation of our criteria[20] and a denial of the fact that in describing the ordinary – 'what we say and imply on specific occasions' – we draw attention to its normativity.[21]

If we are to shun thinking about democracy in purely abstract terms, are perplexed about the way it is used, and yet do not want to fall into an empiricist trap by merely describing current usage – which may involve claims to democracy by all sorts of odious regimes – an approach focusing on criteria may be of use. By spelling out criteria we get to know what any object is. As Cavell puts it, criteria give:

> a sense of how things fall under our concepts, of how we individuate things and name, settle on nameables, of why we call things as we do, as questions of how we determine what counts as instances of our concepts ... To speak is to say what counts.[22]

It is important to note that the point of criteria is not to classify objects that we already know.[23] Rather, the need for criteria only

---

[19] E. Hammer, *Stanley Cavell. Skepticism, Subjectivity and the Ordinary* (Cambridge: Polity, 2002), p. 38.

[20] As Hammer points out, for Wittgenstein criteria are closely akin to our ordinary use of the term: 'Criteria specify and thus define what it means for a thing to have (or to count as having) a given status' (Hammer, *Stanley Cavell*, p. 32.) An example here would be the specifications – popular, universal voting rights, freedom of speech, equality, and so on – according to which we would describe a certain regime as being democratic. However, it should be noted that while criteria 'allow one to determine whether an object is of a specific kind' it tells us nothing of the degree to which that object satisfies criteria (Hammer, *Stanley Cavell*, p. 33).

[21] Normativity in this regard simply implies 'our capacity to make ourselves intelligible by projecting words into new contexts and remain ready to declare and respect the implications of our doing so'. Hammer, *Stanley Cavell*, p. 38.

[22] Cavell in Hammer, *Stanley Cavell*, p. 34.

[23] There are differences of interpretation on this point between Cavell and Mulhall. As Hammer points out: 'For Mulhall, criteria must be structurally in place for us to

arises under unusual, specific circumstances. We are not commonly and continuously aware of our understanding of the criteria for the use of certain concepts. It is only when some perplexity arises that we reflect upon criteria. Hence, as Cavell puts it, the point of eliciting criteria is to reorient ourselves 'when we are lost with respect to our words and to the world they anticipate'.[24] As in Heidegger, for whom the character of equipment is revealed when it no longer functions as we expect – when the tools we use are broken we become aware of the functions they fulfil – so for Cavell we elicit criteria in moments of crisis or perplexity.

This corresponds in an important sense to our political practices: it is when a practice is challenged, or is seen to be inadequate or questionable for some reason, that we are called upon to recount the criteria, to reconsider the point of the practices in which we engage, which we value and defend or criticize. Hence, if we are to think about democracy in these terms, it involves a process of recounting what we are prepared to say, what we are committed to when claiming to be democrats, and a whole host of other activities. Yet it is crucial to note that our criteria are deeply vulnerable: 'since sharing an order of criteria depends on our agreement on an order of judgments (our attunement), they allow or even invite repudiation'.[25] They are not abstract norms that are set up over and above our democratic practices, but are embedded in the community, which is constituted only through the

be able to make judgments. Without such a framework, we would lack the grounds of mutual intelligibility in language. But for Cavell, criteria are simply functions of the judgments we (normal speakers) are prepared to make; there is no level existing independently of our actual or potential judgments by reference to which criteria regulate or justify the intelligibility of those judgments.' In other words, the point of criteria differs markedly for each commentator. For Mulhall, criteria provide 'standards governing the application of concepts'. For Cavell, it is 'to respond to a crisis in our agreement' (Hammer, *Stanley Cavell*, pp. 37–8). My use of the term follows that of Cavell.

[24] Hammer, *Stanley Cavell*, p. 35.

[25] As Hammer notes: 'In explorations of the ordinary, claims made about my life simultaneously purport to be about yours: I take myself as representative of all human beings, and in so doing I make a claim to community. However, there is always a risk of rejection.' Hammer, *Stanley Cavell*, p. 19.

eliciting of claims. As Hammer puts it, 'in eliciting criteria not only do I speak for myself; I also speak for others: speaking for oneself is inevitably speaking for others'.[26] Hence, instead of a wrongheaded attempt to characterize democratic argumentation by listing and categorizing features, assigning them a core or peripheral status, I approach this issue by discussing the treatment of a particular – and one might argue key feature – of democratic argumentation, namely that of equality.[27] I take this treatment to be exemplary of the role ascribed to reason and rhetoric respectively in the different traditions under discussion. Indeed, as will become clear, the particular interpretation of the reason/rhetoric distinction in each of the traditions under consideration is internally related to the manner in which democratic discourse in general, and the role of equality within it, are characterized. As a result, the treatment of equality in each of these pictures gives us an instance of the substance of arguments concerning democracy, as well as of the manner in which these arguments are constituted, and the legitimacy ascribed to different dimensions of argumentation.

EQUALITY, REASON AND RHETORIC

[T]he point of a futural elaboration of the notion of equality would be to hold out the possibility that we do not yet know who or what might make a claim to equality, where and when the doctrine of equality might apply, and that the field of its operation is neither given nor closed.[28]

Deliberativists focus almost exclusively upon the normative guidelines that ought to inform not only the structuring of arguments

---

[26] Hammer, *Stanley Cavell*, p. 36.

[27] Following Wittgenstein, arguments through example are not to be understood as deficient in any way. They are not indirect, nor default options. As Wittgenstein points out: 'When I give a description: "The ground was quite covered with plants" – do you want to say I don't know what I am talking about until I can give a definition of a plant?' L. Wittgenstein, *Philosophical Investigations*, ed. G. E. M. Anscombe and R. Rhees, trans. G. E. M. Anscombe (Oxford: Basil Blackwell, 1958), § 70.

[28] J. Butler, in J. Butler and E. Laclau, 'The uses of equality,' *Diacritics* 27, no. 1 (1995), 5.

themselves, but also the spaces in which they may appear. By contrast, post-structuralists tend to concentrate their efforts on the moment of the emergence of demands, and on the logics of their extension. As noted, this division of tasks is accompanied by a bifurcation in the perceived role of reason and rhetoric in these accounts. The consequences of this division of tasks, and the bifurcation of reason and rhetoric, are multiple. They include an inability to address and account for the emergence and character of democratic demands and argumentation in the round, a failure to characterize properly the intricate qualities of political and democratic argumentation, and an inadequate consideration of the role of imagination in the constitution of such demands. As I will argue, the case of equality in democratic discourse makes this abundantly clear.

The deliberative tradition

Arguments for equality are central to democratic argumentation. This much is undisputed in most discussions of democracy today. Deliberative theorists and post-structuralists agree that equality plays a crucial role in the development and extension of democratic logics. Not surprisingly, there is less agreement on what else could be claimed about equality, its sources and the mechanisms facilitating its expression. Reflecting its procedural emphasis, and based upon the presumption that political equality requires that 'all participants in a process have an equal chance of affecting the outcome', deliberative theorists typically focus on the conditions that need to be in place for equality of participation to be effective in principle.[29] Much effort has

---

[29] J. S. Dryzek, *Deliberative Democracy and Beyond*, Oxford Political Theory (Oxford: Oxford University Press, 2000), p. 172. Cohen also argues that the deliberative interpretation of democracy sees democracy 'as a system of social and political arrangements that institutionally ties the exercise of power to free reasoning among equals'. Equality here includes both formal equality (rules regulating ideal procedures do not single anyone out; each has equal standing at each stage of the deliberative process) and substantive equality (existing distribution of power and resources does not shape their chances to contribute to deliberation). J. Cohen, 'Democracy and liberty', in J. Elster (ed.), *Deliberative*

gone into working through the conditions that would ensure equal opportunities for participation in democratic dialogue, including a focus on the structure of arguments and character of rational discourse that would in principle leave participants open to the viewpoints of others.[30]

It is quite common now to divide deliberativists between an earlier generation of theorists for whom reason remains unchallenged and unchallengeable in its supremacy when conceptualizing democratic discourse, and a later generation who increasingly have come to question the excessive rationalism of this position as they move from a consideration of the idealized conditions of communication to actual instances of democratic contestation. While this division looks plausible when viewed from within this tradition, it looks less crucial once it is placed within the broader panorama of contemporary democratic theory. Let us first, however, concentrate on the views of this latter generation. In addition to questions concerning the possible impact of material inequalities on the deliberation process,[31] as I have noted earlier, authors such as Iris Marion Young and Lynn Sanders have developed the argument for equal conditions of participation by focusing on the question of 'voice'.[32] Both Sanders and Young are

Democracy (Cambridge: Cambridge University Press, 1998), pp. 193–4. See also J. Knight and J. Johnson, 'What sort of political equality does deliberative democracy require?', in J. Bohman and W. Rehg (eds.), *Deliberative Democracy. Essays on Reason and Politics* (Cambridge, Mass.: The MIT Press, 1997), pp. 279–320.

[30] In this respect, much practical work of great value has also been done. See, for instance, O. Renn, T. Webler, and P. Wiedemann (eds.), *Fairness and Competence in Citizen Participation. Evaluating Models for Environmental Discourse* (Dordrecht: Kluwer, 1995). For a critical discussion, see also H. Ward, A. J. Norval, T. Landman, and J. Pretty, 'Open citizens' juries and the politics of sustainability', *Political Studies*, 51 (2003), 282–99.

[31] See N. Fraser and A. Honneth, *Redistribution or Recognition?* (London: Verso, 2003).

[32] Goodin's work on the input-side of democracy could be seen as a contribution to this debate. His emphasis on the role of imagination in making visible other viewpoints highlights aspects escaping the otherwise rationalistic paradigm of much contemporary critical theory. See R. E. Goodin, *Reflective Democracy*, Oxford Political Theory (Oxford: Oxford University Press, 2003), especially ch. 6. See also, L. M. Sanders, 'Against deliberation', *Political Theory* 25, no. 3 (1997); I. M. Young, 'Difference as resource for democratic communication', in Bohman

DEMOCRATIC ARGUMENTATION 67

concerned to emphasize that participation in democratic dialogue will only be equal if there is epistemic equality and an equal consideration of the different narrative forms in which participants may posit their claims. These points are also echoed in the work of Dryzek, who, in addition, aims to formulate some rules or tests to which all forms of communication – including storytelling, rational argumentation, testimony and greeting – should be subject. One such rule stipulates the exclusion of coercion – or the threat thereof – as well as ruling out communication that cannot connect the particular with the general.[33]

However, in a move that echoes a long tradition, none of these theorists are prepared to question the hierarchy established between, on the one hand, rhetorical forms such as testimony, storytelling and so on, and rational argumentation on the other. The need for this arises because of the shift in their work away from idealization to an engagement with the actual processes of democratic argumentation and reason-giving, whether this is in the context of considering the demands of excluded and minority groups or the viewpoints of ecological and green political organizations. These theorists do go further than most deliberative democrats in acknowledging both the potentially constraining character of rational argumentation and the need to accommodate different narrative forms. However, despite this, what are considered to be non-standard, alternative forms of expression are systematically subordinated to what is treated as the standard, namely, rational argumentation. This, I would suggest, renders the accommodation ineffective at best. Dryzek's work is a case in point. Even while recognizing the importance of 'other' forms of communication, usually ascribed to groups such as 'women' and

and Rehg, *Deliberative Democracy*, pp. 383–406. For an empirical account of the role of storytelling in planning processes, see J. Forester, *The Deliberative Practitioner* (Cambridge, Mass.: The MIT Press, 1999).

[33] Dryzek, *Deliberative Democracy*, p. 68. Dryzek prefers to talk of a 'contest of discourses' rather than deliberation simpliciter (p. 74). It should be noted, as Laclau argues, that in fact even the most particularistic demand of necessity must invoke universalistic claims.

'ethnic minorities', he believes it is possible to continue to ground deliberative theory in a critical theory of communication that retains the 'Habermasian antipathy to deception, self-deception, manipulation, strategizing, and coercion'.[34] While the antipathy to deception, manipulation and so on is not in itself problematic,[35] there are several problems with this exclusionary inclusion of the full array of communicative forms. The first concerns the suggestion that it is usually 'marginal' groups who 'resort' to this wider array of rhetorical forms. This preserves, at least in principle, an 'us' who does not need such recourse. This inclusion, which nevertheless retains the dichotomization and hierarchization of reason and rhetoric, is evident also in Dryzek's suggestion that emotions must always, finally, be answerable to reason.[36] In contrast to an earlier tradition, which had the advantage of recognizing the positive contribution of rhetoric to public life, here rhetoric is associated exclusively with emotion and passion, and denigrated in the process. The second problem concerns the retention of a realm of argumentation that is entirely free from, or has an inbuilt immunity to any form of 'distortion'. This, of course, is based upon the idealized conditions specified in the Habermasian approach. Leaving aside the question as to whether even under such idealized conditions the purity and transparency of communication could be guaranteed,[37] the need for an accommodation of wider forms of communication has already moved away from these conditions in significant respects, and cannot

---

[34] Dryzek, *Deliberative Democracy*, p. 54.

[35] The key theoretical issue regarding manipulation, coercion and so on, concerns the basis upon which it is to be differentiated from other forms of communications, and with that, the theory of ideology informing such differentiation.

[36] Dryzek, *Deliberative Democracy*, pp. 53–4.

[37] Here one only needs to think of Derrida's reading of Husserl (see J. Derrida, *Speech and Phenomena*, trans. D. B. Allison (Evanston, Il.: Northwestern University Press, 1973) to problematize the assertion of the possibility of communication that is transparent to itself. See also M. Kohn, 'Language, power, and persuasion: Towards a critique of deliberative democracy', *Constellations* 7, no. 3 (2000), 408–29. For a discussion of the role of humour in dialogic ethics, see S. Basu, 'Dialogic ethics and the virtue of humor', *The Journal of Political Philosophy* 7, no. 4 (1999), 378–403.

therefore call upon insights derived from it in order to safeguard the rationality of communication.

A not dissimilar logic is at work in the more sophisticated account of the discourse of social critics presented by Bohman, who posits his account as a corrective to Habermas', wherein the social critic is 'left with the impossible task of trying to rationally convince the systematically deceived'.[38] Bohman emphasizes the need to take account of the role of persuasion in political discourse, arguing that those who are systematically deceived about their practices cannot recognize the true statements of the critic unless these statements are communicated in a fashion which renders them convincing. According to Bohman, this task is achieved by a class of statements that cut across the strategic/communicative and perlocutionary/ illocutionary distinctions deployed by Habermas. In what he calls 'emancipatory speech', *indirect* means such as irony, metaphor and artistic representation are used to perform perlocutionary acts (e.g., convincing someone) 'in the service of communicative aims, that is, of opening up blocked possibilities of mutual understanding or self-understanding'.[39] Hence, he seeks to move away from sharp distinctions between perlocutions and illocutions, so redrawing the 'philosophical map of reason, with its boundaries between rhetoric and philosophy'.[40] Bohman proposes that we give attention to the possibility of classifying perlocutions, a subject to which I return in the concluding chapter. For now it is sufficient to note that for Bohman one such subset of perlocutions would be emancipatory speech, which consists of 'perlocutionary acts in the service of communicative aims'.[41] In this way, he suggests, we may find a 'proper

---

[38] J. Bohman, 'Emancipation and rhetoric: the perlocutions and illocutions of the social critic', *Philosophy and Rhetoric* 21, no. 3 (1988), 201.

[39] Bohman, 'Emancipation', 199.

[40] Bohman, 'Emancipation', 189. Bohman clearly wants to avoid collapsing these distinctions altogether, something that occurs all too easily within the works of some post-structuralist thinkers.

[41] Bohman, 'Emancipation', 199.

place for strategy, rhetoric, and perlocutions in the sphere of the genuine communicative use of language, that which is oriented to understanding and validity'[42] and so overcome 'the traditional, Platonic enmity to rhetoric'.[43] Bohman also emphasizes the fact that this account breaks with Habermas' quest to hold back rhetoric 'by isolating a purified area of language use oriented to understanding and validity'.[44]

It is clear that Bohman's sophisticated approach, with its nuances and attention to detail, offers several advances. In contrast to Dryzek, who seems content to reassert the possibility of a purified area of language, Bohman sets out to carve out a space for rhetoric that avoids a simplistic denigration, does not equate it with mere manipulation, and emphasizes its positive features – features long recognized in the rhetorical tradition. In particular, the possibility of rhetoric to 'move' someone, or to produce adherence to a particular idea is acknowledged.[45] The social critic also has the task, through her discourse, to overcome instances where there are 'insufficient shared agreements and meanings' and 'speakers cannot achieve their aims by pursuing communication either directly or reflectively'. Here Bohman has located one of the key difficulties in the Habermasian account, namely, the latter's failure to consider situations in which there is an absence of a shared understanding. For Bohman, the social critic must then perform the role of bringing about 'a communicatively shared experience sufficient to disclose the limitations of

---

[42] Bohman, 'Emancipation', 193.   [43] Bohman, 'Emancipation', 185.
[44] Bohman, 'Emancipation', 193.
[45] It should be pointed out that this acknowledgement, of course, was already present even in Plato's writings. Plato, in his later writings, retreated from the absolute antithesis between reason and rhetoric and came to accept 'the necessity of rhetoric as an instrument of moral and political education of the masses' (Fontana et al., Talking Democracy, p. 14). Similarly, Aristotle and Cicero placed rhetoric on an equal footing with philosophy and recognized the value of each form of argument within its own sphere. Hobbes also later also realized that his new science of politics could not be introduced without using rhetorical techniques. See Quentin Skinner, Reason and Rhetoric in the Philosophy of Hobbes (Cambridge: Cambridge University Press, 1996).

forms of public discourse and thereby transform the current social conditions of communicative success'.[46]

While Bohman does suggest that irony and other indirect forms of communication may have a 'jarring effect', he does not have the tools to adequately conceptualize the necessary dislocation that must accompany every institution of a new vocabulary. Neither does he go far enough in thinking through the implications of his position for the conception of subjectivity, and of democratic subjectivity specifically, which informs his analysis. Like Dryzek, Bohman separates out those who are deceived from those who are not. As he notes:

> In fact, rhetoric is not at all like ideology or distorted communication, but it is the employment of strategic means to achieve communicative effects like changes in beliefs, desires, and attitudes. A theory of rhetorical effects ... is precisely what is needed to explain how it is that critics and reformers do things with words and communicate with the self-deceived and deluded.[47]

Here the very account of rhetorical effects continues to rely on a theoretical distinction between those with knowledge of the true and the self-deceived, who have to be moved by special effects, and who are, per definition, not able to be moved by the presentation of (good) reasons.[48] With this distinction, Bohman cuts off the possibility of the use of rhetoric in debates among those who disagree, but who are not 'systematically deceived'. That is, it amounts to a denial

---

[46] J. Bohman, ' "When water chokes": Ideology, communication, and practical rationality', *Constellations* 7, no. 3 (2000), 389. Note that Bohman reformulates the concept of ideology in a manner analogous to many post-structuralist thinkers. However, his conception is still narrower than that of post-structuralists in that it is mainly concerned with the linguistic domain.

[47] Bohman, 'Emancipation', 202.

[48] As Brennan notes, the problem in contemporary politics is often not 'that government provides no reasons, but that its reasons often seem remote from the human beings who must live with their consequences'. This is a consequence of a valorization of abstract reason, cut off from other sources that enrich debate. See W. J. Brennan, 'Reason, passion and "the progress of the law" ', *Cardozo Law Review* 10 (1988), 22 and 11.

of the important role of rhetoric in seeking to persuade others who hold reasonable positions that differ from one's own. What then, it has to be asked, is the picture of democratic subjectivity underlying this distinction? Bohman's retention of a sharp separation here can only be traced back to his reluctance to take on board what could be argued to be the logical consequences of his reformulation of the relation between reason and rhetoric. If, as he suggests, rhetoric, of necessity, accompanies the formulation of arguments that are communicative in intent, but where possibilities of mutual understanding or of self-understanding are blocked in some way, what is it that limits the role of rhetoric to arguments under these specific sets of circumstances? If rhetoric may legitimately be used under these conditions, what prevents its legitimate use under other conditions? This, precisely, as I will show, is the point of departure for post-structuralist theorists and philosophers who argue for what is called a 'generalised rhetoricality'. While, on the whole, these theorists would agree that the effects and presence of rhetoric are more likely to be visible under conditions of crisis, they also insist that rhetoric accompanies argumentation *tout court*.

In conclusion, then, the conception of political equality that operates in deliberative accounts of democracy – understood as each participant having an equal chance to affect an outcome – focuses attention on the requisite conditions that need to be in place for equal participation in deliberation. While it is acknowledged that in practice some inequalities may remain, in principle deliberative theorists aim to be inclusive. This is so despite the exclusionary character of some of the most advanced attempts to articulate a broad and inclusive conception of deliberation. It is also clear that no matter how much lip-service deliberative democrats pay to the importance of rhetoric in the constitution of political argument, it remains at best an instrumental supplement to rational argumentation. Even for those critical theorists who are sceptical of the extreme rationalism underlying much of the work within this paradigm, imagination, voice, narration, metaphor and so on remain external additions to rational argumentation, which retains its priority and remains unmarked by these supplements.

For the argument to advance beyond the gestural inclusion of 'other voices' the reason/rhetoric dichotomy needs to be reworked. What is needed here is the movement from an exclusionary inclusion of rhetoric to an acknowledgement of *rhetoricality* as a general condition of existence.[49] Rhetoricality marks out a generalized rhetoric as a condition of our existence; unlike classical rhetoric, it is not bound to specific institutions and suggests a very different conception of subjectivity from that informing the classical tradition.[50] Its paradigmatic expression is found in Nietzsche, where rhetoric is no longer conceived as a 'doctrine governing the production and analysis of texts', but 'loses its instrumental character and becomes the name for the rootlessness of our being'.[51] Once a generalized rhetoricality is acknowledged, it is possible also to give attention to what is a crucial moment that is precluded from consideration in deliberative theory,

[49] For an insightful account of the demise of classical rhetoric during the Enlightenment and in the Romantic tradition, see, J. Bender and D. E. Wellbery, 'Rhetoricality: On the modernist return of rhetoric', in J. Bender and D. E. Wellbery (eds.), *The Ends of Rhetoric. History, Theory, Practice* (Stanford, Calif.: Stanford University Press, 1990), pp. 3–39. They delineate five conditions of impossibility of rhetoric: transparency and neutrality as values of scientific discourse anchored in objectivity; values of authorship and individual expression in the literary domain, emphasizing subjectivity; liberal political discourse as the language of communal exchange; print and publishing replacing oral traditions; and the emergence of the nation-state and national languages (p. 22). It is only once these conditions are reversed (a loss of faith in scientific objectivity and neutrality; erosion of the value of founding subjectivity in the works of modernist poets, Freud and Heidegger; mass communication exploding the liberal rational model of communication; the dethroning of print by TV and film; explosion of dialects, sociolects and ideolects that replace national languages) (pp. 23–4) that a return to rhetoric becomes possible. But this is a re-turn that alters classical rhetoric. The term they coin for this new form of (engagement with) rhetoric is *rhetoricality* (p. 25). For a further discussion of the decline of rhetoric, see also T. Todorov, *Theories of the Symbol*, trans. Catherine Porter (Ithaca, N.Y.: Cornell University Press, 1984), pp. 60–110.

[50] Hence, it is crucial that there can be no straightforward and simplistic recuperation of the classical rhetorical tradition.

[51] Bender and Wellbery, 'Rhetoricality', p. 27. See also F. Nietzsche, 'On truth and lies in a nonmoral sense (1873)', in K. Ansell Pearson and D. Large (eds.), *The Nietzsche Reader* (Oxford: Blackwell Publishing, 2006), pp. 114–23.

namely, the moment of the *emergence* of demands for equality, and the specific rhetorical forms used in their constitution. Here the focus will shift, first, to the 'eruption' of egalitarian demands, and then to a consideration of the rhetorical mechanisms of their constitution. The constitutive role of conflict and struggle also becomes evident in this context. Finally, I turn to the importance of imagination in the constitution of new political demands.

THE POST-STRUCTURALIST TRADITION
Equality as eruption

> The history of democratic rights is not that of a cumulative acquisition toward the telos of communicative transparency, but a history of *singular* solutions to the dialectic of equality and inequality, a series of locally situated inscriptions of equality into the realm of inequality.[52]

How can the articulation of demands for equality, and similarly for freedom, be characterized so as to take account of their paradoxical character, of the fact that for them to be demanded, they must have existed, but the demands themselves must bring them into existence? Rancière's account of the verification of equality provides us with a possible way to capture this paradox, which remains unacknowledged in the deliberative tradition. Let us turn for a moment to the example of Mary Wollstonecraft, who argues that, given that men and women are created equally, women should be accorded the same rights as men. As she puts it:

> But if women are to be excluded, without having a voice, from a participation of the natural rights of mankind, prove first, to ward off the charge of injustice and inconsistency, that they want reason ...[53]

---

[52] J.-P. Deranty, 'Jacques Rancière's contribution to the ethics of recognition', *Political Theory* 31, no. 1 (2003), 153, emphasis added.

[53] M. Wollstonecraft, *Vindication of the Rights of Woman*, ed. with introduction M. Brody (London: Penguin Books, 1983), p. 88.

[T]he nature of reason must be the same in all, if it be an emanation of divinity, the tie that connects the creature with the Creator.[54]

How should one understand these claims? It is possible, though not usual, to read the *Vindication of the Rights of Woman* as an intervention in a social order that demonstrates or verifies equality not by noting logical inconsistencies, but by making a claim that exposes a wrong. On this reading, Wollstonecraft's text makes visible and puts into question the logic structuring the ordering of society. Hence the 'natural order' is disrupted by those who previously had no voice, whose voices could not be heard within the existing distribution of places and hierarchies in society. In Rancière's terms, this is the moment of politics, in which 'the logic of the characteristic of equality takes the form of processing of a wrong, in which politics becomes the argument of a basic wrong that ties in with some established dispute in the distribution of jobs, roles and places'.[55]

Such political action produces new subjects. However, they are not created *ex nihilo*. Rather, new subjects come into being through a transformation of the 'natural order of the allocation of functions and places into instances of *experience* of dispute'.[56] Hence, through challenging the naturalness of a place, a space for a new subjectivity is forged in struggle.[57] In Mary Wollstonecraft's discourse this occurs when she replaces the appellation 'ladies'[58] with that of 'women'. 'Ladies' captures all that Wollstonecraft associates with the dissipation of the natural characteristics of women as a result of an

---

[54] Wollstonecraft, *Vindication*, p. 142.

[55] J. Rancière, *Disagreement. Politics and Philosophy*, trans. J. Rose (Minneapolis: University of Minnesota Press, 1999), p. 35.

[56] Rancière, *Disagreement*, p. 36.

[57] Hence, political struggle for Rancière is not a conflict between already defined groups. Rather, 'it is an opposition of logics that count the parties and parts of the community in different ways'. J. Rancière, 'Ten theses on politics', *Theory and Event*, trans. D. Panagia, 5, no. 3 (2001) (http://muse.jhu.edu/journals/theory_and_event/v005/5.3ranciere.html).

[58] Wollstonecraft, *Vindication*, p. 81.

enfeebling education. By contrast, the designation 'women' marks the verification of equality, i.e., the place of a dispute with the existing order. This reading can now be contrasted with the standard, broadly liberal interpretation. In the latter case, the *Vindication of the Rights of Women* is argued to demonstrate an inconsistency at the heart of the logic of universal rights: a right based upon the rational character of man is wrongly limited to men. However, this interpretation is possible only once Wollstonecraft's position has become established, or at least acceptable as a possible position in the debate over equality. Hence the account based upon Rancière highlights what needs to be in place for us to read Wollstonecraft under a liberal aspect. To put it differently, the post-structuralist emphasis on accounting for the very process of the emergence of a new demand discloses the conditions of possibility of a liberal perspective.

What occurs in this moment in which something or someone that was neither visible nor audible becomes visible and finds a voice? And what is presupposed by such an account? For Rancière, politics is a matter of aesthetics first and foremost in the non-objectionable sense in that it concerns the visible and the invisible, the logics of the division between the perceptible and the imperceptible, that which supports the visible (the order of the police) and that which disrupts it (the political). The logic of the police distributes bodies within the space of their visibility and it is challenged by a political act that shifts 'a body from the place assigned to it', thus making visible 'what had no business being seen'.[59] Political activity thus takes a particular form. It is:

> a mode of expression that undoes the perceptible divisions of the police order by implementing a basically heterogenous assumption, that of a part of those who have no part, an assumption that, at the end of the day, itself demonstrates the sheer contingency of the order, the equality of any speaking being with any other speaking being.[60]

---

[59] Rancière, *Disagreement*, pp. 29–30. [60] Rancière, *Disagreement*, p. 30.

Those who do not count, and have no qualifications to take part in ruling (*archein*), are the 'poor', not an economically disadvantaged group, but the demos, the part of the community who do not count.[61]

For Rancière, equality is a presupposition, not a 'founding ontological principle but a condition that only functions when it is put into action'.[62] Contra liberal, critical theoretical and deliberative accounts,

> Equality is not a given that politics then presses into service, an essence embodied in the law of a goal politics sets itself the task of attaining. It is a mere assumption that needs to be discerned within the practices implementing it.[63]

Hence, equality is not a substance apart from the practice verifying it. And what makes an action political is not its object, nor as deliberative theorists maintain the place where it is carried out, but its form, which is that of the setting up of a dispute.[64] Nothing is political in itself; it becomes so only where a clash between the police order and an egalitarian logic is set up, thus reconfiguring relations. This means that the demands verifying equality institute a new space of shared meaning. But this is not a space of consensus, as it disrupts the existing social order. The effectiveness of such verification often depends on more than argument. Again, as opposed to deliberative theorists, Rancière notes that 'proving one is correct has never compelled others to recognize they are wrong'. As a result, the 'affirmation of the right to be correct is dependent on the violence of its inscription'. So, for instance the 'reasonable arguments of the strikers of 1833 were audible, their demonstration visible, only

---

[61] Rancière, 'Ten theses on politics'.
[62] J. Rancière, *The Politics of Aesthetics. The Distribution of the Sensible*, trans. G. Rockhill (London: Continuum, 2004), p. 52.
[63] Rancière, *Disagreement*, p. 34.
[64] Rancière, *Disagreement*, p. 32. Rancière argues that equality 'takes effect in lots of circumstances that have nothing political about them ... equality only generates politics when it is implemented in the specific form of a particular case of dissensus'. Rancière, *Politics of Aesthetics*, p. 52.

because the events of 1830, recalling those of 1789, had torn them from the nether world of inarticulate sounds'.[65]

It is not the inherent reasonableness of arguments that wins the day, but a change of perspective, of aspect, forced upon the existing social order, which institutes a new space where meanings may be shared. To repeat: there is not first the shared space in which all reasons and demands may be heard equally and into which new demands can be inscribed, but rather this shared space of reasons needs to be instituted, often through practices other than verbal argumentation. Thus the verification of the presupposition of equality always takes place through the rupturing of a given order by disagreements (mésentente) that challenge existing orders and institute new spaces of meaning, which may become sites of emancipation, or alternatively may become ossified over time.[66] In short, disagreement is not to do with words alone, but with the very ability to see the object of dispute.[67] As Rancière puts it:

> The structures proper to disagreement are those in which discussion of an argument comes down to a dispute over the object of the discussion and over the capacity of those who are making an object of it.[68]

What is at stake here is precisely the possibility of bringing about a change in the way we see things, something explored in some detail in Chapter 3. Here it is necessary to note that the possibility

---

[65] Rancière, *On the Shores of Politics*, trans. L. Heron (London: Verso, 1995), p. 49.

[66] Deranty points out that inscribed moments have a double logic at work in them: they can become ossified and lose their emancipatory quality, or be reclaimed in new contexts. Hence, '[d]emocratic struggles always occur as reiteration of previous inscriptions of equality'. Deranty, 'Jacques Rancière's contribution', 153. See also J. Rancière, *The Names of History*, trans. H. Melehy (Minneapolis: University of Minnesota Press, 1994), ch. 7.

[67] For a critical discussion of Rancière's conception of language, see S. A. Chambers, 'The language of disagreement'. Paper delivered to the Poststructuralism and Radical Politics Conference: 'Fidelity to the Disagreement: Jacques Rancière and the Political', Goldsmiths College, London, 16–17 September 2003 (http://homepages.gold.ac.uk/psrpsg/ranciere.doc).

[68] Rancière, *Disagreement*, p. xii.

of bringing about such a change is in itself dependent upon the object – the wrong – coming into being in the very same moment as the change is brought about. Moreover, this making visible of what was previously unseen, a wrong, restores contingency to social space,[69] and this, for Rancière, is the polemical moment of democracy. Democracy is thus not characterized as a regime or a way of life, but is an interruptive moment in which new subjects come into existence.[70]

Equality as equivalence

Whereas Rancière presupposes the universality of equality and investigates its verification in struggle, for Laclau and Mouffe demands for equality are thoroughly historicized. Arguing that demands for equality and liberty emerge and are made against the horizon of the French Revolution,[71] they concentrate their theoretical effort on explaining *how* these demands are disseminated into more and more areas of social and political life:

> It is only from the moment when the democratic discourse becomes available to articulate the different forms of resistance to subordination that the conditions will exist to make possible the struggle against different types of inequality ... But ... the democratic principle of liberty and equality first had to impose itself as the new matrix of the social imaginary ... This decisive mutation took place two hundred years ago and can be defined in these terms: the logic of equivalence was transformed into the fundamental instrument of the production of the social ... the Declaration of the Rights of Man, would provide the discursive

---

[69] M. J. Shapiro, 'Radicalizing democratic theory: social space in Connolly, Deleuze and Rancière', Paper delivered to the Poststructuralism and Radical Politics Conference: 'Fidelity to the Disagreement: Jacques Rancière and the Political', Goldsmiths College, London, 16–17 September 2003 (http://homepages.gold.ac.uk/psrpsg/ranciere.doc).

[70] Rancière, *Disagreement*, p. 101.

[71] See, in particular, the discussion of equality and liberty in E. Laclau and C. Mouffe, *Hegemony and Socialist Strategy. Towards a Radical Democratic Politics* (London: Verso, 1985), ch. 4.

conditions which made it possible to propose the different forms of inequality as illegitimate and anti-natural, and thus make them equivalent as forms of oppression. Here lay the profound subversive power of the democratic discourse, which would allow the spread of equality and liberty into increasingly wider domains.[72]

As I have shown in Chapter 1, the argument takes the form of a process of universalization through the drawing of equivalences. Hence, we are concerned with the mechanisms and modes of argumentation conducive to the establishment of equivalences and, more specifically, an investigation of the demands of democratic forms of argumentation, as well as the role of rhetoric in these processes. In the first case, we need to investigate the establishment of democratic equivalences, insofar as the equality of participants in dialogue constitutes one of the key conditions for democratic conversation and interaction.

Laclau and Mouffe's conceptualization of chains of equivalences that forge links between demands which are not necessarily connected draws upon Saussurian linguistics, with its distinction between syntagms and paradigms, predicated on a non-referential and non-essentialist conception of language and relations among elements more generally.[73] The creation of equivalences occurs through processes of articulation, which bring together elements that have no necessary belonging. It is only through the creation of equivalences that a set of relational differences can be drawn together into a totality, and defined against something it is not. An example that is frequently employed by Laclau, namely that of an oppressive regime against which demands from different sectors of society are articulated,[74] makes this clear. The separate, differential demands that emanate from a variety of different sectors of society are unified through their

[72] Laclau and Mouffe, *Hegemony and Socialist Strategy*, pp. 154–5.

[73] For a fuller discussion of this background, see *inter alia* D. Howarth, *Discourse* (Buckingham: Open University Press, 2000), ch. 1. See also N. Helsloot, 'Linguists of all countries ... !', *Journal of Pragmatics* 13 (1989), 547–66.

[74] E. Laclau, *On Populist Reason* (London: Verso, 2005), pp. 130–1.

common opposition to the oppressive regime. In other words, while each of the particular demands is distinctive, they share the fact that they are opposed to a common enemy, which is the oppressive regime. They are rendered equivalent in this respect. The unity of the chain of equivalences is then established by one of the elements of the chain taking on the function of representing the chain as a whole, thus operating as an 'empty' signifier, to use Laclau's terms.[75]

Now, in response to the question how, or on what basis, equivalences are established, Laclau and Mouffe suggest that the latter is the result of historical and thus contingent articulation. There is nothing intrinsic in the elements that predispose them to being articulated together. Take, for instance, the example of 'communist enumeration'.[76] In the wake of the experience of fascism in Europe and the anti-colonial revolutions, communist thinkers had to come to terms with the need to characterize the plurality of antagonisms that emerged at the time but which could not be reduced to a class character. The strategy of 'communist enumeration' was one that strove to remain formally on a classist terrain, while simultaneously seeking to incorporate the democratic demands of the masses. It divided society between the dominant and popular sectors, and established this division through an enumeration of their constitutive class sectors. For example, on the side of the popular sectors were included 'the working class, the peasantry, the petty bourgeoisie, progressive fractions of the national bourgeoisie' and so on. Now, as Laclau and Mouffe point out, this enumeration does not merely affirm the literal presence of certain classes or class fractions at the popular pole; it also establishes their equivalence in the common confrontation with the dominant pole.[77] Hence, the equivalence

---

[75] E. Laclau, 'Structure, history and the political', in J. Butler, E. Laclau and S. Žižek, *Contingency, Hegemony, Universality. Contemporary Dialogues on the Left, Phronesis* (London: Verso, 2000), p. 210.

[76] Laclau and Mouffe, *Hegemony and Socialist Strategy*, p. 63.

[77] They point out that equivalence 'is never tautological, as the substitutability it establishes among certain objects is valid only for determinate positions within a given structural context. In this sense, equivalence displaces the identity

between different class sectors 'supposes the operation of the
principle of analogy among literally diverse contents', which amounts
to a 'metaphorical transposition'.[78] From a strictly classist point of
view then, there is no identity between the enumerated sectors; yet,
'the relation of equivalence established among them, in the context of
their opposition to the dominant pole, constructs a "popular" discursive position that is irreducible to class positions'.[79] From this
example it also becomes clear that the non-essentialism of the elements is supplemented with a historico-political restraining condition. Laclau argues that certain historical horizons do, at the very
least, limit what elements may be articulated together.[80] Hence,
attention should always be given to the availability of elements,
and the manner in which such elements may potentially limit the
process of articulation.[81] Nevertheless, it should also be noted that
the limitations imposed by any given context are always in principle
subject to dislocation, thus making possible the articulation of

---

which makes it possible, from the objects themselves to the contexts of their
appearance ... This ... means that in the relation of equivalence the identity of the
object is split: on the one hand, it maintains its own "literal" sense; on the other, it
symbolizes the contextual position for which it is a substitutable element'. Laclau
and Mouffe, *Hegemony and Socialist Strategy*, p. 63.

[78] Laclau and Mouffe, *Hegemony and Socialist Strategy*, p. 110. The hegemonic
relation, characterized in rhetorical terms, is essentially metonymic in character
insofar as it depends upon displacements; insofar as hegemony tries to re-totalize,
it could be likened to metaphoric totalization. See, Laclau and Mouffe, *Hegemony
and Socialist Strategy*, p. 141; and E. Laclau, 'Paul de Man and the Politics of
Rhetoric', *Pretexts* 7, no. 2 (1998), 159.

[79] Laclau and Mouffe, *Hegemony and Socialist Strategy*, p. 63.

[80] Laclau argues that the acceptance of a discourse 'depends upon its credibility, and
this will not be granted if its proposals clash with the basic principles informing the
organization of a group'. Alternatively, 'the more the objective organization of that
group has been dislocated, the more those "basic principles" will have been shattered,
thereby widening the areas of social life that must be reorganized'. E. Laclau, *New
Reflections on the Revolution of Our Time* (London: Verso, 1990), p. 66.

[81] This emphasis echoes central considerations in classical rhetoric. As Fontana
points out: 'the orator cannot persuade without intimate knowledge of the people
he is addressing, and the people cannot respond without understanding (both
rationally and emotionally, that is, in terms of *logos* and of *pathos*) the language of
the orator'. Fontana, Nederman, and Remer, 'Introduction: Deliberative democracy
and the rhetorical turn', p. 16.

elements that may not previously have come into play. Historically this is a matter of investigating the different political horizons impacting upon any one discursive context.

Before moving on to the role of rhetorical devices in the constitution of equivalences and differences, we need to turn to the relationship between chains of equivalence and the articulation of democracy.[82] For Laclau, democracy is grounded on the existence of a democratic subject 'whose emergence depends on the horizontal articulation between equivalential demands':

> An ensemble of equivalential demands articulated by an empty signifier is what constitutes a 'people'. So the very possibility of democracy depends on the constitution of a democratic 'people'.[83]

In this way, the democratic subject emerges in and through the process of making claims, which in turn may come to perform as empty signifiers. It is important to note that the empty signifier plays a dual role in the constitution of a people. On the one hand, it has an active role of representation as it constitutes the people in the process of representing them; it does not simply reflect a pre-given totality. On the other, it represents the people. Since it has to act as a point of identification, it cannot be entirely autonomous from them. Given this, the constitution of 'the people' is the site of a tension. If the totalizing moment – that of equivalence – prevails, representation is destroyed. If, on the other hand, there is a complete autonomization of demands – where difference prevails – the moment of totalization necessary for the constitution of some form of unity would be blocked.[84]

Notwithstanding these important points, Laclau does not further discuss the criteria of what might make a people specifically democratic, or whether there is a point on the continuum of this

---

[82] This should be distinguished from what Laclau calls 'democratic demands'. Such demands, rather peculiarly, are demands that remain isolated, and do not enter into equivalential articulation to constitute a broader subjectivity. Laclau, *On Populist Reason*, p. 74.

[83] Laclau, *On Populist Reason*, p. 171.   [84] Laclau, *On Populist Reason*, p. 162.

tension that would be specifically democratic. He also does not address a crucial dimension of the relation between the making of demands and the constitution of a people, namely the fact that the making of a claim constitutes a relation *between* citizens of a democratic community.[85] What is clear is that for Laclau there is an internal relation between the constitution of chains of equivalence among diverse demands and the possibility of the formation of a democratic community. Moreover, as for Rancière, the interruptive moment that makes visible the contingency of an existing social order is closely associated with the institution of a democratic order. However, contra Rancière, for Laclau it is possible to talk of democracy as an imaginary horizon, a space in which demands for equality and difference may be inscribed. Democracy from this perspective is more concerned with a certain mode of identification – and a particular way of life – than with formal political structures.[86] Yet what exactly this form of life might entail, and what more could be said about the mode of identification appropriate to democratic subjectivity, is left unaddressed. I return to these issues in more detail in Chapters 3 and 4.

Now, Laclau's work on the formation of hegemonic totalities draws *inter alia* from linguistics for its theoretical resources. As suggested above, already in *Hegemony and Socialist Strategy*, the role of rhetoric is asserted against any objectivist, non-symbolic conception of social relations. Laclau and Mouffe argue that one of the main consequences of a break with the discursive/extra-discursive distinction is:

> the abandonment of the thought/reality opposition, and hence a major enlargement of the field of those categories which can account for social relations. Synonymy, metonymy, metaphor are not forms of thought that add a second sense to a primary

---

[85] The absence of an account of the relation between citizens, rather than between citizens and the state is the result of the fact that Laclau models the democratic relation on the basis of an interpretation of populism. I return to this issue in Chapter 4.

[86] Laclau, *On Populist Reason*, p. 169.

constitutive literality of social relations; instead they are part of the primary terrain itself in which the social is constituted.[87]

Here 'rhetoric is not epiphenomenal *vis-à-vis* a self-contained conceptual structure, for no conceptual structure finds its internal cohesion without appealing to rhetorical devices'.[88] In deploying rhetorical analysis, Laclau draws mainly on the figures of metonymy, metaphor and catachresis, arguing for a 'general rhetorization' arising from the fact that in a situation of radical contingency:

> No criterion of analogy is stable; it is always governed by challenging relations of contiguity which no metaphorical totalization can control. Metaphor – and analogy – is at most a 'superstructural' effect of a partial stabilization in relations of contiguity which are not submitted to any literal principle of a priori determination.[89]

Thus, the mutual subversion of metaphor and metonymy is both the condition of success and impossibility of such a general rhetoricality.

I argued earlier that the dichotomy between reason and rhetoric could only be thoroughly dealt with once we move to a terrain of a generalized rhetoricality as suggested by Bender and Wellbery. While Laclau makes this move, it comes at a price. Two issues arise in this regard. The first concerns the fact that rhetoric is now reduced to the operation of a limited number of tropes. This reduction operates in several respects. For instance, in the case of the workings of the logics of equivalence and difference Laclau asserts that only two types of relation can possibly exist between signifying elements: they are relations of substitution (equivalence) and combination (difference).[90]

---

[87] Laclau and Mouffe, *Hegemony and Socialist Strategy*, p. 110.

[88] Laclau, *On Populist Reason*, p. 67.

[89] Laclau, 'Paul de Man and the Politics of Rhetoric', 166.

[90] Laclau, *On Populist Reason*, p. 68. Vickers argues that the reduction of rhetoric to an ever more limited arsenal of figures and tropes in the works of Vico, Hayden White, Roman Jakobsen and De Man serves to impoverish the study of rhetoric, losing much of what the classical tradition could teach us. That this does not necessarily go along with the modern recuperation of rhetoric is evident in the fact that Nietzsche 'was

This restriction also has consequences for conceptualizing the range of possible relations among subjects. These two logics are, more often than not, associated with the creation of the dichotomized positions of 'friend' and 'enemy'.[91] Little space is left for conceptualizing finer distinctions in relation between different subjects. The second issue arises in this regard, and it concerns the need to address the specificity of a democratic rhetoric.[92] While some of Laclau's recent work moves in this direction, especially his writings on identification, which promise a more nuanced understanding of the constitution of subjectivity, more work clearly needs to be done in this area to capture the richness of a transformed rhetorical inheritance and its implications for democratic discourse.[93] Importantly, this work cannot consist only of attention to the uses of tropes and figures in argumentation, since this characterization still retains traces of the reduction of rhetoric to mere 'informal' argumentation.[94] A proper

fully aware of the whole social and political function of classical rhetoric, its powers of persuasion, its use of *movere*, its various genres and categories, and its detailed teaching on the tropes and figures' (Vickers, *In Defence of Rhetoric*, p. 461). Laclau's explicit attention to the political functions echoes that of Nietzsche.

[91] For a fuller analysis of the problems associated with this reduction, see A. J. Norval, 'Future trajectories of research in discourse theory', in D. Howarth, A. J. Norval and Y. Stavrakakis (eds.), *Discourse Theory and Political Analysis* (Manchester: Manchester University Press, 2000).

[92] Vickers, *In Defence of Rhetoric*, p. 461.

[93] There is a large literature dealing with rhetoric and political analysis. See, for instance, the analysis of the role of performativity in the constitution of gender and sexuality (see J. Butler, 'Critically queer', in *Bodies that Matter* (London: Routledge, 1993)); of paradiastole in political discourse (see Q. Skinner, *Reason and Rhetoric in the Philosophy of Hobbes*); of iterability in the constitution of identity (see D. Howarth, 'Complexities of identity/difference: the ideology of black consciousness in South Africa', *Journal of Political Ideologies* 2, no. 1 (1997), 51–78); of naming in politics, drawing on Kripke's work on primal baptism (see S. Žižek, *The Sublime Object of Ideology* (London: Verso, 1989), and Laclau, *On Populist Reason*); of genealogy (see D. Owen, 'Genealogy as perspicuous representation', in C. Heyes (ed.), *The Grammar of Politics. Wittgenstein and Political Philosophy* (Ithaca, N.Y.: Cornell University Press, 2003), pp. 82–96).

[94] Crusius suggests that contemporary rhetorical theory bifurcates between the treatment of rhetoric as informal argumentation, called upon where reason fails (e.g., Perelman, Toulmin), and 'tropists' who see the power of language 'as residing more in image and metaphor than in argument'. The latter group includes Burke and Grassi. See T. W. Crusius, 'Foreword' to Grassi, *Rhetoric as Philosophy*, p. xvii.

revalorization of rhetoric would have to acknowledge its role in opening up new worlds, not only in the rarefied atmosphere of philosophical argumentation, but also in the political world itself. I return to these issues later in the chapter, as well as in the context of the further discussion of the institution of a democratic terrain and the articulation of democratic demands in Chapter 4.

REASONING REWORKED

The recasting of the reason/rhetoric dichotomy requires not only a revalorization of rhetoric, but also a reworking of our understanding of reason.[95] There are many possible ways in which this may be done, ranging from the recuperation of an alternative philosophical tradition[96] to acknowledging that the premises of logic cannot themselves be explained logically. Not unexpectedly, the position I wish briefly to explore here is a Wittgensteinian one. Many commentators on Wittgenstein draw attention to the fact that understanding for him is a practical activity involving the ability to use a general term in various circumstances, and being able to give reasons for and against this or that use. In Wittgenstein himself, the activity of reasoning takes many forms:

> describing examples with similar or related aspects, drawing
> analogies or disanalogies of various kinds, finding precedents,
> exchanging narratives and redescriptions, drawing attention to
> intermediate cases so one can easily pass from the familiar to the
> unfamiliar cases and see the similarities between them: thereby
> being both conventional and creative in the use of the criteria that
> hold our normative vocabulary in place.[97]

---

[95] Hence, the point here is not to do away with the distinction, but to think through the mutual imbrication and difficult relation between different uses of language. As Toulmin notes, 'Rhetoric is not a *rival* to Logic; rather, it puts the logical analysis of arguments into the larger framework of argumentation.' S. Toulmin, *Return to Reason* (Cambridge, Mass.: Harvard University Press, 2001), p. 168.

[96] See, for instance, N. Widder, *Genealogies of Difference* (Urbana: University of Illinois Press, 2002).

[97] J. Tully, 'Political philosophy as a critical activity', *Political Theory* 30, no. 4 (2002), 543–4.

As Tully points out, this is a form of practical reasoning that is not abstracted from everyday use. Instead, it is 'the manifestation of a repertoire of practical, normative abilities, acquired through practice, to use the general term, as well as to go against customary usage, in actual cases'.[98] Hence, a Wittgensteinian approach draws attention away from concerns with reason and *to* the ordinary, and requires a serious engagement with it. However, this does not lead to conservatism and a simple affirmation of the present, as our earlier discussion of criteria makes clear. Instead, it emphasizes the role of imagination, a method of making visible what was before our eyes, yet unnoticed.

Showing in argumentation

Our language can be seen as an ancient city.[99]

As I have so far claimed, reasoning cannot be reduced to deductive reason. Indeed, reasoning itself involves a dimension of *showing*, which escapes conventional characterizations of reasoning and argumentation.[100] This is true of all argumentation.[101] However, in arguments that proceed by analogy, which I shall now turn to in more detail, the dimension of showing predominates. That is, their argumentative structure cannot be stated/said or written in logical form without missing the point. As Lueken argues, analogical arguments, like Wittgenstein's likening of language to an ancient city, project

---

[98] For Tully, since 'it is always possible to invoke a reason and redescribe the accepted application of our political concepts (*paradiastole*), it is always necessary to learn to listen to the other side (*audi alteram partem*), to learn the conditional arguments that support the various sides (*in utramque partem*), and so to be prepared to enter into deliberations with others on how to negotiate an agreeable solution (*negotium*)'. Tully, 'Political philosophy as a critical activity', 543 and 544. Hence, there are certain political consequences that follow from a Wittgensteinian approach.

[99] Wittgenstein, *Philosophical Investigations*, § 18.

[100] This would incorporate, *inter alia*, what Cicero calls *ingenium*, through which 'we surpass what lies before us in our sensory awareness'. Grassi, *Rhetoric as Philosophy*, p. 8.

[101] While showing is present in all argumentation, its argumentative function depends 'upon the character of its relation to what is said'. See G.-L. Lueken, 'On showing in argumentation', *Philosophical Investigations* 20, no. 3 (1997), 220.

a picture onto another domain: 'a picture which carries a web of associations and provides an ongoing source for further conjectures and investigations'.[102] Now, it is important to stress that analogies may, on the one hand, provide support for the thesis that a particular object has a particular property, so proceeding by subsumption. On the other hand, an analogy may establish, develop and even change our way of seeing things.[103] And this emphasis on seeing is not accidental, for showing always involves a dimension of argumentation that reveals something to us, perhaps even disclosing a new world.[104] Hence, the strength of analogical argumentation is that it changes the sense of old questions and generates new ones.[105] It is precisely this characteristic that makes it particularly apt for political argumentation.[106] More specifically, analogical argumentation has four important features, which makes it appropriate for political and ethical argumentation. First, it proceeds from a paradigm case or precedent; second, it is context- and audience-specific; third, it does not presuppose generalizations 'but rather particular instances and persuasive likeness to them'; and, finally, it involves 'extending what is accepted to what is new and unfamiliar by degrees or in stages'.[107] These features are strikingly similar to the emphasis in Roman rhetoric on the concrete occasion, the need to deal with specific matters and with particular questions in the context of the struggle to persuade. The possible argumentative functions of analogy suggested

---

[102] Lueken, 'On showing', 219.   [103] Ibid.

[104] There are obvious parallels here with Heidegger's discussion of the *clearing*, and with Grassi, who connects Heidegger's account of unconcealment with rhetoric understood as *ingenium*, revealing the new and unexpected. Grassi, *Rhetoric as Philosophy*, p. 92.

[105] Lueken, 'On showing', 220.

[106] See, for instance, D. Houghton, *The Role of Analogical Reasoning in Novel Foreign Policy Situations*, Cambridge Studies in International Relations (Cambridge: Cambridge University Press, 2001).

[107] H. Aronovitch, 'The political importance of analogical argument', *Political Studies* 45 (1997), 85–6. See also A. R. Jonsen and S. Toulmin, *The Abuse of Casuistry* (Berkeley: University of California Press, 1988), especially the prologue and ch. 1, which contrasts reasoning based on principles, rules and other general ideas with reasoning focusing on the specific features of a case.

by Lueken need further exploration, for they presuppose not one, but two different models of analogy, and this is precisely what is at stake in the debate between Aronovitch and Panagia on analogical forms of argumentation and their relation to politics, and to democratic politics in particular. In order to explore these issues, I turn to this debate, which has the virtue of exploring these issues in some detail, thus allowing me to begin to draw out what may be involved in talking of 'democratic rhetoric'.

Analogy and the question of likenesses

Analogical argument is eminently apt for politics because analogy and politics both involve building innovatively upon the past by constructively extending precedent.[108]

In analogical argument, the key question concerns the character of extended precedents, and especially for our purposes their relation to imagination and political argumentation. Aronovitch argues that analogical reasoning – in contrast to deductive forms of reasoning,[109] statistical generalization (reasoning from what is known concerning a sample of instances, to a conclusion about a whole class of them) and arguments based on cause and effect (proceeding from a knowledge of either of the elements to an inference about their connectedness) – 'works by relying upon a key likeness or specific parallels between particular situations, persons, entities, and so on'.[110] There are two issues in need of further exploration here, and for Aronovitch they are closely connected. The first concerns the nature of 'similarities' while the second addresses the criteria of success for analogy. To begin

---

[108] Aronovitch, 'The political importance of analogical argument', 78.

[109] Though Aronovitch, on the whole, portrays analogical argument as one form of argument among others, in places he clearly presents it as more suited to politics and better than deductive forms of argument *per se*. For instance, he argues that 'deductive arguments in ethics and politics suffer from a tendency either to leave large gaps between premises and conclusion or to avoid them by traversing only minor and inconsequential distances'. Aronovitch, 'The political importance of analogical argument', 90.

[110] Aronovitch, 'The political importance of analogical argument', 80.

with, Aronovitch suggests that any range of possible subjects may be subject to analogy: particular situations, persons, entities and so forth. Their persuasiveness depends upon 'the compelling quality of the known case(s), and on the likeness involved'.[111] While the emphasis on likeness could easily be read in a naturalistic fashion, for Aronovitch interpretation is central to extending from that which is familiar to that which is unfamiliar. This, in principle, opens the establishment of analogies to debate and contestation: 'the argument for the extension or innovation is itself never uniquely and definitively valid as against alternatives but rather more or less persuasive as compared to them'.[112] And, as he points out, much of political debate 'is indeed a battle over basic imagery and analogies and this is proper to politics for major images and analogies express or suggest fundamental interpretations of a country's past and visions of its future'.[113] Indeed, often more than first principles, metaphors fix the terms for an argument; they are thus essential in motivating and conferring meaning to principles, rather than simply heuristic devices.[114] Examples of such metaphors – or to put it in Wittgensteinian terms, pictures that have the ability to hold us captive[115] – include the social contract and the image of the planet as a global village, to name but two. While they are contestable, 'analogically established values reach back to instances or a series of particulars that are individually secured'.[116] According to Aronovitch, such attachments to particulars and to specific traditions potentially give analogies and analogical forms of argument their grip.

[111] Ibid. [112] Aronovitch, 'The political importance of analogical argument', 86.
[113] Ibid. [114] Aronovitch, 'The political importance of analogical argument', 84.
[115] Wittgenstein, in *On Certainty*, suggests that:'We form *the picture* of the earth as a ball floating free in space and not altering essentially in a hundred years' and that the picture of the earth as a ball 'is a *good* picture, it proves itself everywhere, it is also a simple picture – in short, we work with it without ever doubting it'. See L. Wittgenstein, *On Certainty*, ed. G. E. M. Anscombe and G. H. von Wright, trans. D. Paul and G. E. M. Anscombe (Oxford: Basil Blackwell, 1979), §§ 146 and 147. For a discussion of the role of pictures in Wittgenstein and an account of how pictures hold us captive, see D. Owen, 'Genealogy as perspicuous representation', pp. 82–96.
[116] Aronovitch, 'The political importance of analogical argument', 88.

Apart from the 'fit' between proposed analogies and particular situations, Aronovitch discusses the features of analogical argument that may make it particularly persuasive.[117] It is here that a tension emerges between the recognition of the inescapably provisional character of analogical argument and a fear of relativism.[118] In the course of telling the story of challenges to inequality in the formation of liberalism, Aronovitch concludes with the following claims:

> What is required, therefore, in order to see what Aristotle did not see and to confirm *why he was wrong* is a comparison of traditions in terms of their sequences of particulars and manner of judging likeness and difference. And the critique of bad analogical arguments, as involving, say, an overemphasis on the Athenian-foreigner contrast, is as much a part of what I am recommending as is the constructing of good ones. Through the comparison can be made manifest the greater coherence of one tradition, including coherence with science, and the obstacles to coherence of another, including a false metaphysics. In these ways we simultaneously explain how we arrived at our current notion and also justify it: by explicating a particular sequence of analogical development and the unseating of alternative views it involves.[119]

It is here that one must question the depth of Aronovitch's commitment to analogical forms of argument as probable rather than necessary, as open to debate and contestation, rather than based on

[117] Aronovitch draws on existing work in logic and argumentation to appraise analogical arguments. See I. M. Copi and C. Cohen, *Introduction to Logic*, 9th edn (New York: Macmillan, 1994), pp. 459–63. These criteria include the number of entities between which analogies are said to hold; the number of respects in which the things involved are said to be analogous; the relation between premises and conclusion; the number of disanalogies between instances mentioned in the premises; and relevance, which underlies all other criteria.

[118] Aronovitch suggests that although 'all justification may take us back to the particulars and precedents of one tradition or another, it is not the case that the traditions ... are all on par: we are not awash in a sea of relativism'. Aronovitch, 'The political importance of analogical argument', 89.

[119] Aronovitch, 'The political importance of analogical argument', 90, emphasis added.

'natural properties'. The emphasis on coherence comes very close to precisely the sort of context-transcendent forms of argument that Aronovitch has been at pains to contrast to analogical argumentation.[120] While on the one hand Aronovitch affirms the necessity of the appeal to particulars and the way in which analogical argument establishes linkages between principles and particulars, his narrative is premised upon an account of progress, often found in contemporary liberalism. Moreover, in affirming analogical forms of reasoning as a 'measured approach', which can avoid 'the extremes of conservatism and utopianism through its precedent-based, open-ended and evolving character',[121] he comes very close to conflating a general form of reasoning, which is common within politics to a specific ideological tradition. This is the starting-point of Panagia's critique of Aronovitch's reading of analogical argument.[122] Panagia claims that Aronovitch's emphasis on 'stability, agreement and progressive steps into the future' effectively equates politics and liberalism.

From subsumptive to active analogy

According to Panagia, this equation is problematic since it reduces politics to liberalism. However, he does not question Aronovitch's association between analogical reasoning and, more precisely, a liberal version of deliberative democracy. Instead, Panagia's reading of Kant draws out the role of the *predicative* function of analogy, and attempts to trace out its lineage in neo-Kantian liberalism.[123] Hence,

---

[120] Coherence clearly is central to the tradition of scientific reasoning. However, once different styles of reasoning are considered, the place of coherence itself changes. See Ian Hacking's discussion of 'styles of reasoning', in I. Hacking, 'Language, truth, reason', in M. Hollis and S. Lukes (eds.), *Rationality and Relativism* (Oxford: Basil Blackwell, 1983), pp. 48–66.

[121] Aronovitch, 'The political importance of analogical argument', 92.

[122] Davide Panagia, 'The predicative function in ideology: on the political uses of analogical reasoning in contemporary political thought', *Journal of Political Ideologies* 6, no. 1 (2001), 55–74.

[123] Panagia, 'The predicative function', 56–7.

for Panagia the problem with Aronovitch's argument is not the link between liberalism and analogy, which he wishes to affirm: 'analogical reason is the *sine qua non* of the liberal version of deliberative democracy insofar as this liberalism is indebted to a Kantian ethics of a common sense'.[124] Rather, it is the reduction of politics to liberalism, which negates the possibility of a political thinking not based on analogy.

How does Panagia reach these conclusions? Drawing on Ricoeur, he outlines a distinction between two theories of metaphor, one based on substitution and the other on 'interaction'. Whereas the former concentrates on the passive substitution of one term for another, the latter captures the active, predicative moment of metaphor:

> Metaphor produces meaning not because it passively substitutes one term for another, but because it actively combines terms in such as way as to *produce* the similar.[125]

In contrast to the substitution model, an emphasis on the predicative function – the metaphoricity of metaphor – avoids subsumption[126] and thus retains difference. In this case '[t]wo differences encounter each other in metaphor and the result is an instance of confrontation, contestation and the production of signification'.[127] Understanding metaphor on the basis of interaction thus foregrounds what Ricoeur calls the enigma of metaphor, the fact that difference is retained in the very moment of the establishment of similarity. This is analogous to Laclau's account of the constitution of equivalences,

---

[124] Panagia, 'The predicative function', 67.

[125] Panagia, 'The predicative function', 58, emphasis added.

[126] In Kant, as Panagia points out, judgement is the ability one has to subsume a particular under the concept of the general. 'In determinative judgement the universal law is already given, and therefore this form of judgement can only function as subsumption. In reflective judgement we are only given particular empirical laws; we therefore do not know the universal principles and must determine them through reflective judgement' (p. 62). In the case of the latter, the movement is from particular to universal and the principle allowing this move is that of the 'purposiveness of nature' (p. 63).

[127] Panagia, 'The predicative function', 59.

and contrasts with a Kantian understanding in which natural resemblance forms the basis of analogical reason.[128] Panagia emphasizes the fact that in Kant this forms part of the image of thought as committed to harmony, hence the emphasis on consensus in deliberative theories of democracy. Taking up the contrasting thought of the enigma of metaphor in Ricoeur, Panagia concludes that another kind of political thinking is possible, which is not based on metaphor as subsumption. This thinking is not concerned with that which is similar, but that which is different. While not developed, Panagia invokes the works of Derrida, Deleuze, Foucault and Rancière to point towards democracy as 'interactive moments of rupture within the operation of systems'.[129] In short, Panagia's reading clearly highlights the extent to which a Kantian-inspired conception of politics will tend to be harmonizing rather than disruptive. In addition, his invocation of Ricoeur ensures that another reading of analogy, which is not based on a model of resemblance but emphasizes the moment of enigma – the metaphoricity of metaphor – remains a possibility.[130]

As we have seen in our earlier discussion of Laclau, the space for thinking about politics in general (rather than liberalism and deliberative democracy in particular) in terms of a generalized rhetoricality is opened up once the dependence upon a model of resemblance

[128] Kant addresses the need for analogy in the *Third Critique*. 'Through judgement we encounter the concept of a sensible intuition and transfer that concept onto another object. This establishes a similarity between the two objects and between the rules we use to reflect on the two objects. Thus, with the example of the colour red and the concept of love, a natural resemblance is found between the two such that redness arouses within us an understanding of love.' Panagia, 'The predicative function', 64–5. Panagia, following Ricoeur, attributes the subsumption model, based on resemblance, to Aristotle as well. For a more detailed treatment of analogy and metaphor in Aristotle, see G. E. R. Lloyd, *Polarity and Analogy* (Cambridge: Cambridge University Press, 1966), pp. 405–14.

[129] Panagia, 'The predicative function', 69.

[130] Panagia argues in this respect that we need 'a discussion of the status of the predicative function implicit in all ideologies, as it would seem that it is these predicative elements that allow for movement in thought'. Panagia, 'The predicative function', 70.

is problematized. Several consequences follow from this. If we are indeed in a terrain of a generalized rhetoricality, where similarities and differences cannot be read off from natural resemblances, then any such similarities and differences must be the result of a process of articulation, which is deeply political in character. If this is correct, then also democratic forms of argumentation, as well as democratic forms of community, have to be analysed on the basis of an understanding of politics that privileges contingent articulatory processes,[131] which are always in principle and in practice open to contestation and disruption. Dissensus and struggle then stand at the heart of any thoroughgoing conception of democracy. But, this is not to give up on the normative dimensions of democratic discourse. On the contrary, as is clear in Rancière's rendering of the eruption of demands for equality, it is possible to combine the normative force of a presupposition of equality, with a conception of democracy that places dissensus at its heart, as I shall argue in more detail in Chapter 4.

However, once this is done, far greater attention needs to be given to forms of argumentation and struggle in and through which democracy is instituted and iterated. Here, again, we are not in a no man's land where 'everything goes' as the rhetorical tradition and its extension to the analysis of political discourses, identities and contexts offers rich resources for a rigorous and systematic analysis of the argumentative forms of democracy. Moreover, it is also clear that democratic forms of argumentation cannot be strictly deductive in character since the latter aim to remove the possibility of contestation from the process.[132] Thus insofar as democracy is premised upon the visibility of contingency, no logico-deductive mode of argumentation can be used, either in its defence or as a regulative ideal.

---

[131] It is crucial that an account of articulation includes a treatment of imagination, or following Cicero, *ingenium*.

[132] This does not rule out the possibility of utilizing loosely deductive forms of argumentation, in which the premises are treated as defeasible. I would like to thank David Owen for drawing my attention to this possibility.

The rhetorical dimensions of argumentation – the dimension of showing, as well as the deployment of tropes and figures – and the imagination necessary for its operation, need to be at the heart of any truly democratic conception of argumentation. This emphasis on an awareness of contingency further evokes sensitivity to the particular context and to the need for democratic identification, as well as the constitution of democratic imaginaries. It is to this final issue that we now turn.

DEMOCRATIC IMAGINARIES

In their account of democracy Laclau and Mouffe emphasize the importance of what they call the institution of a democratic imaginary, which emerged historically with the Declaration of the Rights of Man. The democratic imaginary provides a space of inscription, in which demands for equality and freedom can be inscribed and extended to further and further domains. As part of this account, Laclau focuses on the formation of subjectivity and the 'emptiness' that is presupposed by any democratic forms of identification. However, further thought is needed to flesh out the processes through which democratic imaginaries are constituted. And once again it is possible to contrast deliberative and post-structuralist accounts. I start with deliberative democrats.

Deliberation: external and internal

Deliberative democrats require interaction between participants as an essential part of the democratic process because for them such interaction has the virtue of exposing us to the viewpoints of others. In this conception, deliberation conducted in a public forum improves the quality of reasons offered, since all relevant perspectives, interests and information are more likely to be taken into account.[133] This means that deliberation per definition has to be public and

---

[133] J. Bohman, *Public Deliberation. Plurality, Complexity, and Democracy* (Cambridge, Mass.: The MIT Press, 1996), p. 27.

interpersonal. As Bohman argues: 'Deliberation in democracies is interpersonal in a specific, political sense: it is public.' And publicity refers not just to the way citizens deliberate, but also to 'the *type of reasons* they give in deliberating'.[134] Deliberation must be open to all and it must be convincing to everyone. However, beyond these broad, yet already stringent, stipulations,[135] there are several different ways in which such interaction can be envisaged, each setting different standards and ideals for deliberation. These different deliberative models can be characterized as dialogical and reflective respectively. Rather than the standards and ideals of deliberation, of primary interest in this respect are the mechanisms that deliberative theorists envisage for extending alternative political imaginaries.

Bohman holds that a dialogical process of exchanging reasons cannot be settled without interpersonal cooperation and coordination.[136] Deliberation is, in essence, a cooperative activity. The dialogical requirement aims to make certain that it is possible to revise common understandings so as to ensure 'uptake', and this is understood to 'promote deliberation on reasons addressed to others, who are expected to respond to them in dialogue'.[137] The mechanisms summarized by Bohman include attempts to make explicit what is latent in common understandings and shared institutions, such as is found in Rawls's reflective equilibrium; back-and-forth exchanges around differences in

---

[134] Bohman, *Public Deliberation*, p. 25.

[135] As a consequence, 'the only things that ought to be convincing are the reasons offered by or to fellow citizens who also freely exercise their deliberative capacities'. And the audience set certain constraints on public reasons: they must be communicated in such a way that others can understand them, accept them and respond to them. Bohman, *Public Deliberation*, p. 26.

[136] Bohman notes that dialogue is not something we can engage in by ourselves. He holds that it is only in dialogue with others 'that the many diverse capacities for deliberation are exercised jointly' (Bohman, *Public Deliberation*, p. 24). Public deliberation is dialogue with a specific goal, namely that of solving a problem or resolving conflict. It is also important that it is not merely discursive (employing specific regulative standards of justification); it is the mere give and take of reasons (Bohman, *Public Deliberation*, p. 57). It should also be noted that Bohman is critical of some forms of neo-Kantianism and the overly rationalistic views of democracy developed by thinkers such as Habermas (cf. pp. 44–5).

[137] Bohman, *Public Deliberation*, p. 59.

biographical and collective historical experiences, such as proposed by Laden;[138] discourses of application, which are concerned with the use of general norms in specific contexts; the enrichment of norms; shifting and exchanging perspectives so as to enable 'thinking from the standpoint of everyone else'.[139] By deploying these mechanisms Bohman argues that reasons can become generally convincing and thought can be enlarged, as Kant puts it. In addition, attention should also be given to processes that contribute to the ability of democracies to 'promote the emergence and formation of new publics', which may also, crucially, alter the framework of deliberation.[140] As Bohman emphasizes, deliberation within institutions often sets limits on available options, thus stifling democratic renewal. For such renewal to take place, democratic institutions should interact with what he calls 'new publics', which take two main forms – the speech of social critics and the emergence of social movements. In this respect, there is some rapprochement between deliberativists such as Bohman, and post-structuralists such as Rancière and Laclau. Social critics and new social movements have the potential to open up stagnant institutions by introducing new themes and topics and by framing issues in new ways. As we have seen, in 'unblocking' such institutions, Bohman acknowledges that 'irony, jokes, metaphors and other jarring ways of expressing something'[141] may become necessary. Similarly, in the case of social movements, there is a need to go beyond accepted norms and frameworks in order to disclose 'new possibilities of human freedom and transformative agency'.[142] However, it is critical that Bohman limits disclosure by making it 'relative to the limits of existing possibilities of meaning and expression'. When taken together with Bohman's retention of the primacy of reason, this limitation is

---

[138] See A. S. Laden, *Reasonably Radical. Deliberative Liberalism and the Politics of Identity* (Ithaca, N.Y.: Cornell University Press, 2001), p. 196.

[139] Bohman, *Public Deliberation*, p. 40.   [140] Bohman, *Public Deliberation*, p. 198.

[141] Bohman, *Public Deliberation*, p. 205.

[142] Bohman, *Public Deliberation*, p. 213. Disclosure for Bohman does not disclose truth, 'but concerns what makes truth possible'; thus requiring further public testing.

significant. As a result, the radical possibilities of disclosure, which approximate Rancière's conception of polemicization, are subordinated to the broader strictures of his thought.

In contrast to Bohman, for whom deliberation must be an activity in common with others, Goodin argues that others need not be conversationally present. It may only be a matter of making them 'imaginatively' present in the minds of deliberators, so as to inform and expand the democratic imaginary.[143] It is, of course, clear that this 'internal' work does not seek to replace, but rather to supplement external-collective forms of deliberation. Goodin's emphasis on the internal-reflective work that needs to be done in a democracy seeks to revalorize the input-side of democracy, as well as to address some of the practical problems faced by advocates of deliberative forms of democracy.[144] In practical terms, 'democratic deliberation within' asks of participants in the democratic process to assess what is 'the right thing to do, from all perspectives'.[145] It seeks to provide a way to project ourselves into the place of others, with whom we cannot speak, interact or deliberate in person. This requires an imaginative process of engagement that draws on the rich cultural sources available to us in many types of media, from film and television to literature and art. For instance, Goodin cites the important role of autobiographical slave narratives in supporting the abolitionist cause. Similarly, it is often the case that fiction has the ability to engage our imagination in ways that are more effective than historical or reflective essays.[146] And for Goodin this internal reflection is an intrinsic part of the democratic process. However, he fails to address the conditions under which people may be open to such expansion of their imagination, collective or otherwise, and does not account for

---

[143] Goodin, *Reflective Democracy*, p. 171.
[144] In particular, Goodin seeks to address some of the problems that large-scale democracies face in this respect. See his discussion of 'serial deliberation', 'ersatz deliberation', 'emaciated deliberation' and 'blinkered deliberation', in *Reflective Democracy*, pp. 172–8.
[145] Goodin, *Reflective Democracy*, p. 228.
[146] Goodin, *Reflective Democracy*, p. 181.

the norms of communication underlying such an approach. Without some form of dislocation to existing imaginaries, there is little incentive to engage, and even then it is doubtful whether engagement will necessarily take the form of seeing something 'from all perspectives'.

The role of imagination

Post-structuralist political theory in general is well placed to address the question of imagination, focusing as it does on the symbolic resources of politics. However, an affirmation of the essentially symbolic character of political life is not enough to conceptualize that which is required to develop our political imagination in general, and a democratic imaginary in particular. Thus far, we have drawn attention to the role of rhetoric in the constitution of arguments. More specifically, I have emphasized the role of non-subsumptive analogical thinking for constructing equivalences. This discussion has been set in the context of a critique of rationalism as the basis for political argument and judgement. In recuperating the rhetorical dimension of argument and 'being' in general, I have also argued that the requirement of intelligibility requires careful attention to the particular context in which arguments are developed; the individual audiences at which discourses are directed, and the specificity of the kinds of discourse at stake. In contrast to attempts to cast democratic arguments in an *a priori* and universalistic mould, I have argued that the contestability at the heart of democracy should also be reflected in our accounts of democratic argumentation. This is particularly evident in the role that equality plays in democratic discourse. It is undeniable that equality of conditions of participation and speech are laudable ideals. However, this characterization simply miscasts too much of what is at stake in democratic politics. First, it assumes equality and is interested merely in its institutional instantiation instead of investigating its eruption and verification. Secondly, it does not give sufficient attention to the dislocatory experiences needed to provoke an engagement with the viewpoints of others. And finally it tends to assume the existence of a framework of politics in which in principle every voice could be heard, without giving attention to the very structuring of those frameworks and the ways in which the visibility of subjects is structured.

In contrast to the denigration of rhetoric and non-deductive forms of argumentation, I have argued that the contemporary recuperation of the rhetorical tradition gives ample evidence of the possibility of a systematic approach to the analysis of rhetorical forms and their role in the constitution of political subjectivities and imaginaries. Having said this, as Zerilli points out, we should also recognize that we need more than 'the affirmation of contingency'. We need also to be able to think through 'the creation of coherence and meaning that does not efface contingency and thus freedom'.[147] In terms of our earlier discussion of metaphor, we need modes of creating coherence that are not subsuming in character and which give proper place to the role of articulation and imagination in the constitution and maintenance of democratic orders, where maintenance must be understood in terms of maintaining the openness to challenge of any instituted order. In this regard, Zerilli finds in Arendt a conception of judgement not based on determinate judgement and which gives recognition to the productive role of the imagination. Moreover, such judgement for Arendt, as for Cavell, has a disclosive character: it tells us something about, and constructs and/or challenges that community of which we are a part. It is also deeply political in nature:

> The worldly relations that judging creates turn crucially on the ability to see the same thing from multiple points of view, an ability that, in Arendt's telling, is identical with what it means to see politically.[148]

---

[147] L. M. G. Zerilli, ' "We feel our freedom": Imagination and judgment in the thought of Hannah Arendt', *Political Theory* 33, no. 2 (2005), 163.

[148] Zerilli, 'We feel our freedom', 165.

Hence, Arendt shifts the question of political judgement from the epistemological realm to that of politics, which involves 'the exchange of arguments in the sense of opening up the world that has been disclosed to us through language',[149] enabling us to see the world from different perspectives. This form of judgement is arguable in a specific sense: it belongs to *streiten* (to quarrel or to contend) rather than to *disputieren*[150] and it involves imagination in the extension of concepts. Drawing on Kant's treatment of the imagination, Zerilli argues that imagination 'can work on or order material in such a way that we are able to create out of it noncausal associations and even new nature'. Indeed, in line with our earlier discussion and in a similar vein to Laclau she argues that such imagination creates 'new relations between things that have none', such that every 'extension of a political concept always involves an imaginative opening up of the world'.[151] As against most deliberativists' insistence on the presence of others, this imagination involves a third perspective – that of the spectator – which allows one 'to see the same world from one another's standpoint, to see the same in very different and frequently opposing aspects'.[152]

Hence, what we need is an account of the constitution of relations among persons, objects, and practices and so on, which form an articulate network within which things make sense to us. Convincing and persuading one another[153] politically means that I must be able to get another to see the world under the aspect perceived by me, or at the very least to acknowledge the presence of different

---

[149] Zerilli, 'We feel our freedom', 166.

[150] As Zerilli explains: 'Whereas *disputieren* assumes that agreement can be reached through an exchange of arguments constrained by the rules set out by conceptual logic and objective knowledge (as with determinate judgments), *streiten* occurs when concepts are lacking and agreement cannot be reached through the giving of proofs (as with reflective judgment).' Zerilli, 'We feel our freedom', 170.

[151] Zerilli, 'We feel our freedom', 180 and 181. Zerilli points out that Arendt takes rather less from Kant than she could in the discussion of the role of imagination.

[152] Arendt quoted in Zerilli, 'We feel our freedom', 176–7.

[153] Persuasion moves via eloquence, while convincing occurs on the grounds of reasons, broadly conceived.

perspectives as valuable contributions to public life.[154] I turn to
Wittgenstein in the next chapter in order to furnish a more elaborate
account of this process. Once such agreement is gained following
debate and dispute, it would become a naturalized way of seeing the
world. However, as Wittgenstein knew in terms of language, and
Cavell elaborates further, the danger for democratic politics lies precisely in the risk of naturalization and conformism. As Hammer puts
it neatly, conformists 'fail to define their political selves'.[155] The
precise character and the constitution of the 'us' – the democratic
community – is the subject of the next two chapters. Suffice it to say
at this point that democratic argumentation has the character of
being open to challenge and negotiation, contestable in principle, and
hence it cannot be strictly deductive in character, nor does it aim to
reveal a transcendent truth or agreement. Instead, it is disruptive and
like all argumentation relies upon reasons. However, this is a part of a
process of contestation (streiten) rather than (logical) demonstration.
In short, its operation is inevitably rhetorical, since rhetoricality is
not something even reason itself can or should attempt to escape.

---

[154] Here Wittgenstein's account of continuous aspect perception clearly is helpful.
[155] Hammer, *Stanley Cavell*, p. 132.

3 Democratic identification and aspect change

> The creation of democratic forms of individuality is a question of identification with democratic values, and this is a complex process that takes place through a manifold of practices, discourses and language-games.[1]

Understanding the inaugurating moments of democratic subject formation and the practices sustaining such identification requires us to think about the role of, and changes, in political grammars – the latter understood as those horizons delimiting what is intelligible and, hence, what may count as possible reasons in any given context. Wittgenstein's account of aspect change opens up a fruitful way of thinking about these two moments in the context of a consideration of political grammar, while avoiding the pitfalls of either an overly sedimented or a 'heroic' conception of subjectivity within deliberative and post-structuralist positions respectively. Inspired by his emphasis on the practical character of language and grammar, I resist idealized theorizing and a disregard for ordinary political activities and engagements found in much contemporary political theory.[2] However, this does not involve shunning the theorization of democratic practices. Instead, it leads us to engage with the puzzles arising out of the grip of particular pictures on our thinking and to open up new ways of looking at things.[3] The seeing of aspects counters the cognitivism of much of the dominant approaches and shifts attention to activities other than

---

[1] C. Mouffe, *The Democratic Paradox* (London: Verso, 2000), p. 70.

[2] On abstraction and idealization, see O. O'Neill, *Towards Virtue and Justice* (Cambridge: Cambridge University Press, 1996), p. 41. See also M. Freeden, *Ideologies and Political Theory. A Conceptual Approach* (Oxford: Clarendon Press, 1996), p. 3.

[3] Wittgenstein 'created a new style of thinking'. K. T. Fann, *Wittgenstein's Conception of Philosophy* (Berkeley: University of California Press, 1969), pp. 109–10.

thinking in bringing about political change. The paradox of aspect dawning, with its play on both originality and inheritance, offers a guide to rethinking changes in identification, accounting for the new without giving up on intelligibility. The experience of aspect change also foregrounds the moment of the subject, of identification. The accompanying awareness of multiplicity helps to establish the minimum conditions we need in order to get a democratic dialogue under way.

THE GRAMMAR OF POLITICAL VOCABULARIES

Our political vocabularies, insofar as they are rooted in our everyday language, are neither set in stone, nor easily amenable to change. If one is to come to an adequate understanding of the possibilities and limitations to change in those vocabularies, and concomitant changes in subjectivity, one needs to engage not just with specific grammars, but reflect upon the nature of grammar itself. For Wittgenstein, grammar sets the bounds of sense; it is, as Mulhall puts it, 'an articulated network of discriminations that inform our capacity to word the world, to bespeak anything and everything we encounter within it'.[4] Hence, grammar is not itself answerable to facts, but delimits what may count as possible descriptions of how things are. In short, grammar is autonomous: it cannot be falsified and cannot, in itself, be correct or incorrect.[5]

How then may a grammar be challenged? Here an example may be useful. Take, for instance, different conceptions of liberty. If liberty is understood as a human-growth theory, rather than as an unlimited self-determination theory, its surrounding concepts will be limited in a particular way.[6] Notions of equality of opportunity, rather than non-interference, will take centre stage. Thus, the manner in which a

---

[4] S. Mulhall, *Inheritance and Originality. Wittgenstein, Heidegger, Kierkegaard* (Oxford: Clarendon Press, 2001), p. 176.

[5] Grammar is autonomous in the technical sense that it is not amenable to external justification. This does not make it unimportant. See, M. O'Neill, 'Explaining "the hardness of the logical must": Wittgenstein on grammar, arbitrariness and logical necessity', *Philosophical Investigations* 24, no. 1 (2001), 15.

[6] Freeden, *Ideologies and Political Theory*, pp. 68–9, and 77.

central political concept is decontested,[7] limits its political usage. Such deconstestation may not be amenable to falsification and empirical testing.[8] Rather, making visible the grip of a particular (decontestation within a) grammar requires disclosing the specific paths and practices that have been closed off. To put it differently, one needs to treat political grammars in a genealogical fashion.[9] Two elements of Wittgenstein's work in particular can throw further light on thinking through grammatical change. The first concerns his method of engagement with philosophical problems as demonstrated in his own writings.[10] The second is his account of aspect change, which I shall argue, offers a perspicuous way of thinking about grammatical change.

Wittgenstein's method of engagement

Grounded in what he calls a therapeutic practice,[11] Wittgenstein's method of philosophy in his later work demonstrates what may be required in challenging particular 'grammars'. Unlike the *Tractatus*, where Wittgenstein was still enthralled by the prospect of resolving the problems of philosophy once and for all, his later works proceed on the basis of a repeated engagement with the confusions engendered in philosophy by the pictures that hold it captive. This therapeutic task has both a negative and positive dimension.[12] The

---

[7] The term decontestation is drawn from Freeden's work on the morphology of ideology. Once a term is decontested, certain usages are affirmed and others ruled out. The analytical question is then why a specific decontestation, one ordering of the political world rather than another, prevails. Freeden, *Ideologies and Political Theory*, p. 76.

[8] For a similar point, see L. M. G. Zerilli, 'Doing without knowing: feminisms' politics of the ordinary', *Political Theory* 26, no. 4 (1998), 453–4.

[9] See D. Owen, 'Genealogy as perspicuous representation', in C. J. Heyes (ed.), *The Grammar of Politics. Wittgenstein and Political Philosophy* (London: Cornell University Press, 2003), pp. 82–96.

[10] I stress the critical impulse here. See also D. Cornell, ' "Convention" and critique', *Cardozo Law Review* 7 (1986), 679–91; G. Pohlhaus and J. R. Wright, 'Using Wittgenstein critically', *Political Theory* 30, no. 6 (2002), 800–27.

[11] See L. Wittgenstein, *Philosophical Investigations* (Oxford: Basil Blackwell, 1958), §133, § 225.

[12] Wittgenstein's understanding of therapy diverges sharply from Habermas'. See F. R. Dallmayer, 'Critical theory criticized', *Philosophy of the Social Sciences* 2, no. 3 (1972), 221–5.

former draws attention to the confusions engendered by purported philosophical problems, whereas the latter aims to provide a surview of the grammar of the concepts. Two aspects of this approach are of particular interest: the first concerns that which 'drives' the search for therapies, and the second the way that Wittgenstein addresses the problems he has identified.

Though there is not a single 'source', there is an identifiable set of concerns that seem to inform the need for therapies: they include 'the pictures holding us captive', the 'bewitchment of our intelligence by language', the confusions arising when 'language goes on holiday', and so on. As Wittgenstein argues: 'We are interested in language only insofar as it gives us trouble.'[13] This trouble arises, not where one would expect it, not in the use of difficult words or forms of expression. More often than not, Wittgenstein emphasizes that it is the simplicity and familiarity of things that are at the root of our difficulties. In addition to these concerns, Wittgenstein repeatedly invokes occasions on which we do not know how to go on, are perplexed, puzzled or anxious.[14] In all of these cases, there is a certain dislocation or disorientation that inspires the search for resolution.[15]

The manner in which Wittgenstein tackles such problems is enlightening. There is, for a start, no one solution, no one therapy; instead, he proceeds through a variety of means – by giving examples, asking questions, discussing particular cases, and so forth – to clarify and dissolve the problems addressed. Here I wish to concentrate on his use of ordinary, everyday activities. These activities are situated

---

[13] L. Wittgenstein, *Wittgenstein's Lectures, Cambridge 1932–35*, ed. A. Ambrose (Oxford: Basil Blackwell, 1979), p. 97.

[14] 'My talent consists in being capable of being puzzled when the puzzlement has glided off your mind.' Wittgenstein quoted in G. P. Baker and P. M. S. Hacker, *Wittgenstein. Meaning and Understanding, Essays on the Philosophical Investigations*, vol. I (Oxford: Basil Blackwell, 1983), p. 305.

[15] Dislocation here indicates a rupture in sedimented ways of doing things. See E. Laclau, *New Reflections on the Revolution of Our Time* (London: Verso, 1990), pp. 41–4. Cavell suggests the term 'disorientation' for these experiences. S. Cavell, 'The *Investigations*' everyday aesthetics of itself', in T. McCarthy and S. C. Studd (eds.), *Wittgenstein in America* (Oxford: Clarendon Press, 2001), p. 251.

within the context of ordinary daily life and their aims are both to show the work that examples may do, and to recast the status of the phenomenon under discussion such that it provides a clear view of the use of words by drawing out connections:

> A main source of our failure to understand is that we do not command a clear view of the use of words. – Our grammar is lacking in this sort of perspicuity. A perspicuous representation produces just that understanding which consists in 'seeing connexions'.[16]

He shows that this work can be done through recounting ordinary practices in an extraordinary fashion so as to make visible the confusions upon which many accounts of meaning rest. Particularly important here is that he does not adduce new evidence or develop a novel theoretical account of meaning; instead, his examples rearrange what is already apparent. It is worth our while to explore these points further, for each has important consequences for our later argument concerning the ways in which a Wittgenstein-inspired approach may inform discussion of democratic subject formation. Wittgenstein does not bring new evidence to bear, since it is not facts that are at stake here. What matters is the frame within which something may count as a fact. Hence the emphasis on the (re)arrangement of elements which, simultaneously allows us to see something in a different light. In particular, it should be noted here that the elements do not change for Wittgenstein; what changes is the way we see them. This becomes particularly clear in Wittgenstein's reading of Freud's account of the interpretation of dreams where he argues:

> When a dream is interpreted we might say that it is fitted into a context in which it ceases to be puzzling. In a sense the dreamer re-dreams his dream in surroundings such that its aspect changes ... and ... the result is that we say: 'Ah, now I see why it is like that,

---

[16] Wittgenstein, *Philosophical Investigations*, § 122.

how it all comes to be arranged in that way, and what these various bits are ... ' and so on.[17]

Thus, a change of grammar may come about through a rearrangement of elements, such that it provides us with a surview, which, in turn, allows us to notice some aspect of things that has hitherto gone unnoticed:

> the aspect of things that are most important for us are hidden because of their simplicity and familiarity. (One is unable to notice something – because it is always before our eyes.) The real foundations of [our] enquiry do not strike [us] at all.[18]

Before turning to a more detailed treatment of Wittgenstein's discussion of 'seeing aspects' it is important to note the different possibilities inherent in his account of 'noticing connections': the question arises whether it simply entails making visible something which has always already been there, or whether the making visible itself could actually be argued to draw out (new) connections (though these are, of course, not mutually exclusive possibilities). Statements such as 'One is unable to notice something – because it is always before our eyes' suggests that what is noticed is already there; we simply need to become aware of it. On this view, noticing connections occurs 'without discovering something new, by arranging what is already known in a way which clarifies the links or interconnections'.[19] However, it is important that the denial of 'newness' refers specifically to the fact that one does not bring to bear new evidence or facts. Hence, his account is not one that rests on a falsification of other views. Other aspects of his argument suggest that 'clarifying links', 'drawing connections, and 'noticing an aspect' all

---

[17] L. Wittgenstein, *Lectures and Conversations on Aesthetics, Psychology and Religious Belief*, ed. C. Barrett (Oxford: Basil Blackwell, 1989), pp. 45–6.

[18] Wittgenstein, *Philosophical Investigations*, § 129, emphasis added.

[19] H.-J. Glock, *A Wittgenstein Dictionary* (Oxford: Blackwell, 1996), p. 279.

entail a dimension of novel articulation:[20] simply by putting together elements, which were not previously thought of as belonging together, a new set of relations is brought to the fore.[21] And for Wittgenstein, as his treatment of Freudian psychoanalysis shows, this is not a matter of discussion but of persuasion.[22] This articulatory dimension is going to be important in thinking through the political ramifications of his account of aspect seeing.[23]

SEEING ASPECTS

Wittgenstein's interest in aspect perception – in the way in which we 'see' pictures and people – is in how it illuminates important dimensions of our relation to words, understood here as grammar, as how we 'word the world'.[24] Hence, it is not a narrow concern with pictures, but has a far wider reach. As Cavell puts it, 'the topic of our attachment to our words is allegorical of our attachments to ourselves and to other persons'.[25] What is it about aspect perception that allows one to make sense of changes in grammars? As I have argued above, grammar is not subject to extraneous verification since grammar itself provides standards of verification and sets the bounds of sense. Wittgenstein treats matters of verification, justification, and so on,

[20] Articulation refers to a practice of putting together elements that have no necessary belonging. E. Laclau and C. Mouffe, *Hegemony and Socialist Strategy. Towards a Radical Democracy Politics* (London: Verso, 1985), pp. 105–6.

[21] In § 122 Wittgenstein emphasizes 'the importance of finding and inventing connecting links'. See Baker and Hacker, *Meaning and Understanding*, p. 307.

[22] Wittgenstein, *Lectures and Conversations*, § 33, p. 27.

[23] For a detailed discussion of aspect change, see S. Mulhall, *On Being in the World. Wittgenstein and Heidegger on Seeing Aspects* (London: Routledge, 1990).

[24] Mulhall, *On Being in the World*, p. 137, and *Inheritance and Originality*, p. 176. This is important in determining its scope. While some focus particularly on its relevance to art (G. McFee, 'Wittgenstein on art and aspects', *Philosophical Investigations* 22, no. 3 (1999), 262–84) others argue that it has broader significance. See J. Churchill, 'Rat and mole's epiphany of Pan: Wittgenstein on seeing aspects and religious belief', *Philosophical Investigations* 21, no. 4 (1998), 152–72; and A. Baz, 'What's the point of seeing aspects?', *Philosophical Investigations* 23, no. 2 (2000), 97–8.

[25] S. Cavell, *The Claim of Reason. Wittgenstein, Skepticism, Morality, and Tragedy* (Oxford: Oxford University Press, 1982), p. 355.

under the rubric of 'knowing', as against 'seeing'. Knowing always involves analysis, interpretation and description that stand in stark contrast to the grammar of aspect perception, which Wittgenstein further divides into continuous aspect perception and aspect dawning, the latter of which provides a distinctive account of change.[26]

Continuous aspect perception involves 'an immediate, spontaneous reaching for the relevant form of description', where words are used as a simple perceptual report, 'without any awareness that it is one of several options'. For instance, when we look at pictures 'we do not proffer a description of them as if it were one of many possible interpretations'.[27] There is an immediacy in the description offered: 'The focus is ... on the readiness-to-hand of that correct form of description; and this readiness-to-hand is a manifestation of the perceiver's taking for granted the identity of what he perceives.'[28] Hence, continuous aspect perception captures a particular attitude to pictures that is akin to the naturalization that accompanies the sedimentation of grammars. This attitude also has a corollary in what Mulhall calls 'continuous meaning perception' which, for instance, is evident in situations where we know exactly which word it is we wish to deploy at a certain moment.[29] Mulhall argues that the readiness-to-hand of such judgements 'shows the depth to which we have assimilated the principles of organization that structure our language and constitute the specificity of individual word-meaning'.[30] Politically, this is analogous to a situation of hegemony in which we just treat matters in a certain way, where we do not weigh up different alternatives and interpret our practices but simply take them for granted. Hence, in our practices we display an unhesitating attitude, a familiarity, which is indicative of the depth of assimilation of

---

[26] Wittgenstein, *Philosophical Investigations*, p. 194[e]. For Wittgenstein, the aspect blind would treat pictures on an interpretative model, *inferring* from the shape of a face, its expression and so on, that the person is friendly, rather than '*seeing* friendliness of gaze'.

[27] Mulhall, *Being in the World*, p. 22.   [28] Mulhall, *Being in the World*, p. 23.

[29] Mulhall, *Inheritance and Originality*, p. 165.   [30] Ibid.

those practices. Now, it is important that this attitude evident in continuous aspect and meaning perception is a general feature of our human (form of) life. Indeed, without this, no aspect dawning would be possible since no sense of paradox would arise were it not for the experience of continuous aspect perception.[31]

Aspect dawning or change occurs when one realizes that a new kind of characterization of an object or situation may be given, and we see it in those terms:

> I am shewn a picture-rabbit and asked what it is; I say 'It's a rabbit'. Not 'Now it's a rabbit'. I am reporting my perception ... But I may also react ... quite differently. The answer that it is a duck-rabbit is ... the report of a perception; the answer 'Now it's a rabbit' is not ...
>
> The expression of a change of aspect is the expression of a new perception and at the same time of the perception's being unchanged.[32]

Let us begin with a note of caution: though the duck-rabbit example encapsulates the experience of aspect change rather neatly, it should not be taken as paradigmatic, since a fixation on it leads one to miss certain crucial features of the experience while over-emphasizing others. For instance, it underplays the extent to which one takes seeing aspects as having a point,[33] while at the same time creating the impression of a reversible, simple 'flipping' between (just two) different perspectives.[34] Such a 'flipping' between perspectives also suggests that both aspects are either in some sense of equal

---

[31] This is also how Wittgenstein dissolves the sense of paradox arising with aspect dawning. Mulhall, *Inheritance and Originality*, p. 162. Baz takes issue with Mulhall's further claim that Wittgenstein's true interest therefore lies in the notion of '*continuous* aspect seeing'. Adjudicating between these views goes beyond the scope of the present argument. For our purposes, it is enough to note that both emphasize the centrality of aspect seeing to human life and the peculiar nature of being 'occupied' in a particular way when experiencing aspect change.

[32] Wittgenstein, *Philosophical Investigations*, 195e–196e.

[33] An isolated mental experience needs have no point. Baz, 'What's the point', 99.

[34] Cavell, *The Claim of Reason*, p. 354.

value, or of no value at all, whereas politically, a change of aspect often carries with it a great deal of revaluation of a previous perspective.

Among the more general features of the experience of aspect dawning, it is especially crucial to observe that the dawning of an aspect depends upon the drawing of connections. In this sense, the dawning of an aspect is closely connected to providing a surview, that is to say that, by putting objects, words or rules in relation to other objects, words or rules, they are situated in a different context in which sense is made of them. As Wittgenstein puts it: 'When the aspect changes parts of the picture go together which before did not.'[35] This entails seeing something in a different context, one that enables one to make new sense of it: for instance, seeing a radical environmental practice of tying oneself to a tree to prevent the building of a road as part of a web of new forms of democratic resistance. Here there is an articulation between elements that did not belong together before, which means that this experience of aspect change 'calls our attention to the fact that to see anything at all as anything is always, already, to see it in such relations'.[36] The properties of the object are not of key importance here. The relation between it and other objects is.[37] This rules out understanding aspect change on the basis of a cognitive model of the acquisition and accumulation of facts. Rather, aspect change is a shift in perspective that establishes different relations between objects. Looking at Wittgenstein's use of the examples of what he calls 'the Darwinian upheaval' and of Freudian psychoanalysis[38] reinforces these points. Wittgenstein does not regard the reasons why they were accepted as having anything to do with verification or understanding the

---

[35] Wittgenstein, *Philosophical Investigations*, 208^e.

[36] Churchill, 'Rat and Mole's epiphany of Pan', 154.

[37] Wittgenstein, *Philosophical Investigations*, 212^e, 'What I perceive in the dawning of an aspect is not a property of the object, but an internal *relation between it and other objects.*'

[38] Wittgenstein, *Lectures and Conversations*, § 32 and § 33.

causes of one's action.[39] Evidence is not what is at stake here; instead, evidence follows rather than precedes such change. Wittgenstein characterizes such change in the following way:

> I wanted to put that picture before him, and his acceptance of the picture consists in his now being inclined to regard a given case differently: that is, to compare it with this rather than that set of pictures. I have changed his way of looking at things.[40]

Hence, changing one's way of looking at things is not dependent upon a change in the object, but has to do with the relation between objects or words, and with noticing a different relation between these and other objects or words.

This account of coming to regard something differently encapsulates further important insights into the relation between the newness of an aspect dawning and the sense that nothing has changed: the practice or object remains the same, yet it is seen as new. Wittgenstein characterizes the moment of newness by expressions such as seeing something 'in a flash', and 'being struck' by something for the first time.[41] How precisely this moment of newness is understood and how it is configured in relation to existing practices and language use, is of crucial importance. While our ability to do (new) things with words is dependent upon being deeply immersed in our language practices, something more than that is at stake in aspect perception.[42] Where established ways of using words have run out, we are able 'to improvise ways of getting beyond such impasses'[43] and aspect change is one instance of accounting for the ways in

---

[39] See J. Bouveresse, *Wittgenstein Reads Freud*, trans. C. Cosman (Princeton, N.J.: Princeton University Press, 1995), pp. 56–7.

[40] Wittgenstein, *Philosophical Investigations*, § 144.

[41] Mulhall, *Inheritance and Originality*, p. 69.

[42] Just as creative use of language depends upon one's mastery of a language, witnessed in continuous meaning perception, aspect dawning is dependent upon continuous aspect seeing, and indeed shows us something about ordinary ways of seeing and the normal use of words.

[43] Mulhall, *Inheritance and Originality*, p. 69.

which we 'get beyond' or break with established, but tired ways of doing things. It goes beyond the normal practice of 'projecting' a word since such projection proceeds naturally, while in the case of aspect dawning normal directions of projection are broken up or challenged.[44] In this way, Wittgenstein interweaves the novel and what is given in our existing practices by drawing attention to the fact that language is not fixed and unalterable, but inherently open to the future.[45] As Wittgenstein argues, 'new types of language, new language games ... come into existence, and others become obsolete and get forgotten'.[46]

Both creative language use and aspect change bring subjectivity into play.[47] In the case of aspect change, the seeing of connections is accompanied by surprise and the expression of surprise (rather than the reporting of facts)[48] and a peculiar 'occupation' with the object at hand.[49] This first person expression or assent of the subject ('Now I see!') focuses attention on to the extent to which we have drawn new connections and reordered what we know. In making these connections the subject comes to say, 'Now I see!'[50] The moment of subjectivity is most clearly expressed in the reference to Freud's

---

[44] Cavell, *The Claim of Reason*, p. 189. Both Cavell and Mulhall point to the emphasis in Part II of the *Philosophical Investigations* on the 'figurative' uses of words, the *experience* of the meaning of words, the physiognomy of words, etc. which go beyond explanation by appeal to ordinary language games.

[45] Mulhall, *Inheritance and Originality*, p. 71.

[46] Wittgenstein, *Philosophical Investigations*, § 23.

[47] Luntley's recent interpretation of aspect seeing also locates the moment of the subject, and hence of judgement, here. See M. Luntley, *Wittgenstein* (Oxford: Blackwell Publishing, 2003).

[48] Baz, 'What's the point', 109.

[49] Mulhall argues that aspect change 'signals an occupation with the object which is the focus of the experience' (Mulhall, *Being in the World*, p. 12).

[50] The emphasis on 'surprise' solicited in drawing connections serves, in particular, to contrast aspect dawning with a process of interpretation. But note that 'surprise' is not just a feature of Wittgenstein's discussion of aspect dawning. It is already present in Wittgenstein's discussion of rule following. The drawing of connections is not, for Wittgenstein, some subliming moment, behind or beneath the utterance. It is particular circumstances that make sense of them. See, Mulhall, *Inheritance and Originality*, pp. 104–5.

interpretation of dreams discussed earlier and also occurs in Wittgenstein's treatment of mathematical understanding. Here, and in other places, Wittgenstein emphasizes the acceptance of a new picture by someone, evidence of which is borne out not only by verbal expression. For Wittgenstein, as in psychoanalysis, assent may be manifested in other things we are able to do once we have undergone an aspect change: we draw connections differently, see relations differently and so on.[51] In short, we do things differently once we have experienced a change of aspect. Hence, it is a change in sensibility that alters 'some of those deep perspectives in terms of which experience is appropriated, ordered, understood'.[52] Here the role of the subject and her 'occupation with' – what I will call identification-as – the matter at hand is indispensable.

Finally, given the account of change, aspect dawning allows one to step 'beyond the guidance of grammar' without, however, 'giving up on intelligibility'.[53] This is a key insight, since the break introduced is one that is not so radical as to no longer make sense to the subject. This precise putting together of novelty and tradition, of simultaneous contextualization and de-contextualization, is exactly what facilitates overcoming the log-jam between accounts of political subjectivity that are either too historicist or too voluntarist. Things simply are no longer the same; our way of looking at things has changed. But, as I have argued, this is not a break that denies all that has gone before. To the contrary, it is dependent upon what has gone before, but that before is also rearranged – resignified – in important respects. It is precisely this emphasis on rearrangement that allows one to think through a conception of political change that steers a path between radical rupture and continuity.

[51] For a discussion of the psychoanalytic case, see J. Glynos, 'Theory and evidence in the Freudian field: from observation to structure', in L. J. Glynos and Y. Stavrakakis (eds.), *Lacan and Science* (London: Karnac Press, 2002), pp. 13–50.

[52] J. C. Edwards, *Ethics without Philosophy. Wittgenstein and the Moral Life* (Tampa: University Presses of South Florida, 1985), p. 133.

[53] Baz, 'What's the point', 120.

UNDERSTANDING CHANGES IN POLITICAL GRAMMARS
Aspect change – in Rancière's terms, opening up the space where an argument may be heard in the first instance[54] – depends upon a different way of looking and seeing, which allows the subject to say 'Now I see things differently!' It is crucial that one acknowledges this moment of change, since without it there is no way of accounting for the very institution of a new political grammar. However, as I have argued above, this should not be treated as a moment of radical break, but as a rearrangement of elements that makes possible a new way of seeing something. Before exploring the implications for politics more fully, I briefly turn now to the way existing political theory negotiates the institution not only of new political grammars, but democratic political grammars in particular.

Against intellectualism: 'identification-as'

Let me first turn to theorists of deliberative democracy.[55] Much of their appeal derives from the ability to address the perceived need to revitalize political participation through engaging citizens in the decision-making process by means of deliberation; in this sense, it is 'seen as a hopeful way out of the quagmire of civic estrangement'.[56] Given the centrality accorded to the possibility of a change of view being brought about as a result of deliberative interaction,[57] it would not be unreasonable to expect that these accounts of democracy provide a conception of subjectivity that can accommodate and account for such change. Even though one may expect this to be a central theme

[54] J. Rancière, *Disagreement. Politics and Philosophy*, trans. J. Rose (Minneapolis: University of Minnesota Press, 1999), p. 56.

[55] I concentrate on Habermas-inspired accounts of deliberative democracy, though, as I point out later, Rawlsian accounts suffer from similar problems.

[56] E. C. Weeks, 'The practice of deliberative democracy: Results from four large-scale trials', *Public Administration Review* 60, no. 4 (2000), 360.

[57] See *inter alia* D. Pelletier, V. Kraak, C. McCullum, U. Uusitalo and R. Rich, 'The shaping of collective values through deliberative democracy: an empirical case study from New York's North County', *Policy Sciences* 32 (1999), 103–31; C. Sunstein, 'The law of group polarization', *The Journal of Political Philosophy* 10, no. 2 (2002).

occupying deliberative theorists, changes in political subjectivity have received scant attention. Many reasons may be furnished for this. For one thing, theorists of deliberative democracy are not, on the whole, concerned with the subjectivity of participants in the process,[58] but with procedures that may bring about the desired outcomes.

More precisely, their focus is on modes of decision-making within existing democratic systems, rather than the modes of subject formation pertinent to democracy.[59] And, insofar as they do deal with issues that may fall under the rubric of subjectivity and agency, they focus on providing an account that may bolster or improve existing normative commitments. In particular, the proceduralism[60] characteristic of Habermas' version of deliberative democracy forecloses the question of the identity-forming ethos of democracy.[61] It discourages the reactivation of questions concerning identity, as well as reflection on the ethos of democracy, since it presupposes that we follow the rules 'blindly'. This highlights the problem at stake. While, for instance, Habermas' whole account of politics acknowledges that there are circumstances under which the social coordinating mechanisms we take for granted may become disrupted, his answer to these disruptions relies on a model of politics that cannot account for

---

[58] For Habermas, the ' "self" of the self-organizing legal community disappears in the subjectless forms of communication that regulate ... will-formation'. J. Habermas, *Between Facts and Norms. Contributions to a Discourse Theory of Law and Democracy*, trans. William Rehg (Cambridge: Polity Press, 1997), p. 301. A notable exception in this regard is Warren's work on subjectivity. See M. Warren, 'The self in discursive democracy', in S. White (ed.), *The Cambridge Companion to Habermas* (Cambridge: Cambridge University Press, 1995), pp. 167–200.

[59] For a discussion of the presuppositions of the modern subject in liberal theory, see S. White, 'After Critique: Affirming subjectivity in contemporary political theory', *European Journal of Political Theory* 2, no. 2 (2003), 209–26.

[60] The success of deliberative politics 'depends not on a collectively active citizenry, but on the institutionalization of the corresponding procedures and conditions of communication'. Habermas, *Between Facts and Norms*, p. 298.

[61] Habermas grants the necessity of a democratic culture (*Between Facts and Norms*, pp. 487 and 500) but has difficulty incorporating it into his overall argument. See R. J. Bernstein, ' "Laws, morals, and ethics": The retrieval of the democratic ethos', *Cardozo Law Review* 17 (1996), 1127–46; R. Coles, 'Of democracy, discourse, and dirt virtue', *Political Theory* 28 (2000), 553.

the effects of deep dislocations. A Habermasian proceduralist answer to the disruption of sedimented practices calls for more formalization precisely under conditions where the very legitimacy of such procedures themselves may have been called into question.[62] If, instead, one turns one's attention to the characterization of already existing democratic practices, the problem reappears.[63] There is as yet no adequate account of the self that would support 'this image [of a democratically transformable self] as it relates to politics'.[64] Instead, we have an emphasis on the role and requirements of democratic discourse.[65] While suggestive, a rather bloodless conception of participation is put forward which, as I have suggested earlier, relies on rational argumentation and a provision of reasons to bring about change from one mode of thinking about a political problem to another, from purely self-interested motivations to thinking in terms of the general interest.[66]

Indeed, the problems remain even where the formation of citizens through participation is explicitly addressed. Laden's work is a case in point. Unlike most deliberative theorists his Rawlsian

---

[62] Stuart Hampshire, an internal critic of this position, suggests that procedures are also contestable: 'Procedures of conflict resolution within any state are always being criticized and are always changing and are never as fair and unbiased as they ideally might be. But if they are well known and are part of a continuous history, they are acceptable for reasons that Hume explained in his essay "The Ideals of Commonwealth". The institutions and their rituals hold society together, insofar as they are successful and well established in the resolution of moral and political conflicts according to the particular local and national conventions: "this is our peculiar form of governance and we cling to it."' S. Hampshire, *Justice is Conflict* (Princeton, N.J.: Princeton University Press, 2000), p. 26.

[63] See also R. Blaug, 'New theories of discursive democracy', *Philosophy and Social Criticism* 22, no. 1 (1996), 60.

[64] M. Warren, 'Democratic theory and self-transformation', *American Political Science Review* 86, no. 1 (1992), 13.

[65] See *inter alia* O. Renn, T. Webler and P. Wiedemann (eds.), *Fairness and Competence in Citizen Participation* (Dordrecht: Kluwer, 1995).

[66] See S. Benhabib, 'Toward a deliberative model of democratic legitimacy', in S. Benhabib (ed.), *Democracy and Difference. Contesting the Boundaries of the Political* (Princeton, N.J.: Princeton University Press, 1996), pp. 71–2; and J. Fearon, 'Deliberation as discussion', in J. Elster (ed.) *Deliberative Democracy* (Cambridge: Cambridge University Press, 1998), p. 49.

account of deliberative liberalism explicitly emphasizes the constitutive role played by the activity of 'reasonable political delibe-ration' in fostering the reasonableness of citizens.[67] Laden maintains that engagement in the process of reasonable deliberation itself will foster an attitude of reasonableness among citizens, such that they will value not only the particular results of deliberation but also the process itself. These are important and plausible insights. Hence, a key part of his work sets out to address the construction of a common political will where there is none: 'we sometimes engage in delib-eration with someone in the hopes of forming a relationship that does not yet exist'.[68] Laden argues:

> Offering claims in reasonable deliberation ought not to be seen on the model of premises in a practical deduction. Rather, we should see it as *inviting* ... one's deliberative partner to share a world-view – a space of reasons. Such an invitation can be extended both to someone with whom I already share a well-defined and mutually understood relationship and to one with whom I do not yet share anything but the possibility of forming such a relationship.[69]

To capture this sense of (possible) subjectivity, Laden introduces the term 'plural subject' to designate a situation in which people form a relationship and, importantly, have a sense of that relationship and the claims it authorizes.[70] However, as he acknowledges, this does not yet shed light 'on the phenomena of joint action and intention formation'.[71]

---

[67] A. S. Laden, *Reasonably Radical. Deliberative Liberalism and the Politics of Identity* (Ithaca, N.Y.: Cornell University Press, 2001), p. 195. Following Rawls, Laden holds reasonableness to be 'a willingness to engage in reasonable political deliberation when faced with political conflicts and to abide by the outcome of that deliberation' (p. 194).

[68] Laden, *Reasonably Radical*, 95. Laden's emphasis on the fact that practical reasonableness is not deductive in character is important, given the concerns expressed in Chapter 2 on the character of the rationality that informs deliberative argumentation.

[69] Laden, *Reasonably Radical*, p. 95, emphasis added.

[70] Laden, *Reasonably Radical*, pp. 95–6.   [71] Laden, *Reasonably Radical*, p. 95.

As I have argued, this will depend upon an account of identification that should include a treatment of both the disruptive moments responsible for a loosening of the grip of existing grammars – hence propelling us towards a genealogical self-awareness – and the moment of grip, which involves instituting a new political grammar. Neither of these receives particular attention in Laden's account. There is no doubt, as he suggests in drawing on Tully's genealogical approach, that becoming aware of one's own cultural background, and drawing the attention of one's dialogical partners to those factors and how it shapes important aspects of one's life, is a key part of the process, which must do much of the work of pulling us into the formation of a common space of reasons or political grammar. However, unlike in Wittgenstein and Foucault, he offers no developed account of this process. An 'invitation' to participate in a 'space of reasons' simply does not carry the force necessary to induce participants to become involved in what is no doubt a demanding process of critical self-examination, nor does it capture anything of the sense of dislocation and provocation that might inspire the process of aspect change in the first place. We need to turn to a theorist who draws more strongly on Foucault and Nietzsche to find a more elaborate account of the character of genealogical self-awareness. In the context of a discussion of Wittgenstein's suggestion that grammatical pictures 'hold us captive', Owen argues that such self-reflection involves the following four features: the identification of a picture that holds us captive; a redescription of this picture 'that contrasts it with another way of seeing the issue in order to free us from captivity to this picture', 'an account of how we have become held captive by this picture', and, being motivated 'to engage in the practical working out of this reorientation of ourselves as agents'.[72] Hence, it is only once a picture is called into question that we are in a position to assess its value for us and to

---

[72] D. Owen, 'Genealogy as perspicuous representation', 95. Owen draws these conclusions from a consideration of examples of genealogical self-reflection in Nietzsche and Foucault.

question or rethink the ways in which it has previously guided our judgements and activities in the world.[73] This calling into question of a particular picture, it should be noted, cannot be willed. Rather, it results from a dislocation, as I have suggested earlier, from some event or happening which ruptures the grammar ordering our political life and impairs our ability to make sense of our world and our actions and commitments within it.[74] It should, moreover, be noted that our responses to such dislocations cannot simply be 'read off' from the grammars that have previously guided and inspired our actions. Insofar as they are dislocated, they too fail in varying degrees to act as sufficient guides, and stand in need of rearticulation, of being refashioned.

Finally, once (re)engaged in a particular 'space of reasons', the way in which practices contribute to the shaping of one's own and a common identity also stands in need of further elaboration. While drawing upon Tully, Laden underestimates the distance between his dialogical and Tully's more genealogical approach.[75] In the case of the former, most of the work will be done through 'reasonable deliberation' while in the case of the latter, a far wider range of practices will have to be drawn upon, and these will almost certainly undercut the limitations Laden places upon what may count as political deliberation. For Laden, political deliberation as distinct from other political activities, 'takes place in political fora, it concerns political topics, and it takes place among people insofar as they are political agents'.[76] It is thus a strictly delimited, narrow set of activities, rather than a wider repertoire of practical abilities, skills and activities.[77]

---

[73] Owen, 'Genealogy as perspicuous representation', 84–5.

[74] Owen suggests that we think of such moments as a disjuncture between 'our ways of making sense of ourselves, on the one hand, and our cares and commitments, on the other'. Owen, 'Genealogy as perspicuous representation', 84.

[75] For an elaboration of these differences, see J. Tully, 'Wittgenstein and political philosophy: Understanding practices of critical reflection', in Heyes (ed.), *The Grammar of Politics*, pp. 17–42.

[76] Laden also notes that it is plural in that all participants do not need to share the same conception of citizenship. Laden, *Reasonably Radical*, p. 100.

[77] J. Tully, 'Political philosophy as a critical activity', *Political Theory* 30, no. 4 (2002), 543.

In short, though Laden is acutely aware of what is needed, his ability to address the problem is limited by the strictures shared by most deliberative democrats, including *inter alia* a too narrow conception of reason-giving and a lack of attention to the role of practices in facilitating the grip of political grammars. Concerning the former, as Wittgenstein points out, even the process of providing reasons involves a moment of change which cannot be accounted for in terms of the provision of reasons themselves.[78] One can provide reasons *ad nauseam*, but sooner or later reasons give out: 'giving grounds ... come to an end sometime'. However, the end is not 'an ungrounded presupposition; it is an *ungrounded way of acting*'.[79] It is at this point that the act of identification, occurring during aspect change, assumes its relevance. The subject becomes a democratic subject, not simply because she is rationally convinced it is the better option, though that may be part of the story, but rather because she participates in democratic practices, which retroactively orient her to identify as democratic subject (or in Laden's case, as reasonable citizen, which would entail a further determination).

This moment of subjective assent ('I am a democrat!') involves a process of identification – a picture gripping us, being occupied by something – that escapes the linguistic reductionism and excessively rational, disembodied account of much deliberative democratic theory. This 'identification-as' is the embodied act of a subject passionately involved in an activity that structures her political life and participation in a certain way.[80] As Tully has shown with respect

---

[78] See G.-L. Lueken, 'On showing in argumentation', *Philosophical Investigations* 20, no. 3 (1997), 205–23.

[79] L. Wittgenstein, *On Certainty*, ed. G. E. M. Anscombe and G. H. von Wright, trans. D. Paul and G. E. M. Anscombe (Oxford: Basil Blackwell, 1979), § 110, emphasis added.

[80] For a recent discussion of the role of passion in politics and its exclusion from liberal conceptions of politics, see *inter alia* C. Hall, ' "Passion and constraint": The marginalization of passion in liberal political theory', *Philosophy and Social Criticism* 28, no. 6 (2002), 727–48; and A. Abizadeh, 'Banishing the particular: Rousseau on rhetoric, *patrie*, and the passions', *Political Theory* 29, no. 4 (2001), 556–82.

to modern constitutionalism, allegiance to a particular political grammar entails engagement in a range of practices, including contestation, negotiation and voicing violently conflicting demands, to name but a few.[81] And as I have argued previously, dimensions of argumentation, such as persuasion and rhetoric, as well as bodily, materialized inscriptions are key to this process.[82] Needless to say, these are precisely the dimensions that are either explicitly excluded or marginalized in deliberative thought.[83]

The themes of passionate engagement with something, and persuasion occur repeatedly in Wittgenstein's writings, and often in the same context. In *On Certainty* Wittgenstein remarks that:

> Where two principles really do meet which cannot be reconciled with one another, then each man declares the other a fool and heretic.
>
> I would say I would 'combat' the other man, – but I wouldn't give him reasons? Certainly; but how far do they go? At the end of reasons comes persuasion.[84]

In his discussion of religious belief, he suggests that it is 'something like a passionate commitment to a system of reference ... It's passionately seizing hold of this interpretation.'[85]

Hence, even within the most rarified of contexts, such as those described by deliberative democrats, identification must be understood in its richest sense, as including a wide range of phenomena and practices that must be accounted for, both in the moment of

---

[81] J. Tully, *Strange Multiplicity. Constitutionalism in an Age of Diversity* (Cambridge: Cambridge University Press, 1995).

[82] See J. Meehan, 'Feminism and Habermas' discourse ethics', *Philosophy and Social Criticism* 26, no. 3 (2000), 43; W. E. Connolly, *The Ethos of Pluralization* (Minneapolis: University of Minnesota Press, 1995), p. 13; Warren, 'The self in discursive democracy', 194–5.

[83] See, for instance, Bohman's treatment of metaphor. J. Bohman, *Public Deliberation. Pluralism, Complexity, and Democracy* (Cambridge, Mass.: The MIT Press, 1996), p. 205.

[84] Wittgenstein, *On Certainty*, §§ 611 and 612. See also Wittgenstein, *Lectures and Conversations*, §§ 35, 27.

[85] Wittgenstein, *Culture and Value*, p. 64e.

constitution and ongoing participation. As I have argued earlier, it is precisely as a result of the reconfiguration of such practices, in seeing them differently, that newness emerges. And this can be brought about by a multitude of means: from rhetorical persuasion to violent upheaval. Thus, a Wittgensteinian approach draws attention to the practices shaping our (political) life, and in so doing draws our attention away from the bewitchment of theoretical reasoning. As in Heidegger, theoretical reasoning for Wittgenstein is a secondary activity. So long as our models of political grammars are inspired by an attempt to represent how things are *sub specie aeternitatis*, we will remain insensitive to the multiplicity of practices supporting and deepening democratic life.[86]

Seeing pictures as pictures

This brings me to a further key characteristic of the account of aspect change provided by Wittgenstein. Aspect change allows one to notice that one is now seeing something, not just in terms of this or that picture but also as a picture. Where aspect change occurs, what becomes visible is not just the presence of a different understanding of things, but an awareness of the multiplicity of aspects under which something can be seen. As Wittgenstein points out:

> If you search in a figure (1) for another figure (2), and then find it, you see (1) in a new way. Not only can you give a new kind of description of it, but noticing the second figure was a new visual experience.[87]

What are its political consequences? When one comes to see a picture as a picture, this releases one from the captivity of seeing something under just one aspect.[88] Being aware of a political grammar as a

---

[86] See Tully, 'Wittgenstein and political philosophy'.

[87] Wittgenstein, *Philosophical Investigations*, 199ᵉ.

[88] Wittgenstein, *Philosophical Investigations*, § 144. This is akin to the 'unconcealing event' in Heidegger. See Edwards, *Ethics without Philosophy*, p. 213.

grammar is, similarly, indicative of an awareness of multiplicity. Moreover, this highlights the fact that 'things can never be quite the same again'; once I have seen both the duck and the rabbit, I cannot return to the point where I was aware of only one of these aspects. Politically, this awareness of multiplicity, of a variety of viewpoints could foster a greater degree of openness in political life. As Tully suggests, if we reflect critically on our 'well-trodden ways of thought and action' we may render them 'less indubitably foundational, and thereby disclosing possibilities of thinking and acting differently'.[89] It could, but does not necessarily do so. There is nothing axiomatic in the move to seeing our practices as just that – one set of practices among others – to regarding that practice as on a par with other practices. While this problem does not arise for Wittgenstein – seeing a duck is not better than seeing a rabbit, and I would not necessarily be more attached to one than to the other – politically the issue is more complicated. While the duck-rabbit has no point and nothing hangs on whether I notice one or another,[90] coming to understand my dreams differently, or moving from one conception of understanding life to another, has consequences. Just so with politics. A change in political identification involves a change in understanding one's self and one's place in relation to others and to a set of wider practices. This raises a further set of questions, not all of which are elaborated by Wittgenstein (and one should not expect them to be).

The first point to note concerns the dislocation or disorientation that may give rise to the need for new identifications, the use of new words, and new ways of depicting practices. For Wittgenstein this moment arises when I no longer know how to go on, when 'established ways of using words have run out'. Politically, this occurs when the 'social coordinating mechanisms' of a society have broken down; when sedimented practices are questioned; when traditional

---

[89] Tully, 'Wittgenstein and political philosophy', pp. 41–2.

[90] An absence of the ability to perceive aspects has consequences, both for the way in which we inhabit and work with language, and more broadly, for our relations to others.

ways of doing things become disrupted. And as with language, so with politics. Language has within it the resources for change, yet some rearrangement of elements will be necessary and new connections need to be established. New sense has to be made of something; it has to be new, yet it still has to be intelligible. If we lack the new, we are forever trapped in tradition; if tradition is entirely absent, the new will be unintelligible. This points to the need for an account of change that avoids these two extremes.

Mulhall argues that language for Wittgenstein is 'a human edifice and subject to a variety of unpredictable but retrospectively comprehensible modes of alteration, extension, and expansion in response to human needs and purposes'.[91] The key question here concerns precisely what the character of such 'retrospective comprehensibility' might be, and the degree to which it involves a subordination of newness to existing rationalities.[92] On the reading of Wittgenstein provided here, such retrospective comprehensibility would be brought about through the process of establishing connections and rearticulating elements. Thus, against the view of aspect dawning mistakenly drawn from the duck-rabbit example, becoming aware of an aspect is not a matter of wilfully 'flipping' between different perspectives. Being able to see different perspectives depends crucially on becoming alerted to the broader background against which they are or become intelligible. Politically these questions can also only be addressed with extensive knowledge of specific grammars, the situations under which they become dislocated and the wider conditions for the emergence and transformation of particular grammars. Whereas in the case of ducks and rabbits, this awareness of connections depends upon, for instance, having seen live ducks and rabbits, politically it takes a more complex form in which the rearticulations may be both more unexpected and more imaginative, as

---

[91] Mulhall, *Inheritance and Originality*, p. 70.

[92] Such 'retrospective comprehensibility' cannot be of the order of a rational or progressive telos working itself out through history.

I have suggested at the end of the previous chapter.[93] This process is always retroactive; interpretation and elaboration follows the initial moment of establishing connections, of coming to see something in a particular way.[94] If a grammar gives us the ability to 'word the world', a new grammar opens up fresh worlds in which different objects and projects may appear and old ones may be ruled out.[95] Hence, there is a futural element that does not determine what is possible, but nevertheless shapes and frames the terrain in which we operate.

Thinking about subjectivity in relation to political grammars also raises distinctive questions. The place opened for 'the human voice' is not one of a pre-constituted mode of political subjectification.[96] Rather, it is a space in which the possibility of subjectivity emerges, and its very point is to establish and/or to disarticulate existing communities. 'Identification-as', insofar as it entails both the moment of subjective identification and an emphasis on intelligibility, serves to make a practice mine, and claims, constitutes or affirms my place in a community.[97] In Chapter 4 I elaborate the implications of these suggestions for our understanding of democratic subjectivity. At this stage it is sufficient to note, as Owen points out, that 'it is through the exercise of one's political voice that one

---

[93] The articulation of new rights, for instance, often solicits laughter. See B. Honig, 'The time of rights', keynote address, Sixth Essex Graduate Conference in Political Theory, 13–14 May 2005. This would be an instance of novel articulation, which is both unexpected and uncomfortable – hence the laughter – and yet intelligible.

[94] Just as for Wittgenstein being able to ask for an ostensive definition presupposes a vast practical ability of working with words, some of which at root is based on ostensive training, so in politics. A vast array of 'training' precedes knowing how to do something politically. Nevertheless, nothing can replace the moment of saying 'Now I know how to go on!'

[95] Politically, there clearly are cases where a shift in perspective may rule out holding onto another or a previous perspective. One can think here of the case of racist identification, which must be shed once one moves to a democratic identification.

[96] Hence, this 'voice' cannot be equated, in any simple fashion, with a liberal conception of subjectivity.

[97] This making mine entails, following Cavell, 'that I am answerable not merely to it, but for it' thus evoking a sense of community. Mulhall, summarizes the point thus: 'I cannot work out my political identity alone.' S. Mulhall, 'Promising, consent, and citizenship', Political Theory 25, no. 2 (1997), 184. I return to these issues in Chapter 4.

discovers (ongoingly) where one stands politically ... and how one stands politically in relation to others (the depth and extent of one's agreement with others)'.[98]

Finally, the effects of this experience of the dawning in politics also raise particular issues. Where political grammars are concerned, it is always possible simply to say: 'We know this is our practice, and it is different from yours, but we still regard ours as a superior way of doing things!' Nevertheless, getting an open and democratic dialogue on the way has, as a minimum precondition, that initial awareness, that sense of the contingency of one's own position.[99] All else depends upon a particular political articulation. But, it needs emphasizing, such articulation always takes place within the web of already existing, if dislocated, grammars. As Wittgenstein puts it, we are 'back to the rough ground'. Here the democratic subject needs to continue to argue and work for her own position, to take responsibility for it, precisely because it is not guaranteed. An awareness of this opening facilitated by aspect change, is a precondition for the inauguration and support of a democratic grammar.

Against heroism

Whereas deliberative theories tend to foreclose the moment of subjective identification, post-structuralists focus precisely on this question. For both Laclau and Žižek, for instance, dislocation opens up a space for subjectivity. Žižek argues in this respect that ' "subject" is a name for that unfathomable X called upon, suddenly made accountable, thrown into a position of responsibility, into the urgency

---

[98] D. Owen, 'Cultural diversity and the conversation of justice', *Political Theory* 27, no. 5 (1999), 587. There are, of course, also limits to political identification, raising the question of withdrawal of consent, and the exercise of dissent. See also Mulhall, 'Promising', 184–5.

[99] Tully calls this 'diversity awareness'. Commenting on Tully, Laden argues that in order to 'open ourselves up to hearing other points of view, we need to come to understand why our point of view is itself a point of view and not an all-encompassing vision of reality'. Laden, *Reasonably Radical*, p. 195.

of decision in such a moment of undecidability'.[100] Similarly, for Laclau dislocation 'is the source of freedom ... not the freedom of a subject with a positive identity – in which case it would just be a structural locus; rather it is ... the freedom of a structural fault which can only construct an identity through acts of identification'.[101] In both, the concern is to counter substantive and deterministic conceptions of subjectivity, and thus both draw a distinction between 'subject positions' and 'the subject'. The former, derived from Foucault, captures the extent to which we occupy sedimented structural positions as a result of our everyday participation in the grammar of politics and social life. We are, for instance, citizens, parents, members of various associations, and so on. The latter emphasizes the disruption of these positions and is conceived as the moment in which new political grammars may be instituted through acts of identification.[102] Hence, the subject is 'present' only on those occasions, which one could argue are quite rare, when decisions are taken and new paths are opened up. Nevertheless, it is a 'presence' that is almost always retroactive: that is, it is usually only after the fact that we could say a decision had been taken, a political act had taken place.[103] Žižek puts it the following way: 'An act is never fully "present", the subjects are never fully aware that what they are doing "now" is the foundation of a new symbolic order – it is only afterwards

---

[100] S. Žižek, *For They Know Not What They Do. Environment as a Political Factor* (London: Verso, 1991), p. 189.

[101] Laclau, *New Reflections*, p. 60.

[102] Subjects only become aware retrospectively of founding new symbolic orders. Žižek, *For They Know Not What They Do*, p. 222.

[103] Žižek also notes, importantly, that the meaning of ideological terms are fixed retroactively: 'the effect of meaning is always produced backwards, *après coup*. Signifiers which are still in a "floating" state – whose signification is not yet fixed – follow one another. Then, at a certain point ... some signifier fixes retroactively the meaning of the chain ... To grasp this fully, we have only to remember the above-mentioned example of ideological "quilting": in the ideological space float signifiers like "freedom", "state", "justice", "peace" ... and then their chain is supplemented with some master-signifier ("Communism") which retroactively determines their (Communist) meaning: "freedom" is effective only through surmounting the bourgeois formal freedom', and so on. See S. Žižek, *The Sublime Object of Ideology* (London: Verso, 1989), pp. 101–2.

that they take note of the true dimension of what they have already done.'[104] Hence, the act is performative: 'it defines its own conditions; retroactively produces the grounds which justify it'.[105]

This account, in its emphasis on the productive role of dislocation, resonates well with a number of aspects of the argument concerning 'identification-as' that I have developed above. Wittgenstein's account of aspect seeing involves a change of perspective in the subject, which recedes once identification with a new subject position is in place. In Wittgenstein's terminology, this is the difference between the exclamation 'It's a rabbit!' and a description of a rabbit. While Wittgenstein in his later work does not explicitly address the question of subjectivity,[106] his remarks could be argued to presuppose something akin to the characterization of the moment of subjectivity offered by post-structuralists such as Žižek and Laclau. In his account of rule following, as much as in the characterization of aspect seeing, the moment of the subject emerges when 'I do not know how to go on', when existing practices no longer make sense, when we are perplexed and puzzled by something, and when new articulations are called for. As I have argued earlier, this puzzlement is what drives his investigations.

Now, the post-structuralist accounts offered by Žižek and Laclau are extremely helpful in breaking the log-jam of determinism and substantivism. In terms of more specific identifications, the arguments they offer suggest that if the subject emerges as a result of a dislocation of a grammar or social imaginary, there is nothing that predisposes the development of a response to such dislocation in a particular direction.[107] As a result, a democratic identification

[104] S. Žižek, *For They Know Not What They Do*, p. 222.
[105] Žižek, *For They Know Not What They Do*, p. 192.
[106] See P. M. S. Hacker, *Wittgenstein on Human Nature* (London: Phoenix Paperback, 1997).
[107] See A. J. Norval, 'Hegemony after deconstruction: The consequences of undecidability', *Journal of Political Ideologies* 9, no. 2 (2004), 139–57.

will arise from a specific contingent political articulation.[108] Two problems arise at this point. The first concerns insufficient attention to the precise character of a democratic identification and the second relates to dimensions of the argument that may very well have counter-democratic implications.

The point can be illustrated by referring to the role of the 'ethical act' in bringing about changes in 'the coordinates' of social reality, or fashioning a rearticulation of a symbolic order.[109] For Žižek, in particular, the emphasis on the register of the 'real' in Lacan – that which cannot be represented symbolically – and dislocation intervenes to counter a certain perceived pragmatism, conventionalism and incrementalism in contemporary political theorizing. Nothing other than a radical break, an ethical act, or a deep dislocation will be sufficient to counter these contemporary 'evils' and the accommodation with the existing order that they encourage. In short, the call is for a new form of 'heroic' politics[110] that remains, I would argue, inimical to the thought of democracy and, more generally, runs the risk of failing the intelligibility test. This problem will have to be resolved if one is to capture both the moment of the institution of a democratic ethos which, no doubt, may involve moments of rupture, and the need, on an ongoing basis, to reactivate it and to become democratic subjects anew. As we have seen, this difficult negotiation between the new and the existing context is precisely what is at stake in aspect dawning. We need to look at these issues in more detail to be able to provide an account of democratic subject formation that will accommodate moments of change and dislocation, so going beyond the bounds of grammar without 'giving up on intelligibility'.[111]

---

[108] See E. Laclau, 'Glimpsing the future: A reply', in S. Critchley and O. Marchart (eds.), *Laclau. A Critical Reader* (London: Routledge, 2004), p. 298.

[109] See S. Žižek, 'Melancholy and the act', *Critical Inquiry* 26 (2000), 657–81.

[110] Žižek renounces any appeal to existing norms. See S. Žižek, 'Holding the place', in J. Butler, E. Laclau and S. Žižek, *Contingency, Hegemony, Universality* (London: Verso, 2000), p. 326.

[111] Baz, 'What's the point', 99.

ASPECT DAWNING AND ASPECT CHANGE

As I have argued, thinking about democratic subjectivity requires both an account of moments when we first become democrats, and the activities necessary to sustain those identifications. The pictures of democracy we have looked at thus far fail on both these counts, though for very different reasons. We may begin to address these lacunae by unpacking what I argue to be differences – in degree, rather than in kind – between aspect dawning and aspect change. Though Wittgenstein draws no such distinction, there is enough in his account of aspect change to warrant reflecting on differences in emphasis so as to enable us to think through in more detail what is at stake in grammatical change.

As we have already seen, noticing an aspect change for the first time – let us reserve this experience for the term 'aspect dawning' – contains an element of surprise and exclamation:[112] 'Now it is a rabbit!' We have also seen that this is not an ordinary perceptual report. Now, the air of paradox accompanying aspect dawning is constituted of both the element of surprise and now noticing that the figure has not changed. This second feature is equally helpful to clarify the nature of changes in political grammar. Here the emphasis is on what is continuous yet discontinuous with a previous way of looking at something: seeing the duck-aspect of the duck-rabbit is different from the perceptual state before the aspect dawning occurred. Yet, it differs from the moment of aspect dawning itself. If aspect dawning connotes the new, that element of initial surprise, when a novel set of connections or articulations offer us a picture that allows us to make some sense of a disruptive experience, aspect change may be utilized to capture the sense in which the initial moment of dawning could be reactivated at a later stage. In terms of political subjectivity it is important to capture both these dimensions. The

---

[112] Kuhn also points out that scientists speak of 'the "lightening flash" that "inundates" a previously obscure puzzle, enabling its components to be seen in a new way'. T. S. Kuhn, *The Structure of Scientific Revolutions* (Chicago: University of Chicago Press, 1970), p. 122.

former may be used to think about that first moment of assuming democratic subjectivity: 'Now I am a democrat!' The second is a point of reactivation, which involves remembering anew why I am a democrat. For democratic theory, these two moments have quite different, though related, implications.

The institution of a democratic order today is often treated under the rubric of 'transitions to democracy', and tends to focus on top-down elite-negotiated changes from authoritarian to democratic regimes.[113] However, this literature singularly fails to deal with the processes through which people become democrats, including the sorts of activities in which they participate and how they come to identify themselves as democrats. Similarly, literature that assumes as a backdrop a certain picture of modernity, disenchantment and individualization tends to ignore the need for an account of the moment of institution and its iteration.[114] By contrast, an earlier contractarian literature, which dealt with the paradoxes of the institution of democratic regimes, at least had the advantage of acknowledging some of the difficult issues at stake here. Rousseau's famous lawgiver, who recognizes the need to address the problem of how a not-yet democratic people will come to make the laws instituting a new democratic order, is a case in point.[115] Rousseau deals with both the retroactive character of the institution of a democratic regime and its futural elements, of which the imagination of the social contract is a key aspect.[116] To be a democrat, to identify as a democrat and to live out the ethos of democratic activities, I already have to have become such in order to be able to say, 'I am a

---

[113] For a critical review of transition studies, see D. Howarth, 'Paradigms gained? A critique of theories and explanations of democratic transition in South Africa', in D. R. Howarth and A. J. Norval, *South Africa in Transition* (London: Macmillan, 1998), pp. 182–214.

[114] Iteration is here understood on the Derridean model: repetition always involves a degree of alteration. See J. Derrida, *Limited Inc.* (Evanston, Ill.: Northwestern University Press, 1988).

[115] J. J. Rousseau, *The Social Contract* (London: Penguin Classics, 1968), pp. 86–7.

[116] These are intimately tied up together, but I will here concentrate on the former.

democrat!' Nothing can replace that moment of identification. Yet, these inaugurative moments should not be understood as moments in which new forms of subjectivity are created *ex nihilo*. More often than not, there has been a prolonged period of preparation for such moments, and the role of a genealogical account of these processes is absolutely crucial. South Africa is a case in point. The elections of May 1994, which so captured the international imagination, did so precisely because they signified an inaugural, exclamatory moment. Queuing in the baking sun for hours on end in order to vote condensed the moment in which all South Africans could claim their status as equal subjects of a new democracy. 'We are all democrats now!' 'We are all equal now!' 'We are all humans now!' As I have suggested, this new sense of subjectivity needs to be understood in the context of my earlier arguments. First, no amount of factual description could account for it. Evident here was an aspect dawning in the full sense of the term. As against expectations right up until the election itself, the political grammar of apartheid was replaced by identification as democrats. Old perspectives had been revalued and ruled out of court as new relations were set up. Secondly, this occurred very much in the context of engaging in a set of practical activities: queuing, waiting, talking to others, voting and, prior to that, taking part in protest activities, both at grassroots and union level. It was, in many senses, a bodily experience of claiming a new status. Thirdly, that very act of common participation was indicative of already engaging in a novel set of practices structured by the new grammar. Intolerance of difference was replaced by a new openness; a right to occupy a position rather than the position. A new form of subjectivity, and hence of community, had come into being.

Nevertheless, such forms of subjectivity need recurrent activation if the force of a democratic ethos is to be sustained and deepened. While much literature bemoans the passivity and disinterest marking the citizenry of democratic regimes, little attention is given to what may bring about resurgence in democratic activity as evidenced in protests associated with the anti-globalization movement;

new forms of environmental activism; and, most recently, anti-war protests. Though there is a growing literature claiming that deliberative practices could potentially bring about renewal of democratic subjectivity,[117] the mechanisms at work in the production and sustaining of democratic subjectivities are not addressed. I have suggested that the idea of aspect change may be informative in this respect, since it allows us to conceptualize the sense of renewal and the grip it may have on us. It entails a rediscovery of the dawning of an aspect; and it allows us to capture the reactivation of an already present identification necessary to sustaining the ethos of democracy.

We have also seen that for Wittgenstein, aspect dawning and aspect change entail an occupation with the object at hand. In political terms, I have suggested we think of this as 'identification-as'. This identification, in the wake of either aspect dawning or aspect change, entails awareness of the picture as picture. This making visible of the contingency of the picture one identifies with, and of the multiplicity of aspects under which it could be seen, is not also indicative of a weakening of identification with the particular practice under discussion. Identifying as a democrat means simultaneously that I allow space for the other and for her identification. This, however, does not in the least weaken my identification. To the contrary, it could strengthen it. Should such identification with a particular political grammar become sedimented, we would have a situation akin to what Wittgenstein understood by continuous aspect perception. In these circumstances, grammars are decontested and we have a hegemonic political grammar. No interpretation is needed and there are no exclamatory moments. Here proceduralism may very well provide an accurate picture of democratic activities. Procedures for taking decisions are in place, and tend to be uncontested. However, once these grammars become problematized through either

---

[117] See, for instance, T. Akkerman, 'Urban debates and deliberative democracy', *Acta Politika* 1 (2001), 71–87; B. Ackerman and J. S. Fishkin, 'Deliberation day', *The Journal of Political Philosophy* 10, no. 2 (2002), 129–52.

dislocating experiences or ongoing contestations by disaffected groups the different dimensions of aspect dawning and change again enter the picture.

CONCLUSION

For the later Wittgenstein, the problems of philosophy are not (dis)-solved through great and sudden insights as Wittgenstein's practice attests. He returns to problems again and again, approaching them from different directions. This way of engaging with philosophy and its puzzles is suggestive when thinking about the nature of democratic identification. While an initial change to democracy may be akin to a sudden insight in certain respects, institutionalizing a democratic ethos requires an ongoing re-enactment and re-engagement with democratic practices. If democracy is conceived as a never-ending struggle, then the mode of subjectivity supporting it must be one that can take account of this. Hence the emphasis on a re-engagement and reactivation of democratic practices. As we know, the simple repetition of practices, while necessary, may in the long run fail to sustain democratic identification. This is why moments of reactivation are necessary. They may take different forms, ranging from new forms of political engagement (such as direct action protest) to the vicarious participation in struggles for democracy far away. They all capture something of what I have characterized as aspect change, which involves the recognition of the discontinuous within the continuous and vice versa. Challenges to traditional forms of political participation, identifying with democrats marching through the streets of Prague, or sitting glued to the television watching Mandela's release from prison, all contribute to a renewal of our own democratic identifications and may have the effect of reinvigorating local democratic practices.

This reinvigoration depends, of course, on the dislocation of our current grammars. However, even where changes are quite radical, such as in the transitions from authoritarian to democratic regimes, and where one could speak of aspect dawning, I have argued the dislocation need not take the form of a 'great event'. More often than not, it will take the form of a multitude of different practices which, when taken together, make possible a different way of looking at things. To put it differently, in order to identify as a democrat, there are many practices and knowledges that already need to be in place. This means that abstract models of 'the subject', 'radical subjectivity' and so on, on this reading, remain too tied to a modernist conception of politics. Both a heroic politics and a strong conception of the subject as creator, as a 'radical' moment of founding, are rooted in a model of democratic change closer to a revolution than a radical democratic conception.[118]

Becoming a democrat (again) is not to be understood on the basis of a cognitive model. This is why it is not sufficient to argue that to overcome the democratic deficit we simply need to 'educate' citizens better or to improve the quality of our argumentation, though both of these may be necessary. It is also why it is not sufficient to think that simply presenting 'the facts of a case' in a rarified context will make us all democrats. Democrats need to become democrats, repeatedly, and this requires identification and persuasion. It is here, as I have suggested, that the role of persuasion and rhetoric becomes central to any account of democratic subjectivity. The importance of assent on the part of the subject should not be underestimated either. However, as I have argued, such assent should not be understood primarily on the basis of a model of rational reason-giving. One of the key contributions of the later Wittgenstein is his emphasis on seeing things aright. The ability of the subject to see new connections and to envisage a new political grammar would count here as evidence of the subject's assent. Indeed, Wittgenstein's account of 'seeing' and 'looking' alerts us to the fact of the importance of activities other than 'thinking' in bringing about political change (the role of stories,

---

[118] For an insightful treatment of the different modalities of the act of founding, see B. Honig, *Democracy and the Foreigner* (Princeton, N.J.: Princeton University Press, 2001).

narratives, anecdotes, engaging in activities, and so forth). Aspect dawning and change also draw our attention to the key role that 'identification-as' plays in the constitution and maintenance of political identities in general. More specifically, it highlights and makes visible a multiplicity of perspectives, which are crucial to the formation and reiteration of a democratic ethos. The character of this democratic ethos and its implications for the way in which we think about relations between citizens need further exploration. This is the subject matter of the next chapter, where I draw on Wittgenstein-inspired accounts to supplement the picture of democratic subjectivity within post-structuralist accounts of agonistic democracy.

4 Democratic subjectivity: the promise of democratic community

The price of liberty is our subjection to eternal vigilance.[1]

Democratic theory today needs to address a number of concerns relating to the question of 'voice'. This, I have suggested, has been treated in two distinctive ways in contemporary democratic theory. For deliberative democrats, it is a matter of equality in the process of deliberation, though, as critics like Sanders have argued, this approach largely ignores the issue of epistemic authority, of who may be heard within the constraints of rational argumentation. In contrast, for post-structuralists, 'voice' is thematized precisely from the perspective of those excluded from the polity. The latter approach constitutes an advance over the former. However, its reach is hampered by the sharp division it introduces between 'the declared political community and the community that defines itself as excluded from this community'.[2] Hence, even as the possibility of the existence of a 'common stage' and 'the existence and status of those present on it'[3] is at stake here, theoretical effort has gone almost exclusively into thinking about this problem from the point of view of those barred from the domain of the visible. This leaves the terrain of what is called variously 'the police', 'the situation' and 'politics' virtually untouched by the analysis.[4] However, if, as Rancière

[1] S. Cavell, *Conditions Handsome and Unhandsome. The Constitution of Emersonian Perfectionism*, The Carus Lectures, 1988 (Chicago: University of Chicago Press, 1990), p. 125.

[2] J. Rancière, *Disagreement. Politics and Philosophy*, trans. J. Rose (Minneapolis: University of Minnesota Press, 1999), p. 38.

[3] Rancière, *Disagreement*, p. 26.

[4] As discussed in Chapter 2, for Rancière, the term 'police' designates the terrain of the social, of constituted rules, what Badiou calls the 'situation' and what for Laclau

acknowledges, 'one kind of police may be infinitely preferable to another',[5] then we need to be able to think through more clearly what it means to suggest that politics 'acts on the police', that it reshapes places and changes words.[6] This clearly also has consequences for the way we think about subjectivity since the bifurcation between politics and the police is replicated also in Rancière's discussion of political subjectivity. For him, the irruption of politics is always a matter of subjectification through *dis*identification, a removal from the naturalness of place, rather than one of identification. Identification is always a matter of the police, of an identified part of the community.[7] By contrast, Laclau's emphasis on and theorization of the process of identification in the constitution of political subjectivity contests the idea that any identification must already, simpliciter, form part of 'the police' order. The emphasis on dislocation, which does the work achieved in Rancière's writings by the category of disidentification, serves to conceptualize the rupture needed to be able to think the possibility of a distancing and questioning of an existing order. Rancière does acknowledge the constitution of new subjects 'that take the wrong upon themselves' as well as the fact that there is a need to 'invent new forms and new names for it'. As he argues:

> Political subjectification redefines the field of experience that gave to each their identity with their lot. It decomposes and recomposes the relationships between the ways of doing, of being, and of saying that define the perceptible organization of the community ... A political subject is not a group that 'becomes aware' of itself, finds its voice, imposes its weight on society. It is an operator that connects and disconnects different areas, regions, identities.[8]

---

constitutes 'institutional politics'. See A. Badiou, *Ethics. An Essay on the Understanding of Evil*, trans. Peter Hallward (London: Verso, 2001), p. lvi; and E. Laclau, 'Glimpsing the future', in S. Critchley and O. Marchart (eds.) *Laclau. A Critical Reader* (London: Routledge, 2004), p. 298.

[5] Rancière, *Disagreement*, p. 31.   [6] Rancière, *Disagreement*, p. 33.
[7] Here the contrast between Rancière and Laclau emerges at its sharpest, though, as I have argued, they are, nevertheless, not incompatible.
[8] Rancière, *Disagreement*, p. 40.

Despite this, Rancière does not treat the invention of new names at any length. This necessary invention of new names is precisely what Laclau regards as the central concern of politics. Laclau argues in this respect that if

> the unity of social actors were the result of a logical link subsuming various subject positions under a unified conceptual category, 'naming' would simply involve choosing an arbitrary label for an object whose unity was ensured by *a priori* means. If, however, the unity of the social agent is the result of a plurality of social demands coming together through equivalential (metonymic) relations of contiguity, the contingent moment of naming has an absolutely central and constitutive role.[9]

The question for us must be one of how these insights are related to and affect a democratic conception of political subjectivity and community.

Much attention has recently been given to new modes of democratic participation, but as soon as one delves somewhat deeper, it quickly becomes clear that there is little agreement on what such community might amount to. This is not only evident in the dispute between deliberativist and post-structuralist approaches to democracy. There are also rather divergent accounts of democratic community and subjectivity within each of these broad approaches. This chapter starts with the suggestion that there is at least some agreement across different approaches; one could claim today that there is a consensus that democratic community cannot be thought about in substantive terms. That is, that there is no substance that underlies community. However, having acknowledged the absence of substance as an adequate basis from which to think about community – political community and democratic community – and hence, subjectivity, there are many different ways in which accounts of community may be and are developed.

---

[9] E. Laclau, *On Populist Reason* (London: Verso, 2005), 227.

One of the most prevalent and influential post-structuralist versions of community is that articulated in the works of Laclau and Mouffe, who set out to provide an explicitly non-essentialist theoretical account of the formation of subjectivity. This chapter starts with an engagement with the aspects of their writings on subjectivity relating directly to the demands of thinking through the features of *democratic* forms of identification. As already argued, their work provides an important advance on essentialist accounts of identity. They rightly emphasize the significance of identification for and the political character of all identity formation. However, they remain rather more tentative on the details of democratic forms of identification and subjectivity. In order to advance the argument and to clearly articulate a conception of a *democratic* community we need to be able to specify in more detail some intuitions, present in different aspects of their respective writings, pertaining to the relations *between* subject-citizens. I set out to deepen these insights by drawing on Wittgenstein, Cavell and Derrida. In so doing, I flesh out a picture of democratic subjectivity and community that is neither teleological nor essentialist, that acknowledges the contingency and non-necessity of identity so important in Laclau and Mouffe's works, yet seeks to make visible the distinctively normative dimensions of such community.[10] In short, in this chapter I wish to defend what I call, following Owen, a processual perfectionist account of democracy and democratic identity,[11] in the sense understood by Cavell and found in a different form in the writings of Derrida, to which I now turn.

---

[10] I use the term normative in the sense given to it in Cavell's work, implying 'our capacity to make ourselves intelligible by projecting words into new contexts and remain ready to declare and respect the implications of doing so'. E. Hammer, *Stanley Cavell. Skepticism, Subjectivity, and the Ordinary* (Cambridge: Polity Press, 2002), p. 38. Hence, it is intimately tied to the grammars of our political practices.

[11] See D. Owen, 'Democracy, perfectionism and "undetermined messianic hope" ', in C. Mouffe and L. Nagl (eds.), *The Legacy of Wittgenstein: Pragmatism and Deconstruction* (Frankfurt am Main: Peter Lang, 2001), pp. 139–56.

THE PROMISE OF DEMOCRACY

> Is it possible to think and to implement democracy, that which would keep the old name 'democracy', while uprooting from it all those figures of friendship ... which prescribe fraternity. Is it possible, in assuming a certain faithful memory of democratic reason and reason *tout court* – I would even say the Enlightenment of a certain *Aufklärung* (thus leaving open the abyss which is again opening today under these words) – not to found, where it is no longer a matter of *founding*, but to open to the future, or rather to the 'to come', of a certain democracy?[12]

In exploring Derrida's account of 'democracy to come', it is necessary to elucidate his understanding of the 'to come', and its consequences for democratic community. In short, I will show that this (impossible) future, a future that never arrives, announced in the 'to come', has the structure of a promise: like a promise, it is a means by which an imagined future can intervene in and act upon the present. Hence, the appeal to democracy to come has consequences in the present; it is not something infinitely deferred, with no discernible impact upon the now. Thus, it has a certain urgency.

How then should we understand the 'to come' in 'democracy to come'? It does not mean only that the perfect democracy does not exist and, that insofar as it is infinitely deferred, 'it will always remain to come'.[13] It suggests that democracy will never exist, in the sense of a present existence. This is not because it is deferred but because it is, and remains aporetic in its structure.[14] As Derrida points out, 'democracy to come' is a phrase without a verb, and it is undecidable between two possibilities. On the one hand, it could be treated as a

---

[12] J. Derrida, *Politics of Friendship*, trans. George Collins (London: Verso, 1997), p. 306.

[13] J. Derrida, *Rogues. Two Essays on Reason*, trans. P.-A. Brault and M. Naas (Stanford: Stanford University Press, 2005), p. 73.

[14] Derrida describes this aporetic structure as follows: '(force *without* force, incalculable singularity *and* calculable equality, ... heteronomy *and* autonomy, indivisible sovereignty *and* divisible or shared sovereignty, ... and so on)'. Derrida, *Rogues*, p. 86.

neutral, constative analysis of a concept. Then it would be describing what the concept of democracy implies, and has always implied (memory, promise, the event to come, historicity, perfectibility). On the other hand, it could be treated as a performative, in which case it functions much more like an attempt to win over, to gain conviction, or adherence. In this sense democracy to come functions as a call – a call to action and engagement – and not as an infinite deferral.

Derrida is also at pains to emphasize that democracy to come should not be confused with the regulative idea in the Kantian sense. He expresses several reservations regarding the regulative idea, including that it is used rather too loosely; and that it remains of the 'order of the possible'. If treated as 'an ideal possible that is infinitely deferred' democracy to come would still share in a form that is not 'wholly freed from all teleological ends'.[15] What remains to be decided/done does not, for Derrida, consist 'in following, applying, or carrying out a norm or rule'. Like Wittgenstein, Derrida holds that if we were to have such determinable rules, what must be done would be dictated in advance.[16] Then, as we know, there no longer will be space for decisions.[17] In contrast to the regulative idea, Derrida emphasizes several dimensions of democracy to come that resist such a determinacy. It is in this sense that the impossible – what remains foreign 'to the order of the "I can" ' – assumes its centrality, since it captures the importance of the event, of what is not foreseeable. This also serves the function of holding open the relation to the future.

For Derrida the futurity of democracy is captured in the claim that democracy has the structure of a promise, 'a promise that is kept in memory, that is handed down ... inherited, claimed and taken up'.[18]

---

[15] Derrida, *Rogues*, p. 84.   [16] *Ibid.*
[17] For a more detailed discussion of undecidability, the decision and democracy to come, in relation to Laclau's work on Derrida, see A. J. Norval, 'Hegemony after deconstruction: The consequences of undecidability', *Journal of Political Ideologies* 9 (June 2004), 139–57.
[18] Derrida, *Rogues*, p. 85.

Hence, the promise emphasizes a tradition,[19] that which is handed down, and a certain conception of community, a community that claims and takes up that tradition. Such taking up, it should be recalled, will always be a taking up or reactivation with a difference; it can never be a mere repetition.[20] As I will argue shortly, this taking up of a tradition involves making claims, which constitute community anew.[21] It is now necessary to look at each of these elements in greater detail. The promise of democracy encapsulates reference to the future in two distinct senses. On the one hand, it refers to the 'to come' of the event, of what is unforeseen, and hence, of what cannot be determined in a programmatic (or any other) way. Hence, as noted earlier, this account is non-teleological; it does not have an endpoint 'in some perfect state of self-realization, but rather, is an ongoing process of struggle'.[22] The promise of democracy here is a holding open of the future, against our contemporary practices and claims to democracy. It suggests that another future is possible, that there is more to democracy than what is called democracy today. An integral part of this process of keeping open the future and, hence, of democracy, are the critical practices associated with democracy. As Derrida puts it,

> The expression 'democracy to come' does indeed translate or call for a militant and interminable political critique. A weapon aimed at the enemies of democracy, it protests against all naïveté and every

---

[19] More concretely, Derrida puts it this way: 'The idea of the promise is inscribed in the idea of a democracy: equality, freedom, freedom of speech, freedom of the press – all these things are inscribed as promises within democracy.' 'Politics and friendship: A discussion with Jacques Derrida', Centre for Modern French Thought, University of Sussex, 1 December 1997. At (www.hydra.umn.edu/derrida/pol+fr.html).

[20] For Derrida, repetition always involves alteration, captured in the term 'iterability'.

[21] As for Wittgenstein, the constitution of the new takes place with reference to tradition, captured also in the reference to 'elders' in Cavell.

[22] Owen suggests this as one of the affinities between Foucault's and Cavell's respective accounts of perfectionism. As I will argue later more fully, Derrida and post-structuralist theories of democracy more generally share much of this understanding of perfectionism. See D. Owen, 'Perfectionism, parrhesia and the care of the self: Foucault and Cavell on ethics and politics', in A. Norris (ed.), *The Claim to Community. Essays on Stanley Cavell and Political Philosophy* (Stanford, Calif.: Stanford University Press, 2006), p. 137.

political abuse, every rhetoric that would present as a present or existing democracy, as a de facto democracy, what remains inadequate to the democratic demand ... But beyond this active and interminable critique, the expression 'democracy to come' takes into account the absolute and intrinsic historicity of the only system that welcomes in itself, in its very concept, that expression of autoimmunity called the right to self-critique and perfectibility.[23]

Hence, there are two sense in which critical practices are understood here: first, as the ongoing critical engagement with every empirical democracy and with states and orders claiming that appellation, and, secondly, the dimension of critique which is essential to democracy and only to democracy as 'constitutional paradigm'. Though seemingly familiar, Derrida gives the latter an unfamiliar twist through the emphasis on autoimmunity, to which I will return below. It is important to note that this account of the importance and character of critical practices thus far concurs with Cavell's characterization of perfectibility. As I will argue, in both there is a questioning of the programmatic, an emphasis on the open-endedness of critique, and recognition of the fact that these emphases also have consequences for our conception of what may constitute a democratic community. Though no doubt there are different inflections in Cavell and Derrida, both are at pains to call attention to the impossibility of fully constituted communities, at peace with themselves. As we will see shortly, Cavell's emphasis on self-transformation and aversion, on the struggle against conformism resonates with Derrida's accentuation, generally, of deconstruction as a form of 'bad conscience' and with the emphasis on continual interrogation which must characterize democratic 'citizenship', with democracy being concerned with 'being out of joint', with the interruption of relation, which must put into question every traditional conception of community.[24]

---

[23] Derrida, *Rogues*, pp. 86–7.
[24] Derrida, *Rogues*, p. 88.

This then brings us to the second sense in which the promise emphasizes futurity, namely, the holding open of the democratic community, which, for Derrida, must extend beyond the nation-state. This opening up of the question of democratic community raises at least two further difficult issues: that of hospitability and that of autoimmunity, or the risks posed to and by democratic community. Let us turn to hospitality first. The theme of hospitality gives a particular inflexion to the question of democratic community, that is, of who counts.[25] Democracy for Derrida extends beyond the nation-state, beyond conceptions of citizenship, since 'if we dissociate democracy from the name of a regime we can then give this name "democracy" to any kind of experience in which there is equality, justice, equity, respect for singularity of the other at work'.[26] The first opening of my relation to the other is captured by Derrida in the theme of 'hospitality',[27] an unconditional injunction to welcome the other that, nevertheless, must be negotiated, given the risks of an unconditional welcoming and given the need to avoid assimilation, one-way communication and acculturation. Unconditional hospitality

---

[25] For Derrida, the question of counting and of number stands at the heart of democracy. He argues: 'I refer to counting and to taking account of number because the question of democracy is in many respects, if not entirely, as we have known since Plato and Aristotle, the question of calculation, of numerical calculation, of equality according to number. Along with equality (*to ison*) according to value or worth (*kat'axian*), equality according to number is one of two kinds of equality ... Hence the calculation of units, that is, what are called voices or votes [*voix*] in democracy ... What is a voice or a vote?' Derrida, *Rogues*, pp. 29–30. Derrida further suggests that as 'soon as everyone ... is equally ... free, equality becomes an integral part of freedom and is thus no longer calculable. This equality in freedom no longer has anything to do with numerical equality or equality according to worth ... It is itself an incalculable and incommensurable equality'. Derrida, *Rogues*, p. 49.

[26] 'Politics and friendship: A discussion with Jacques Derrida', Centre for Modern French Thought, University of Sussex, 1 December 1997.

[27] It should be noted that Derrida opposes hospitality to tolerance, which limits the welcome. G. Borradori, *Philosophy in a Time of Terror. Dialogues with Jürgen Habermas and Jacques Derrida* (Chicago: University of Chicago Press, 2003), pp. 127–8. For the same reason, Derrida also refuses the term 'cosmopolitanism', which is also conditional. For a general discussion of hospitality in Derrida's writing, see A. J. P. Thomson, *Deconstruction and Democracy*, Continuum Studies in Continental Philosophy (London: Continuum, 2005), pp. 89–100.

does not wait upon an invitation. Rather, it is in advance 'open to someone who is neither expected nor invited'; it is hospitality of visitation rather than of invitation.[28] While this is practically impossible, as Derrida recognizes, it has the function of exposing us to the idea of the alterity of the other, to the idea of 'someone who enters our lives without having been invited'.

This goes to the heart of democracy to come, conceived as call, as promise. As Caputo puts it, 'If we dare not say of this democracy that "it is" we cannot avoid saying that "it calls".'[29] It summons us, with the urgency that Derrida repeatedly emphasizes. And, in contrast with a long philosophical tradition, Derrida regards this call as issuing forth from the other, the stranger, the immigrant, the *voyous*,[30] the voice of the other in me. What these terms capture, above all, is the subversion of the self that is at work here, and hence it also entails a reworking of autonomy and a questioning of sovereignty.[31] The call of democracy exposes me to the other, sets me in relation to an other, necessarily, in much the same sense as that envisaged by Cavell. However, in neither case does this exposure lead to a comfortable, safe sense of community; rather it does its work precisely in the sense that it undoes relation as it reconfigures it.[32]

[28] Derrida in Borradori, *Philosophy in a Time of Terror*, p. 129.

[29] J. D. Caputo, 'Without sovereignty, without being: unconditionality, the coming God and Derrida's democracy to come', *Journal for Cultural and Religious Theory* 4 (2003), 14.

[30] There is an interesting structural similarity between Derrida's treatment of the *voyou* and Laclau's recuperation of populism. Both authors point to the difficult yet crucial role the excluded, the other, the popular plays in the constitution of democracy. See Derrida, *Rogues*, pp. 63–70 and Laclau, *On Populist Reason*.

[31] I do not deal with the question of sovereignty here, which is a central theme of *Rogues*. For an insightful discussion of the question of sovereignty in Derrida and Habermas, see R. Gasché, ' "In the name of reason": The deconstruction of sovereignty', *Research in Phenomenology* 34, no. 1 (2004), 289–303.

[32] As Derrida suggests with reference to international institutions such as the International Criminal Court, and the Declaration of Human Rights: 'this presupposes an extension of the democracy beyond nation-state sovereignty, beyond citizenship. This would come about though the creation of an international juridico-political space that, without doing away with every reference to sovereignty, never stops innovating and inventing new distributions and forms of sharing' (*Rogues*, p. 87).

This characterization of democracy to come also highlights the risks inherent in democracy. In Derrida's late works, these risks are described empirically as well as accounted for theoretically. Empirically the focus is very much on cases in our contemporary world where democracy is put at risk in the name of saving democracy from itself. Examples here range from the suspension of the second round of elections in Algeria in 1992 to the measures introduced in the name of the safeguarding of democracy in the post-9/11 world. Conceptually, this sense of the threat of democracy to itself is captured in the use of the term 'autoimmunity', which has a number of senses in Derrida.[33] Here it is important to note that the sense referred to earlier, in which autoimmunity refers to the possibility of democracy perfecting itself (through the right to auto-critique) is inseparable from its fragility (its openness also exposes it to the 'threat' of those wishing to put it to an end, from within). In the latter case, the suicidal tendency is precisely the attempt to close off critique in the name of a defence of democracy itself. It is important that in the latter case, the attack comes from within, not from some clearly 'external' others. Democracy attacks a part of itself (elections) in order to protect itself in the long run. However, as Derrida suggests, it is by no means certain that this would be successful.

The autoimmune topology operates both in space and in time. The former 'dictates that democracy be *sent off* [*renvoyer*] elsewhere, that it be excluded or rejected, expelled under the pretext of protecting it', for instance, as is familiar to us now, by 'sending off to the outside the domestic enemies of democracy'. The latter suggests a putting off till later – in the case of elections, for instance.[34] In fact, Derrida suggests that this double 'sending off/putting off' is inscribed

---

[33] The term appears with slightly different senses in different texts. See also S. Hadad, 'Derrida and democracy at risk', *Contretemps* 4 (2004), 29–44. However, its meaning derives clearly from the biological sciences, where it describes a phenomenon in which a body's immune system turns on its own cells, destroying it from within. See also A. Thomson, 'What's to become of "democracy to come"?', *Postmodern Culture* 15 (2005).

[34] Derrida, *Rogues*, pp. 35–6.

in democracy itself, a democracy without concept 'devoid of sameness and ipseity', for, following Plato: 'what is lacking in democracy is proper meaning ... Democracy is defined, as the very ideal of democracy, by this lack of the proper and the selfsame.'[35] Democracy, for Derrida, is what it is only in this *différance*: 'it is interminable in its incompletion'. It is this openness that inaugurates both the call of and the risks to democracy; an urgency to institute, advance and reconstitute it, again and again. Now, this perfectionism also informs the account of radical democracy and non-substantive political community articulated in the works of Laclau and Mouffe. It is to a detailed consideration of their writings on democracy that I now turn.

RADICAL AND PLURAL DEMOCRACY

In Chapter 1 I discussed Laclau and Mouffe's account of radical democracy from the point of view of the place of disagreement and the process of the universalization of interests, and in Chapter 2 I have looked at the role of the articulation of equivalences in this account. It is now necessary to draw out, in more detail, their understanding of radical democracy as an ongoing process, which, I will argue, could be characterized as a perfectionist account which is processual in character. This aspect of their account is most clearly visible in the manner in which they characterize the horizon of democracy. I have already noted the role of imagination in this respect. A radical democratic politics, Laclau and Mouffe argue, is 'a form of politics which is founded not upon dogmatic postulation of any "essence of the social", but, on the contrary, on affirmation of the contingency and ambiguity of every "essence", and on the con-stitutive character of social division and antagonism'.[36] It should be noted that the emphasis here is upon the *form* of democratic politics, not some substance of democracy that can be specified in advance of

---

[35] Derrida, *Rogues*, pp. 36–7.
[36] E. Laclau and C. Mouffe, *Hegemony and Socialist Strategy. Towards a Radical Democratic Politics* (London: Verso, 1985), p. 193.

and in separation of any struggle giving it its contents. Their further specification of what they understand by a radical and plural democracy confirms this insight. They argue that:

> Pluralism is *radical* only to the extent that each term of this plurality of identities finds within itself the principle of its own validity ... and this radical pluralism is *democratic* to the extent that the autoconstitutivity of each of its terms is the result of displacements of the egalitarian imaginary. Hence, the project for a radical and plural democracy, *in a primary sense*, is nothing other than the struggle for maximum autonomization of spheres on the basis of the generalization of the equivalential-egalitarian logic.[37]

Hence, radical democracy depends in essence upon a process of extension of demands, which turn relations of subordination into relations of oppression, so making visible the subversive potential of democracy.[38]

Now, a number of commentators have, at least implicitly if not explicitly, questioned the emphasis in Laclau and Mouffe's work on the form of (democratic) politics, arguing that it does not provide enough by way of specifying the substance of democracy.[39] These criticisms range from a demand for the specification of a precise

---

[37] Laclau and Mouffe, *Hegemony and Socialist Strategy*, p. 167.

[38] Relations of subordination are those relations in which one is subject to the decision of another. It is only once democratic discourse becomes available that subordination could be articulated as illegitimate. Hence, relations of subordination come to be seen as, and challenged as relations of oppression. See Laclau and Mouffe, *Hegemony and Socialist Strategy*, pp. 153–4.

[39] See, for instance, the views expressed by Brockelman and Wiley, both of whom in different ways call for a more clearly articulated 'programme' to be specified. T. Brockelman, 'The failure of the radical democratic imaginary: Žižek versus Laclau and Mouffe on vestigial utopia', *Philosophy and Social Criticism* 29 (2003), 183–208; J. Wiley, 'Review essay: the impasse of radical democracy', *Philosophy and Social Criticism* 28 (2002), 483–8. A rather more nuanced critique is developed by Dallmayr, who argues for a conception of democracy that is not simply directed towards domination, 'but toward a tensional balance between presence and absence, liberty and equality: that is a struggle for mutual recognition'. See F. Dallmayr, 'Laclau and hegemony: Some (post) Hegelian caveats', in S. Critchley and O. Marchart (eds.), *Laclau. A Critical Reader* (Abingdon: Routledge, 2004), pp. 50–1.

political programme, a blueprint for a radical democratic politics, to noting the gap between 'the incompleteness of the social' and the argument for a (democratic) politics of emancipation.[40] Laclau repeatedly responds to these and similar points by arguing that there is 'no possibility of deriving a normative injunction to keep open the gap ... from the ontological existence of that gap ... The democratic widening of the gap is itself a contingent decision which is not anchored in any necessary grounding.'[41] While I concur that more needs to be said about democracy, it is crucial that the emphasis on form and the experience of constitutive contingency of our values and forms of social organization contains, for Laclau and Mouffe, an injunction similar to the one expressed by Derrida, namely, that democracy is never fully instituted, and that it remains to be struggled for. As Keenan puts it: 'The recognition of the limits, gaps, dislocation, and openness that constitute the general *field* of politics ... is understood to produce a new, more democratic practice of politics ... ensuring that nothing gets *too* decided or *fully* institutionalized'.[42] Hence the demand that we take responsibility for our freedom and for the fact that 'we ourselves are the exclusive creators of our world'.[43] We now turn to a discussion of the question of the democratic 'we' in Laclau and Mouffe.

IDENTITY AS NEGATIVITY

In their critique of conceiving of identity in essentialist forms, first developed in response to reductionism in the Marxist tradition and later in opposition to communitarian approaches, Laclau and Mouffe privilege negativity in the constitution of any form of identity, collective or otherwise. In a nutshell, the argument can be summarized

---

[40] See J. Sumič, 'Anachronism of emancipation or fidelity to politics', in Critchley and Marchart (eds.), *Laclau. A Critical Reader*, p. 197.

[41] See, for instance, E. Laclau, 'Glimpsing the future', in Critchley and Marchart (eds.), *Laclau. A Critical Reader*, p. 291.

[42] A. Keenan, *Democracy in Question. Democratic Openness in a Time of Political Closure* (Stanford, Calif.: Stanford University Press, 2003), p. 135.

[43] Laclau, *New Reflections*, p. 173.

as follows: if there is no positive, substantive basis to identity, then identity must be given in opposition to something that is excluded from it. As Mouffe puts it:

> It is vital to recognize that, since to construct a 'we' it is necessary to distinguish it from a 'them', and that all forms of consensus are based upon acts of exclusion, the possibility of the political community is at the same time the condition of impossibility of its full realization.[44]

Hence, the unity of such an identity clearly cannot be found in a set of positive characteristics. Instead, it is constituted through the operation of hegemonic practices producing empty signifiers, which represent the absent unity of community. The mutually constitutive role of the logics of equivalence and difference is crucial as each limits the operation of the other in the constitution of identity. However, they are not accorded the same weight in this process since, for Laclau, the unity of the series must ultimately be produced out of equivalential relations. (This emphasis privileges the moment of frontier formation and hence of antagonism.) It is only when one of the elements occupying a position of equivalence comes to incarnate the series, that its unity is established. This is the role of the empty signifier, which becomes the signifier of the whole chain.[45] Now, while this theorization is supplemented with a discussion of identification, further elaboration is needed if one is to provide an account of *democratic* forms of identification. Some of this work can be achieved by giving attention to *how* the identification is held[46] and on its 'directionality' (for want of a better term). It raises questions, in general terms, as to whether and how democratic identification

---

[44] C. Mouffe, 'Democratic politics and the question of identity', in J. Rajchman (ed.), *The Identity in Question* (London: Routledge, 1995), p. 36.

[45] Laclau, *On Populist Reason*, p. 133.

[46] This is an issue that is also explored in J. Glynos and D. Howarth, *Logics of Critical Explanation in Social and Political Theory* (London: Routledge, 2007).

differs from non-democratic forms of identification, and how we might begin to conceptualize these differences.

Democracy and demands

It could be argued that two areas of recent theorizing in Laclau and Mouffe's work set out to address some of these concerns.[47] I will look at these in turn. Laclau, in *On Populist Reason* and in more recent writings, argues that the minimal unit of social analysis is the category of 'demand', which presupposes that a social group is not a homogeneous group or referent, but rather 'that its unity should ... be conceived as an articulation of heterogeneous demands'. Demands, for Laclau, tend to start as requests, addressed to the institutions of power. When those demands are ignored or not responded to, these requests are turned into claims, which may be addressed to or against institutions. This process involves both the constitution of the identity of the claimants and that of the 'enemy', the addressee of the claim, and it is constituted through the establishment of equivalences between claims. The position of democracy in respect of these claims is characterized as follows:

> Democracy is grounded only on the existence of a democratic
> subject, whose emergence depends on the historical articulation
> between equivalential demands. An ensemble of equivalent
> demands articulated by an empty signifier is what constitutes a
> 'people'. So the very possibility of democracy depends upon the
> constitution of a 'democratic people'.[48]

For the time being, it is sufficient to note that democracy and democratic identifications receive their determination only through the articulation of equivalential demands to/against institutions. I will return to the question as to whether this is specification is sufficient to distinguish democratic from other forms of identification.

[47] See especially C. Mouffe, *The Democratic Paradox* (London: Verso, 2000).
[48] Laclau, *On Populist Reason*, p. 171.

From antagonisms to adversarial relations

Mouffe's work in recent years has focused on the development of an analysis of democratic relations between subjects (and this already marks an important difference from Laclau, who tends to focus on the articulation of demands to an other, usually a state or institution of power). In the course of these writings, she distinguishes between antagonistic and agonistic relations.[49] Antagonism is an ineliminable feature of political life for Mouffe, as for Laclau. In addition, however, for Mouffe the key task of democratic politics is to create conditions that would make the emergence of antagonisms less likely.[50] This is the project of 'agonistic pluralism'. Mouffe puts it this way:

> I propose to distinguish between two forms of antagonism,
> antagonism proper – which takes place between enemies, that is,
> persons who have no common symbolic space – and what I call
> 'agonism', which is a different mode of manifestation of
> antagonism because it involves a relation not between enemies but
> between 'adversaries', 'adversaries' being defined in a paradoxical
> way as 'friendly enemies', that is persons who are friends because
> they share a common symbolic space but also enemies because
> they want to organize this common symbolic space in a different
> way.[51]

Several issues in respect of this distinction stand in need of further discussion. I will only outline them here briefly. The first concerns the characterization of the democratic relation as 'adversarial', with contestation taking place *within* accepted symbolic boundaries.[52]

---

[49] See C. Mouffe, 'Politics, democratic action, and solidarity', *Inquiry* 39 (1995), 105. It should be noted that this conceptualization problematizes the characterization of antagonism as theorized in their earlier work, *Hegemony and Socialist Strategy*. There antagonism was also considered to be an intrinsic part of political life. However, precisely for that reason, the aim of a radical democratic politics was *not* to eliminate antagonism, but indeed to proliferate sites of antagonism; to politicize hitherto naturalized relations.

[50] Mouffe, *The Democratic Paradox*, p. 13.   [51] Ibid.

[52] See also C. Mouffe, 'Politics and passion: The stakes of democracy', Centre for the Study of Democracy Perspectives, 2002.

There is at least a question as to whether this portrayal is sufficiently open to contestation and, hence, sufficiently democratic. Given that it is a relation that is specified as being established within an *already shared* symbolic order, it seems to rule out contestation about the boundaries and formation of the space itself at the same time as Mouffe affirms the importance of confrontation and questioning of power relations.[53] The second concerns the dual role antagonism plays in this account. On the one hand, Mouffe affirms with Laclau, that 'antagonism proper' is constitutive of politics. On the other hand, the democratic relation demands that this primary antagonism be turned into agonism, into an adversarial relation. The desire both to retain and to problematize antagonism – in the double figuration, 'antagonism proper' and 'agonism' – raises a set of further questions.[54] So as to get a better grip on them, it is useful to place this account alongside Laclau and Mouffe's earlier theorization of 'radical and plural democracy'. In this earlier account, antagonism is regarded as the *differentia specifica* of their conception of democracy.[55] The emphasis on antagonistic relations and their constitution through the drawing of political frontiers is what distinguishes their account both from liberal democratic theorists such as Rawls and from others, such as Habermas, who position themselves within the radical democratic tradition. This centrality given to the moment of the political derives, respectively, from their use of Sorel and Schmitt.[56] In Mouffe's work

---

[53] Mouffe holds, correctly in my view, that we cannot rid ourselves of relations of power. Mouffe, *The Democratic Paradox*, p. 22. Hence, there is no possibility of a final reconciliation or suturing, to use a Lacanian term, of community.

[54] Drawing on Schmitt, Mouffe argues that 'the identity of a democratic political community hinges on the possibility of drawing a frontier between "us" and "them" ' and she suggests that democrats would be ill-advised to dismiss this insight because of a dislike for Schmitt (Mouffe, *The Democratic Paradox*, p. 43). One may argue, however, that it is necessary to make a distinction between the individuation of identity and its political articulation in the form of a frontier. For a discussion of this issue, see A. J. Norval, 'Frontiers in question', *Acta Philosophica* 2 (1997), 51–76.

[55] This is the position as articulated in *Hegemony and Socialist Strategy*. Both Laclau and Mouffe subsequently redefine their positions in later writings.

[56] Laclau tends to draw on Sorel, while Mouffe's reference point in this respect is Schmitt.

the earlier emphasis on antagonism (proper) is now accompanied by an attempt to work out the characterization of democratic relations between subjects, namely, 'adversarial' relations. Once we move onto this terrain, and it is an important shift, antagonism now is something to be *overcome*.

But is it possible both to assert and maintain the primacy of antagonism, *and* to argue for its domestication in adversarial relations? This route is promising only if one divides the terrain in which the different forms of antagonism may appear. Antagonism (proper) would occur in the constitution of the political field as such; it would accompany the institution of *any* political regime, including also (but not exclusively) that of democracy, while the agonism could be reserved to capture moments of antagonism occurring *within* the already constituted terrain of the democratic regime. In the former case, there is *no* shared symbolic space since it is precisely a symbolic space that is being instituted, while in the latter one assumes the existence of such a space and proceeds to analyse the relations that obtain between democratic citizens. There are, however, two potential difficulties with this account. First, it lacks a clear conceptualization of the movement from one set of relations to another; there is no discussion of the transformation of 'enemies' into 'adversaries'. Second, the characterization of adversarial relations is now argued simply to be about differences within a common space.[57] However, this seems to take the edge off their earlier account of contemporary politics and the point of radical democracy, which is to politicize existing relations, and, hence, to problematize the constitution and shape of that common political space, even while it puts it into question. If this edge is done away with, there is little left to distinguish between Mouffe's and, for instance, more liberal

---

[57] There is a third problem, namely, that antagonism is now characterized as something occurring where there is no common symbolic space. This is clearly untenable on their own account of antagonism, which must at least share or constitute in the process of conflict, the sharing of a set of concerns over which the antagonism takes place.

approaches.[58] Hence, the need both to retain and to do away with antagonism through its management.[59]

Bringing Wittgenstein back in

It is interesting to pursue some of the other intellectual sources on which Mouffe draws so as to see whether insights drawn from these make visible aspects of agonism not captured in the wider discussion drawing on Schmitt. In the development of her argument concerning agonistic pluralism and democracy Mouffe also draws on Wittgenstein in important respects. In particular, she emphasizes the insights for democratic identification we may draw from his attention to practices, discourses and language games.[60] Referring to Wittgenstein's conception of agreement established on a form of life, Mouffe suggests that 'it allows us to grasp the conditions of emergence of a democratic consensus'.[61] More specifically, she characterizes her own theorization of agonistic pluralism as Wittgensteinian in that it explores the political analogue to his account of rule following. Emphasizing the openness and plurality of rules, Mouffe suggests that we think of the democratic game along similar lines:

> If we follow his [Wittgenstein's] lead, we should acknowledge and valorize the diversity of ways in which the 'democratic game' can be played, instead of trying to reduce this diversity to a uniform model of citizenship. This would mean fostering a plurality of forms of being a democratic citizen and creating the institutions

---

[58] See W. E. Connolly, 'Twilight of the idols', *Philosophy and Social Criticism* 21 (1995), 127–37.

[59] It should be noted that this problem does not arise for Laclau, at least not in the same way. This is so for two reasons. First, Laclau, unlike Mouffe is not concerned with furnishing a conception of democratic subjectivity, other than suggesting that such subjectivity is aligned with the populist interruption of power relations. Second, Laclau tends to treat discussions concerned with the organization of democratic life as 'administrative' or 'institutional' problems. Questions arising in this terrain are often characterized as merely 'ontic' by Laclau, in contrast to his interest in the ontology of the political. See, Laclau, 'Glimpsing the future', p. 298.

[60] Mouffe, *The Democratic Paradox*, pp. 67–76.

[61] Mouffe, *The Democratic Paradox*, p. 70.

that would make it possible to follow the democratic rules in a plurality of ways.[62]

Hence, like Tully to whom I turn shortly, Mouffe here emphasizes the multiplicity of voices constitutive of a pluralist society, voices that should not be harnessed into a single position, into harmony and consensus.

Having drawn out the dimensions on which there is a convergence of purpose in Mouffe and Wittgenstein, one can, nevertheless, not brush over areas of potential divergence. The core of this potential divergence concerns whether the emphasis on exclusion as a necessary moment of identity formation in Mouffe's writing is easily reconcilable with an understanding of identity based upon a Wittgensteinian approach. Although both could, in broad terms, be characterized as 'anti-essentialist', their different critiques have divergent consequences for our understanding of identity in general, and subjectivity in particular. The former, with its emphasis on negativity, gives an account of what is excluded in the formation of an identity, while the latter focuses on the plurality and multiplicity of the identity in question.

Some remarks of Wittgenstein's suggest that an articulation between these positions is at least not entirely out of the question. In this respect, Wittgenstein's comments on drawing boundaries are illuminating:

> For I *can* give the concept 'number' rigid limits in this way, that is, use the word 'number' for a rigidly limited concept, but I can also use it so that the extension of the concept is *not* closed by a frontier. And this is how we use the word 'game'. For how is the concept of a game bounded? ... Can you give the boundary? No. You can *draw* one; for none has so far been drawn.[63]

---

[62] Mouffe, *The Democratic Paradox*, p. 73.

[63] Wittgenstein, *Philosophical Investigations* (Oxford: Basil Blackwell, 1958), § 68.

It should be noted here that for Wittgenstein the drawing of boundaries is a specific practice, which is called for under precise circumstances and for particular purposes. But it is not a general claim concerning the individuation of identity. As I will argue shortly, for Wittgenstein the individuation of identity does not entail negativity. Hence, were this approach to be deployed, it would involve at least an attenuation of a strong emphasis on negativity as an ontological category, and would require recasting antagonism as a precise type of ontical political logic.[64] In this case antagonism and the workings of frontiers would be present sometimes, even often, in the constitution of *political* boundaries, but it would be one among several possibilities, depending upon the precise political logics at work. (It is also possible to combine this recasting of antagonism with Laclau's later writings, where antagonism becomes one possible response to the dislocation of the subject which, I have argued earlier, comes very close to the sense of disquietude inspiring Wittgenstein's writings.[65])

A further issue regarding Mouffe's use of Wittgenstein arises at this point. She acknowledges, with Cavell, that the notion of responsibility plays a key role in Wittgenstein's account of practices.[66] However, this dimension of Wittgenstein's thought remains unexplored. Again, this raises the question as to whether a Wittgensteinian approach entails something more than merely a formal method.

---

[64] I have developed the detail of this argument elsewhere. See Norval, 'Frontiers in question' and A. J. Norval, 'Future trajectories of research in discourse theory', in D. Howarth, A. J. Norval and Y. Stavrakakis (eds.), *Discourse Theory and Political Analysis* (Manchester: Manchester University Press, 2000), pp. 219–36.

[65] In *New Reflections* Laclau gives up on the ontological primacy of antagonism and argues, instead, for the ontological primacy of dislocation. See E. Laclau, *New Reflections on the Revolution of Our Time* (London: Verso, 1990), p. 39. These issues clearly cannot be explored in full here. Suffice it to say that there is at least a possibility of a fruitful articulation between Laclau and Mouffe's writings – both jointly and respectively – and insights drawn from Wittgenstein. However, as I have indicated throughout, this does require considerable conceptual reworking of their earlier writings, as well as of some of the positions articulated in their more recent works.

[66] While Laclau also draws on Wittgenstein, there is no engagement with these questions in his reading of Wittgenstein. Similarly, his reading of Derrida also takes issue with accounts of Derrida that take up questions of responsibility, and so on.

Mouffe herself suggests something of the sort in her use of his account of rules and its potential for thinking through the idea of the multiplicity of the ways in which democratic games may be played. However, these implications are not followed through or developed and are not used to elaborate and deepen the account of democratic subjectivity. This is precisely what is done in other accounts, such as those developed by Tully and Cavell, who seek, in quite different ways, to adumbrate a Wittgensteinian approach.

OVERLAPPING ASPECTIVAL IDENTITY

Tully, like Laclau and Mouffe, starts from a problematization of essentialist views.[67] In the context of developing his critique of modern constitutionalism, Tully argues that concepts such as the people, popular sovereignty and citizenship all tend to presuppose the uniformity of the nation-state. In contrast to this view, which would see the nation 'fitting into its own shape' as Tully puts it, he suggests that cultures overlap and are 'densely interdependent in their formation and identity'. Like Derrida, Tully argues that cultures are not internally homogeneous. 'They are continually contested, imagined and re-imagined, transformed and negotiated, both by their members and through their interaction with others.'[68] Hence, identity, unlike a 'billiard ball', works more like a network of similarities, overlapping, criss-crossing and open to negotiation.

Tully draws on Wittgenstein for these general insights and, more specifically, on the way Wittgenstein goes about dislodging the assumption that a concept is identical to itself in every instance.[69] Such assumptions about unity, according to Tully, are mistaken and presuppose that the theorists and citizens who use the language 'look

<hr/>

[67] J. Tully, *Strange Multiplicity. Constitutionalism in an Age of Diversity* (Cambridge: Cambridge University Press, 1995), p. 13.

[68] Tully, *Strange Multiplicity*, p. 11.

[69] ' "A thing is identical with itself." There is no finer example of a useless proposition ... It is as if in imagination we put a thing into its own shape and saw that it fitted.' Wittgenstein, *Philosophical Investigations*, § 216. Quoted in Tully, *Strange Multiplicity*, p. 199.

for and insist upon a uniformity and unity that the diverse and aspectival constitutional phenomena it is supposed to represent do not exhibit'.[70] Identity and the meaning of any culture is *aspectival* rather than essential. Hence, Tully argues that identity changes 'as it is approached from different paths and different aspects come into view'. Cultural diversity is 'a tangled labyrinth of intertwining cultural differences and similarities, not a panopticon of fixed, independent and incommensurable worldviews in which we are either prisoners or cosmopolitan spectators in the central tower'.[71]

This view of identity draws deeply on Wittgenstein's treatment of language games and family resemblances, an understanding of identity that does not rely on an exclusionary logic for its constitution. In the context of heading off the suggestion that there is an essence to language games, Wittgenstein suggests that:

> Instead of producing something common to all that we call
> language, I am saying that these phenomena have no one thing in
> common which makes us use the same word for all, – but that they
> are *related* to one another in many different ways.[72]

There is no one characteristic that is shared by all; rather, many threads run through a fibre, contributing to its strength or unity, but without one of the threads running the whole length.[73] As Wittgenstein says, there is a complicated network of similarities overlapping and criss-crossing.[74] What sort of conception of identity is provided here?

This conception of identity is clearly non-essentialist: there is no singular essence to a game, no one characteristic that would make a game identifiable as a game. Does this leave us with a conception of identity that is inordinately vague, without boundaries? For Wittgenstein, the answers to these questions are clear: 'the

---

[70] Ibid. [71] Tully, *Strange Multiplicity*, p. 11.
[72] Wittgenstein, *Philosophical Investigations*, § 65.
[73] Wittgenstein, *Philosophical Investigations*, § 67.
[74] Wittgenstein, *Philosophical Investigations*, § 66.

extension of the concept is *not* closed by a frontier'.[75] But does this not make it unusable? Not all uses of a concept require sharp boundaries, and in certain instances, where a specific practice requires it, we may *draw* such boundaries.[76] Explaining and understanding the unity of a concept, however, can and does proceed in many other ways than demanding and providing *Merkmal* definitions.[77] One can see things in a particular way, under a particular aspect; use terms according to rules given in certain practices; deploy the practice of pointing to something; and so forth. There is a multitude of ways in which the identity of terms is defined practically, and there are equally many instances where sharp definition is not a prerequisite for appropriate use. It could be concluded safely, following Wittgenstein, that the absence of a sharply defined boundary does not impede our use and understandings of concepts.

However, there are more important consequences following from this approach to identity. It facilitates consideration of the particular characteristics contributing to a concept such as game, retaining an emphasis upon multiplicity, without attributing to them an essentialist status. Hence games may involve winning and losing as in chess, but there may also be games where there is no winning and losing; they may involve and require certain skills, or games may be devoid of the requirement for skill, focusing instead on providing enjoyment and amusement. In none of the cases are games reductively characterized, either by way of essentialist gestures or by way of exclusionary identification. Characterizing identity here is less a matter of opposing it to something else than of a rich account

---

[75] Wittgenstein, *Philosophical Investigations*, § 68.

[76] It is precisely here that a rapprochement between Wittgenstein and Mouffe becomes possible. However, that depends upon a very clear conceptual distinction between the individuation of identity – which may take place in different ways – and a subsequent drawing of boundaries or frontiers for different, sometimes political purposes.

[77] A *Merkmal* definition analyses terms into a conjunction of characteristic marks, and is one kind of definition in terms of necessary and sufficient conditions. See G. P. Baker and P. M. S. Hacker, *Wittgenstein. Meaning and Understanding, Essays on the Philosophical Investigations*, vol. I (Oxford: Basil Blackwell, 1980), p. 37.

of overlapping similarities and differences. This depiction comes close to Derrida's account of iterability: the practice of repetition–alteration constitutes the identity of a term, without one singular characteristic being repeated as an essence.[78] What such an account allows us to do is to focus attention and analytical skill on these rich and complex dimensions of identity, all of which contribute to the individuation of identity, yet none of which could be said to form *the* essence of (an) identity.

Now, a further question regarding this account of identity needs to be posed, and that concerns its relation to a broadly liberal democratic conception of political identity. For Tully there is a complicated interplay between acknowledging the reality of our actual intertwined identities and the defence of a (liberal) conception of openness. This is evident in Tully's own writings, as well as in the manner in which his work has been taken up more broadly. Tully argues that recognition of the inter-twinedness of identity could foster a dialogical spirit of mutual recognition and accommodation of cultural diversity.[79] His discussion of constitutionalism makes this abundantly clear. He argues, on the basis of his earlier account of identity, that a survey of the composite languages of constitutionalism alerts us to the fact that constitutions are not 'fixed and unchangeable agreements reached at some foundational moment, but chains of continual intercultural negotiations and agreements'.[80] The aspectival view remains crucial here. It can be realized in circumstances where participation takes the form of a practical dialogue in which partial and complementary narratives are exchanged,[81] with the result that one's own ways are made to seem strange and unfamiliar, opened up to critical interrogation, reinterpretation and negotiation. As Tully puts it,

---

[78] For Derrida's treatment of iterability, see J. Derrida, *Limited Inc.* (Evanston, Ill.: Northwestern University Press, 1988). For a deployment of these insights in the analysis of the formation of political identities, see D. Howarth, 'Complexities of identity/difference: The ideology of black consciousness in South Africa', *Journal of Political Ideologies* 2 (1997), 51–78.

[79] Tully, *Strange Multiplicity*, p. 209.   [80] Tully, *Strange Multiplicity*, p. 183.

[81] Ibid.

When subjects not only act in accord with the rules but also stand back and try to call a rule into question and negotiate its modification, they problematise this mode of acting together and its constitutive forms of relational subjectivity. This is the context in which political philosophy as a critical activity begins, especially when these voices of democratic freedom are silenced, ignored, deemed unreasonable, or marginalised.[82]

Commenting on Tully, Laden argues that such 'diversity awareness' is achieved through an open-ended process of negotiation, providing us with a particular view on *how* an identity is held:

> In order to open ourselves up to the hearing other points of view, we need to come to understand why our point of view is itself a point of view and not an all-encompassing vision of reality. Negotiation ... provides what might be called the narrative inducement to overcome diversity blindness.[83]

However, neither Tully nor Laden give sufficient attention to the conflict and dislocation necessary to foster the need for opening oneself to another's argument. Nevertheless, it is clear that this conception of identity, importantly, does facilitate attention to the diversity of voices and practices that goes into making up what appear to be unitary conceptions (of nationhood, citizenship, constitutions and so on) structuring modern political life. Given that, it is clear that Wittgenstein's work does not come without commitments, it is necessary to explore this further, and to investigate the implications for a democratic politics in general, and more specifically, for the relations that hold between democratic subjects.

---

[82] Tully, *Strange Multiplicity*, p. 206. Drawing on Foucault in a different context, Tully makes a similar point: J. Tully, 'Political philosophy as critical activity', *Political Theory* 30 (2002), 541.

[83] A. S. Laden, *Reasonably Radical. Deliberative Liberalism and the Politics of Identity* (Ithaca, N.Y.: Cornell University Press, 2001), p. 195.

AVERSIVE IDENTITY

> [F]or Wittgenstein philosophy comes to grief not in denying
> what we all know to be true, but in its effort to escape those
> human forms of life which alone provide the coherence of our
> expression.[84]

There are different accounts of what an ethic inspired by Wittgenstein might entail, and these may highlight different, if not always compatible, dimensions of our subjectivity. Nevertheless, almost all draw attention to Wittgenstein's emphasis on the ordinary, and our quintessential human forms of life. Here I will start to draw out an ethic of responsiveness from this account, before moving on to a more detailed discussion of Cavell's reading of the ordinary and its implications for political community.

Wittgenstein's work contains an incipient ethics, one that is grounded on practical engagement as a fundamental form of human relation.[85] This is evident *inter alia* in his discussion of the way in which humans come to recognize, understand and relate to 'pain behaviour'.[86] 'Knowing one's pain' and 'recognizing' another as being in pain does not proceed on the basis of an attribution of characteristics

---

[84] S. Cavell, *Must We Mean What We Say?* (Oxford: Charles Scribner's Sons, 1976), p. 61.

[85] This reading is based upon arguments and themes developed more fully in the work of, in particular, Stanley Cavell and Stephen Mulhall. See S. Cavell, *The Claim of Reason. Wittgenstein, Skepticism, Morality, and Tragedy* (New York: Oxford University Press, 1982), and S. Mulhall, *On Being in the World. Wittgenstein and Heidegger on Seeing Aspects* (London: Routledge, 1990). See also D. Sparti, 'Responsiveness as responsibility: Cavell's reading of Wittgenstein and King Lear as a source for an ethics of interpersonal relationships', *Philosophy and Social Criticism* 26 (2000), 81–107. I have also drawn inspiration from reading J. C. Edwards, *Ethics without Philosophy. Wittgenstein and the Moral Life* (Tampa: University Presses of South Florida, 1985). Cavell points out that though there is something like a moral or religious urgency present throughout the *Philosophical Investigations*, 'the ethical is not in these works accorded the standing of a separate field of philosophical study'. S. Cavell, *This New Yet Unapproachable America* (Albuquerque, N. Mex.: Living Batch Press, 1989), p. 11.

[86] For Wittgenstein this discussion forms part of his problematization of the inner/outer distinction. See P. M. S. Hacker, *Wittgenstein. Meaning and Mind. Part 1: Essays* (Oxford: Blackwell, 1990).

or mental states. It is not a cognitive, epistemic process.[87] Rather, it is a matter of being able to respond to the distinct behavioural criteria of pain, anger, thinking and so on, which includes not only avowals, facial expressions and gestures, but also surroundings and the occasions of these expressions.[88] And for Wittgenstein, one learns to recognize these criteria in practice and to respond to them. I do not say 'His face was sad, so he too was probably sad.' If I did respond to someone's sadness in this fashion, one would feel that there was something seriously amiss. From Wittgenstein's perspective, such a person would suffer from aspect-blindness. Mulhall characterizes it in the following manner:

> The aspect-blind cannot see (or regard) human behaviour in terms
> of the fine shades, the variety and the flexibility which our
> psychological concepts pick out and presuppose. They are
> incapable of applying our psychological concepts directly and
> unhesitatingly to behaviour and must instead infer its freight of
> human significance ... In this sense, the aspect-blind would be
> blind to an aspect of the *humanity* of human behaviour.[89]

The need to *infer* the meaning of an act or attitude from an expression of a face by the aspect-blind contrasts to the unhesitating responses we could normally be expected to have.[90] This, on Mulhall's reading

---

[87] There is nothing wrong with ordinary talk of 'knowing one's pain'. The problem arises when that talk is translated into a philosophical problem, trying to determine under which conditions I can be certain that another is in pain.

[88] See also P. M. S. Hacker, *Insight and Illusion* (Oxford: Clarendon Press, 1972), especially ch. x, for a discussion of criteria in this context.

[89] Mulhall, *Being in the World*, p. 86.

[90] For Wittgenstein these are 'primitive reactions' forming part of our 'natural history'. See Wittgenstein, *Philosophical Investigations*, §185. As Sparti points out, while Wittgenstein does not claim that 'the meaning of a given bodily expression is obvious, he does assume both that the expressions of our bodies enhance the language of human connectedness, and that the living human body is a primitive, i.e. is used as a paradigmatic criterion when we extend the ascription of psychological predicates to objects or to non-human sentient beings'. Sparti, 'Responsiveness as responsibility', 103.

of Wittgenstein and Cavell, has further consequences for our relations to others:

> If ... the attitude of attachment to our words mirrors our attachment to ourselves and other persons (a suggestion reinforced by noting that linguistic behaviour is a sophisticated domain of human behaviour in general), then those who lack the attachment to words will have a counterpart in those lacking the analogous attachment to others. Since the former attitude of attachment can be partly characterized as a familiarity with – an unhesitating capacity to move around within – language, and its lack as a form of linguistic stumbling ... we are led to conclude that an aspect-blind person's behaviour in relation to other persons is to be imagined as equally a matter of hesitation, stumbling.[91]

As I have argued in Chapter 3, what is crucial here is an 'unhesitating response', or lack of it. It is in this respect that Wittgenstein's conception of language as a practice can be said to contain an incipient ethics:

> Just as our responses are the smallest events that can be 'moves' in our language games, so can our caring responses become the smallest unit of our morality. Our *responsibility* to others lies in our *responsiveness* to them. Our responsibility, in other words, lies in the fact that if we can be blind (hidden) to the others, we can also acknowledge them.[92]

However, it is important that we will *not always* acknowledge others or respond to them; nor even that we ought to: the central concept of acknowledgement 'does not describe a given response but is, rather, a category in terms of which such responses are evaluated'.[93] Now, it

---

[91] Mulhall, *Being in the World*, pp. 88–9.

[92] Sparti, 'Responsiveness as responsibility', 91.

[93] Hammer, *Stanley Cavell*, p. 64. Hammer continues to point out that regardless 'of whether we respond or not, the structure of acknowledgement is in place; the other's demand for recognition, even if unheeded, puts us in a position of responsibility'.

should be made clear that this reading of Wittgenstein regards an ethics, not as a theory, but as a 'bent that emerges especially by understanding the place of acknowledgement and ethical responsiveness in our practical life'.[94] Importantly, this moment of response is not based upon an assumed shared, primordial 'humanity'. Rather, we need to work to regain and rediscover responsiveness.[95] Responsiveness and responsibility form a key part of Cavell's reading of Wittgenstein, which also offers one of the most politically developed readings that draw upon his writings.

Here I seek to flesh out an account of democratic subjectivity by focusing in detail on what it demands in terms of our relations to others and, hence, of democratic community. It is in this context that Cavell's work is particularly illuminating. He seeks to counter claims of subjectivism when dealing with the ordinary, while drawing attention to the fact of individual responsibility for and the invoking of community in the claims we make. In brief, in speaking we take up positions *vis-à-vis* others, and these positions encompass obligations and expectations.[96] Individuals thus bear responsibility for their responses and judgements within a shared form of life.[97] It is of crucial importance that the rules of language, or of a game, do not determine

---

[94] Sparti, 'Responsiveness as responsibility', 81.

[95] Sparti, 'Responsiveness as responsibility', 99.

[96] Hammer, *Stanley Cavell*, p. 8. As Cavell puts it: 'the point is to determine *what* position you are taking, that is to say, *what position you are taking responsibility for* – and whether it is one I can respect. What is at stake in such discussions is not ... whether you know our world, but whether, or to what extent, we are to live in the same moral universe. What is at stake ... [is] the nature or quality of our relationship to one another'. Cavell, *The Claim of Reason*, p. 268.

[97] Cavell argues that: 'You cannot use words to do what we do with them until you are initiate of the forms of life which give those words the point and shape they have in our lives.' Cavell, *The Claim of Reason*, p. 184. And, as Cavell points out, forms of life are not *merely* conventional in the sense that a particular culture has found them convenient. Instead, the conventional is 'those forms of life which are normal to any group of creatures we call human, any group about whom we will say, for example, that they *have* a past to which they respond, or a geographical environment which they manipulate or exploit in certain ways for certain humanly comprehensible motives. Here the array of "conventions" are not patterns of life which differentiate human beings from one another, but those exigencies of conduct and feeling which all humans share.' Cavell, *The Claim of Reason*, p. 111. See also S. Mulhall, *Stanley*

what we can and may do: just as there are always projections of words that are unusual, so there may be moves in a game that may not be obvious. What matters here is that 'we are able to say, how and to what extent we are able to make sense in a particular case'.[98] Each of us is responsible. We cannot escape responsibility by pointing to the rules of a game, or some objective framework within which we are operating.

In the course of his discussion of aesthetic and moral judgement, reflection and conduct, Cavell develops his account of community, invoked in the making of claims. These insights are extended to thinking about political community in his readings of Rousseau and Rawls, in particular. In this context, Cavell suggests that what we learn from the social contract teachings is the beginning of an answer to the question concerning with whom I am in community. Hence, the social contract is not about mere obedience, but is rather about membership of a polis, which implies that:

> I recognize others to have consented with me, and hence that I
> consent to political equality. Second, that I recognize the society and
> its government, so constituted as mine; which means that I am
> answerable not merely to it, but for it. So far, then, as I recognize
> myself to be exercising my responsibility for it, my obedience to it is
> obedience to my own laws ... the polis is the field within which I work
> out my political identity and it is the creation of (political) freedom.[99]

Thus, from the start Cavell shifts attention away from the 'legislating voice' to a conversational voice, the voice in which community is invoked.[100] However, there is cause to proceed slowly here, so as to avoid a too quick rapprochement between Cavell's invocation of voice and the treatment of voice in the deliberative tradition. In the

---

Cavell. *Philosophy's Recounting of the Ordinary* (Oxford: Clarendon Press, 1994), p. 67 on the role of our relation to our elders/native tongue.

[98] Hammer, *Stanley Cavell*, p. 21.   [99] Cavell, *The Claim of Reason*, p. 23.

[100] This distinction in respect of Cavell's writing is developed further in A. Norris, 'Political revisions: Stanley Cavell and political philosophy', *Political Theory* 30 (2002), 828–32.

latter, demands for inclusion of different voices proceed in the name of the completion of an already constituted community, and such voices are always ultimately subordinated to a limiting conception of rationality and a narrowing focus on argumentation as constituting the nodal point of political life.

For Cavell, by contrast, what is at stake is precisely the *founding* of community, its *invocation* in the claims we make, and what we can say, and what others can say for us in such voicing of claims. And it is crucial that for Cavell argumentation is not at the heart of political life; rather, 'the issue is not to win an argument ... but *to manifest for the other another way*'.[101] As Hammer puts it:

> The task of speaking, of having a voice, does not coincide simply with uttering one's thoughts in such a way that others may rationally be convinced by one's position; rather, the hero of Cavell's vision of democracy is only able to attain the goal of demonstrating to others the partiality of her society's arrangements by offering herself and her position, as representing an alternative self *for* those others.[102]

To see what exactly this entails and how Cavell develops this understanding of voice, it is important to look further at his account of (political) community and its roots in his understanding of perfectionism.

As for Rancière, Cavell's account of the forging of political community, both in giving assent to and in its withdrawal, is an aesthetic one, which emphasizes the shaping of my own identity and its consequences for and in relation to political community.[103] As Mulhall puts it:

> Politics here appears as an arena in which the self defines or creates itself; political autonomy is an aspect of human autonomy as such,

---

[101] Cavell, *Conditions Handsome and Unhandsome*, p. 31.

[102] Hammer, *Stanley Cavell*, pp. 132–3.

[103] In this respect, see R. Shusterman, 'Putnam and Cavell on the ethics of democracy', *Political Theory* 25 (1997), 193–214.

and insofar as I exercise my political responsibilities, I must think of myself as shaping or forming my (political) identity. But this process of self-definition is essentially communal; the field within which it can alone be achieved is constituted insofar as I recognize others, and they recognize me, as fellow-members ... I cannot work out my political identity alone.[104]

Just as central to the emphasis on the invocation of community are the possibilities of rebuff and dissent. In Cavell's philosophy, community is not known *a priori*; it is *disclosive*: 'for whom you speak and by whom you are spoken for' is not given, but is disclosed in the act of making and staking claims. It also means that one risks rebuff 'of those for whom you claimed to be speaking', as well as having to rebuff 'those who claimed to speak for you'.[105] Cavell furthermore distinguishes between the withdrawal of one's consent and dissent. The former involves both saying 'It is no longer mine' and 'It is no longer ours', since just as consent required acknowledgement of others, so does its withdrawal. By contrast, dissent is a dispute about the content of consent. Hence, to dissent is still to exercise one's political voice.[106] Dissent, rather than a rejection of political responsibility, seeks to investigate the extent to which my voice is in fact speaking for others, and whether others speak for me.[107]

It is in this emphasis on voice and the interminable interplay between dissent and assent that Cavell's account comes closest to the agonism proposed by post-structuralist theorists of democracy, and it is precisely in this sense that it could enrich our understanding of agonistic democracy. In particular, Cavell's emphasis on *exemplarity* provides a picture of democratic responsiveness and responsibility, supplementing the account of radical democracy offered by Laclau

---

[104] S. Mulhall, 'Promising, consent, and citizenship: Rawls and Cavell on morality and politics', *Political Theory* 25 (1997), 184.

[105] Cavell, *The Claim of Reason*, p. 27.

[106] Not speaking for oneself politically is 'having nothing (political) to say'. Cavell, *The Claim of Reason*, p. 28.

[107] Hammer, *Stanley Cavell*, p. 131.

and Mouffe. To see precisely how Cavell's may supplement their account, we need to look more closely at this characterization of perfectionism and how it relates to democracy.[108] Perfectionism for Cavell, drawing on Emerson in particular, is not an alternative theory but an outlook,[109] a dimension of the moral life that spans Western life and concerns.[110] Following Emerson and Nietzsche, Cavell characterizes perfectionism as *aversive thinking*, that is, aversion to conformism. Politically, conformism entails a forgetting of the need to define oneself: 'the conformist, by failing to estrange himself from prevailing opinion (as well as from himself), lets the community speak for him, yet without interrogating its right to do so'.[111] Without the ability to criticize and animate our existing institutions, and the imagination to change and challenge them, democratic institutions risk becoming fossilized and sclerotic. As Cavell puts it, 'the mission of Perfectionism generally, in a world of false (and false calls for) democracy, is the discovery of the possibility of democracy, which to exist has recurrently to be (re)discovered'.[112] Democracy, for Cavell, is not a matter of reaching agreement, as it is for deliberative theorists. Rather, the emphasis is on disagreements, on 'separateness of positions', and on ongoing conversations and differences of position.[113] The task of keeping our political institutions alert and alive to change and challenge is, at least in part, that of individuals having an ethic, a striving to better themselves, and so society, by overcoming habit. Fostering an aversive identity is a crucial part of this process.

Hence, oppositional, critical thinking consists in the ability to withstand conformism and to respond to the *inevitable failures* of

---

[108] Cavell, *Unapproachable America*, p. 11.
[109] Shusterman questions whether Cavell could incorporate the body into his conception of voice. See Shusterman, 'Putnam and Cavell', 213, endnote 22.
[110] Cavell, *Conditions Handsome and Unhandsome*, p. 2.
[111] Hammer, *Stanley Cavell*, p. 132.
[112] Cavell, *Conditions Handsome and Unhandsome*, p. 17.
[113] Cavell, *Conditions Handsome and Unhandsome*, pp. 24–5.

democracy without falling back onto cynicism.[114] Conformism makes slaves of us. Escaping this slavishness depends upon being dissatisfied with our current selves or the state things. The desire for that which exceeds our current state (of self and of society) arises from this self-dissatisfaction.[115] Now it is important that Cavell's account does not rest on a picture of the individual self as isolated. This self, in contrast with the liberal conception of an autonomous, self-contained self is always already divided, riven[116] and dependent upon other human beings, since the self cannot fulfil itself without regard for others.[117] The self is both an attained self and a self striving for another, next self.[118] This search for a next self is emphatically not teleological. Here Cavell sharply differs from those commentators such as Rawls, who treat perfectionism as teleological doctrine. There is no singular vision of what the good is that is striven for, nor any question of imposing one's own conception of the good onto others.[119] There is also no question of the self being isolated from others. As Cavell notes, Emerson's writing, upon which he draws, 'works out the conditions for my recognizing my difference from others as a function of my recognizing my difference from myself'.[120] As noted earlier, the

---

[114] Cavell, *Conditions Handsome and Unhandsome*, p. 36. Emerson calls oppositional thinking aversive thinking.

[115] Cavell, *Conditions Handsome and Unhandsome*, pp. 47 and 51. Cavell elaborates
these themes in response to Rawls's reading of perfectionism, which he takes to
task for an impoverished account of Nietzsche. I return to this theme in the
concluding chapter.

[116] For Cavell, drawing on Emerson, the subject is divided or inherently doubled. This
is a consequence of his picture of the self 'as a process of becoming or failing to
become – of being committed to one's attained self and thereby blind to the
attractions of one's further or unattained self, or of being committed to one's next
self and so avoiding conformity with one's present self'. Mulhall, *Stanley Cavell*,
p. 299. It is in this sense that Cavell's conception of the subject comes into sharp
contrast to a liberal conception. The emphasis on dependence – on others and on
language – contrasts with a liberal stress on autonomy as starting point. By
contrast, for Cavell autonomy is always something to be attained, and if attained,
always threatened and precarious. See Mulhall, *Stanley Cavell*, pp. 292–310.

[117] Shusterman, 'Putnam and Cavell', 204.

[118] The term 'next' for Cavell denotes both a future self and a self besides the current self.

[119] Cavell, *Conditions Handsome and Unhandsome*, p. 46.

[120] Cavell, *Conditions Handsome and Unhandsome*, p. 53.

working out of any identity can only occur in the context of my relations to others:

> Emerson's turn is to make my partiality the sign and incentive of my siding with the next or further self, which means siding against my attained perfection (or conformity), sidings which require the recognition of an other – the acknowledgement of a relationship – in which this sign is manifest.[121]

It is, furthermore, crucial that for Cavell this perfectionism is essential to life in a constitutional democracy.[122] Contrasting Emersonian perfectionism to aristocratic and elitist forms of perfectionism, Cavell suggests that it is tied to democracy in a very particular way: as preparation to withstand the failures of democracy, by keeping 'democratic hope alive in the face of disappointment with it'.[123] He argues that it is inevitable that we will be disappointed in democracy, 'in its failures by the light of its own principles of justice'.[124] In this, Cavell departs from much current writing on democracy, which tends to treat it in an unequivocally triumphalist manner as unproblematic panacea for all ills in contemporary society. Instead, his picture of democracy emphasizes and takes account of the multiplicity of ways in which democracy may fail to achieve what it promises. This has important consequences for democratic subjectivity. The consent we give to society, on this reading, is one that recognizes and emphasizes the existing inequities in society, and our consent to them. Mulhall captures precisely what is at stake here:

> Thinking of the polis as mine ensures that I am *implicated* in whatever the polis is and does: for even if its structures and pronouncements do not embody what I am prepared to recognize as my (political) will, my membership entails that they are made in my name and so are ones for which I am answerable.[125]

---

[121] Cavell, *Conditions Handsome and Unhandsome*, p. 31.
[122] Cavell, *Conditions Handsome and Unhandsome*, p. 9.
[123] Cavell, *Conditions Handsome and Unhandsome*, p. 56.   [124] Ibid.
[125] Mulhall, *Stanley Cavell*, p. 58 (emphasis added).

Hence the urgency and weightiness with which Cavell invests the question of voice. Yet, while this could be cause for despair, his account of perfectionism is accompanied by an incessant call, the call of exemplarity.

Exemplarity plays a crucial role in Cavell, in the account given of both aesthetic and moral discourse, and is already clearly present in his characterization of the appeal to ordinary language as an exemplification of language such that others, a new generation, 'may learn it from you, may come to say what you say'.[126] The treatment of aesthetic, moral and political discourse by Cavell all raise questions about how we are to go on, about how to exercise one's judgement in a new context,[127] yet they are raised slightly differently in each context. In the case of aesthetic discourse, the aim is to elicit agreement on the (aesthetic) status of a particular object.[128] Here the movement is from a subjective judgement to a claim to speak for others. In the case of moral discourse, there is no claim to universality. Rather, the emphasis is on mutual respect for individual differences. Political discourse shares elements of both of these discourses. With aesthetics, it claims to speak for others, and with moral discourse there is the emphasis on respect for individual differences. Hence, political discourse combines the emphasis on self-knowledge as a means to achieve community and vice versa.

There may be events, persons, or movements that are politically analogous in status to the aesthetic object in coming to be regarded as exemplary. This is achieved through an extension of its grammar. Conversely, there may be dimensions of achieved political community through which I may learn something about myself, and the positions I hold in respect of a concrete political issue. In each of these cases, the role of the exemplar is crucial. It should be noted, however, that the exemplar is not given, and there is nothing

---

[126] Cavell, *Conditions Handsome and Unhandsome*, p. 24.
[127] Mulhall, *Stanley Cavell*, p. 65.
[128] My discussion of the distinctive characteristics of these discourses relies heavily on Mulhall's excellent treatment in *Stanley Cavell*, chs 2 and 3.

automatic in becoming exemplary. All this depends upon a process of engagement, of affirming consent and expressing dissent, which is the activity of a democratic community. Indeed, Cavell in his discussion of Nietzsche, argues that the exemplar acts as access to another realm. The exemplar 'is not grounded in the relation between the instance and the class of instances it stands for but in the relation between the instance and the individual other – for example, myself – for whom it does the standing, for whom it is a sign'.[129] In this sense, the exemplar acts as a *call*, as a reminder of another self, and another state of things, capturing both the dissatisfaction discussed earlier, and the possibility of another self, another way of doing things. This central insight, as we have seen, is also present in Derrida's account of 'democracy to come'.

At this point it is crucial to re-emphasize the importance of Cavell's characterization of the claims made in speaking. As noted earlier, for Laclau (democratic) community comes into being through 'the horizontal articulation of equivalential demands', and for Mouffe in adversarial relation between members of the polity.[130] It is here that the emphasis in Cavell on the effects and implications of my making a claim comes into force: making a claim tells us something about the character of the community invoked and contested. It implies relations of equality, and not only of equivalence.[131] It characterizes the place of assent and dissent as internal to the constitution of a democratic community. And it provides us with a clear account of the place of the individual within the account of community, and the responsibility of each for his or her claims. While Laclau's account alerts us to the importance of identification and provides us with a picture of the process of articulation and the role it may play

---

[129] Cavell, *Conditions Handsome and Unhandsome*, pp. 50–1.

[130] As pointed out earlier, while Mouffe quotes Cavell approvingly on the importance of making claims and the responsibility that comes with it, she does not take on board the broader context within which Cavell develops this point.

[131] While equivalence between elements may make them equal in their common opposition to something outside of them to which they are opposed, it does not tell us (enough) about equality.

in the constitution of democratic demands, Cavell's approach draws out and develops Wittgensteinian intuitions about the importance of not reducing our understanding of community to what we share in our exclusion of, or opposition to, the other. In so doing, Cavell provides us with a deeper and nuanced account of what democratic subjectivity – both individually and communally – might entail.

Exemplarity: Nora and the inchoate political voice

This account of democratic subjectivity highlights two important aspects of democratic identification absent from other treatments of the matter. These are, first, the sort of responses one may expect within societies with a democratic ethos and, second, a discussion of the actual process of the emergence of new claims within such an order. In both cases, Cavell's insights deepen our understanding of what a democratic grammar might entail. This is particularly evident in his discussion of the sense of injustice experienced by Nora in *The Doll's House*. Nora has to find her own voice, in contradistinction to the one Thorvald attributes to her and through which he seeks to control her. The deprivation of voice she suffers and the difficulties she faces in expressing her inchoate sense of injustice, arises from 'the work of moral consensus itself, spoken for by the respectable Thorvalds of the world (in us)'.[132] What is at stake here is a denial of the validity of her sense of injustice – Thorvald accuses her of speaking like a child, of being ill and of not understanding the world she lives in – and the charges she brings against the social order itself.[133] It is worth quoting Cavell at length here:

> I am taking Nora's enactments of change and departure to
> exemplify that over the field on which moral justifications come to
> an end, and justice, as it stands, has done what it can, specific
> wrong may not be claimable; yet the misery is such that, on the

---

[132] Cavell, *Conditions Handsome and Unhandsome*, p. xxxvii.
[133] Cavell, *Conditions Handsome and Unhandsome*, p. 109.

other side, right is not assertible; instead something must be shown. This is the field of Moral Perfectionism ... In the field of moral encounter ... the exhaustion of justifications, the sense of something unacceptable, is reached first by the one out of authority ... the position of the victim; there is a cause ... Then the alternative to persisting in the claim to be right cannot be ... to say. 'This is simply what I do,' and wait; which is to say, that would not provide an alternative, but a reiteration of right. The alternative would be to find myself dissatisfied with what I do.

Then, if, as is overwhelmingly likely, I continue to consent to the way things are, what must be shown, acknowledged, is that my consent ... compromises me; that I know change is called for and to be striven for, beginning with myself. But then I must also show, on pain of self-corruption worse than compromise, that I continue to consent to the way things are, without reason, with only my intuition that our collective distance from perfect justice is, though in moments painful to the point of intolerable, still habitable.

It is worth reflecting further on this reading, for it draws out some of the complexity inherent in the making of claims and the difficulty of expression of senses of injustice that do not fit the parameters of current moral and political discourse. Through the example of Nora, Cavell captures the experience of a sense of injustice that is inexpressible in the terms of prevailing discourse, but where misery is clearly unmistakable. What does one make of such an experience in a context governed by a democratic grammar? Nora stands as an exemplar. She embodies a claim exceeding existing discourse, one that acts as a call to open ourselves up to other, foreign possibilities. Consequently, there are no readily available responses to her. The given terms of discourse would simply require of her to submit herself to an intolerable denial of her voice. Hence, it is not satisfactory simply to repeat the 'this is just the way we do things here'. In denying the possibility of this response, Cavell alerts us to the fact that Nora's claim, even if it fails to find expression in the dominant discourse, nevertheless has an impact upon it. The sense of wrong must be acknowledged. At the very least, one will have to restate the terms and reasons for the denial of the claim. In this case, one will have become aware of the painful distance from 'perfect justice' in the current order, forcing reflection on the fact that my consent to society is not only to what Cavell calls its 'successes or graces'; 'it reaches into every corner of society's failure or ugliness'.[134] This acknowledgement of society's distance from perfect justice, for Cavell, signals a disposition that allows for

> civil life to go on in the face of broken promises, conflict of interest, discrimination ... It also means that I recognize that at some time my sense of my society's distance from the reign of perfect justice, and of my implication in its distance, may become intolerable. Then if an argument should not take place (under present conditions?), what should take its place? (I assume that constitutional debate is not here in order.)[135]

It is precisely here that an (aspect) change is required, which, as is clear from the position expressed by Cavell, as well as in our earlier discussion of aspect change, cannot simply be of the order of argumentation. The dislocation resulting from Nora's presence – nothing remains the same in the wake of her 'enactments of change and departure' – calls for a response, a re-examination and reiteration of the dominant position, hence provoking an engagement with her claims. At worst, this will result in a reassertion of the dominant position, at best, it may lead to a rearticulation of it. However, even in the worst case, the prevailing order cannot simply be reasserted: it will be marked by the engagement. Closure cannot be complete here. And while, in this particular case, 'constitutional debate' may not be in order, in others, it may well be given that we assume responsibility not only for the contents of the polity, but for its very shape.[136]

---

[134] Cavell, *Conditions Handsome and Unhandsome*, p. 107.

[135] Cavell, *Conditions Handsome and Unhandsome*, p. 110.

[136] Tully explores the complexities of democratic change and its relation to constitutionalism, and suggests that contemporary constitutional struggles are

The exemplar, and its promise, plays a crucial role in opening up and in making visible its contours. Cavell thinks this promise through the figure of perfectionism and the self's openness to a further self, in oneself and in others, 'which means, being one who lives in promise ... which in turn means expecting oneself to be, making oneself intelligible as an inhabitant now also of a further realm',[137] and it is precisely in this sense that his perfectionism, which for him is 'the condition of democratic morality', resonates so strongly with Derrida's account of 'democracy to come'.

CONCLUSION

> In order for an emerging people to appreciate the healthy maxims of politics ... the effect would have to become cause; the social spirit should be the result of the institution which would have to preside over the founding of the institution itself; and men would have to be prior to the laws what they ought to become by means of laws.[138]

The formation of any democratic community has both retrospective and prospective dimensions. However, these dimensions should not be understood in any simplistic chronological order since the retrospective and the prospective are implicated in one another through a trace structure.[139] This is clearly captured in Rousseau's paradox of the institution of the democratic community: 'men' have to be prior to the law what they ought to become by means of the law. The formation of a democratic subject relies upon a set of practices being drawn together retroactively. But this drawing together of an already

groping towards a situation in which 'a constitution can be both the foundation of democracy and, at the same time, subject to democratic discussion and change in practice'. This would be the spirit expressed by *Haida Gwaii*. See Tully, *Strange Multiplicity*, p. 29.

[137] Cavell, *Conditions Handsome and Unhandsome*, p. 125.

[138] Rousseau, quoted in W. E. Connolly, *The Ethos of Pluralization* (Minneapolis: University of Minnesota Press, 1995), p. 138.

[139] Derrida discusses the trace structure of time in his reading of Husserl, in *Speech and Phenomena*, trans. David B. Allison (Evanston, Ill.: Northwestern University Press, 1973).

existing set of practices cannot occur without reference to the promise of democracy: its futural element is thus crucial, but nevertheless, must remain precarious.

This emphasis on the precariousness of identity, its provisional and never fully achieved character, is one shared by Laclau, Mouffe, Tully, Cavell, Wittgenstein and Derrida alike. However, they highlight different aspects of this experience. Laclau and Mouffe both tend to treat it in predominantly 'analytical' terms. That is, the emphasis on and recognition of contingency and precariousness does not translate into any further normative commitments. The contingency of identity simply suggests an in principle openness that could be articulated in any political direction. Hence, their respective accounts of democracy do not use or draw in any particular fashion upon this insight. This is not the case with Cavell's and Derrida's accounts since both are at pains to draw a link between the never fully achieved character of identity and democracy.

A similar divergence in argument is present with respect to their emphasis on the relationality of identity. All these theorists argue for and deploy a relational conception of identity in their writings. But it is only Tully, Cavell, and Derrida who develop relationality in a normative direction. As noted earlier, while Mouffe goes a long way in this direction, she refrains from taking on board the wider implications of Cavell and Wittgenstein's thought. However, this said, it should be noted that her work diverges from Laclau's in that she specifically addresses herself to the question of relations *between* citizens in the development of her account of democracy. This stands in some contrast to Laclau, for whom populism acts as the exemplar in relation to which any thought of democracy needs to be developed. Given this presupposition, the emphasis remains on the division between the people and oppressive regimes. From this starting-point, it is difficult to see how a more nuanced conception of democratic relations could be fleshed out. Investigating the logics of horizontal relations, and their theoretical presuppositions, are crucial to a conception of democracy which emphasizes not only the contingent contextual articulations, with which we historically have come to associate democracy, but also what we may need to suppose, given the grammar of democracy.

Democracy, in these terms, should be thought of as a form of life rather than a regime, its defence in terms of the development of an ethos, rather than a set of institutions, though this is clearly not to deny that creative thought about the latter is needed. All of this pre-supposes that we have a clear idea and characterization of the relation between subjects, which we would call, given our criteria, democratic. This brings us back to the question raised at the start of the chapter. The real issue, when treating identification in democratic terms, is *how* such identification is held. Here relationality and contingency together take centre stage. To put it differently, the key to differ-entiating between a democratic, and other forms of identification, is in the manner in which such identification is held. Cavell draws out some of the implications for democratic subjectivity. Aversive identity is based precisely upon a problematization of the given, of prevailing opinion, and it is closely tied in with self-definition, which, we have seen, is essentially communal in character. This is the moment of the political *within* already constituted democratic regimes.

Several important consequences follow from this. The first is that whatever takes place within democratic regimes cannot be rele-gated to the 'administration of things'. There is no absolute distinction to be drawn between the moment of the political – as the institution of a regime – and politics as the sedimentation of that institution. Things are more complicated than this, as Tully's work on constitutionalism has clearly shown. Democracy and democratic identity are not given once and for all, fully constituted and then simply subject to admini-stration. To the contrary, as both Cavell and Derrida make clear, democracy is to be conceived of as an ongoing project of renewal. Hence the emphasis on the role of disagreement, dissatisfaction, and as Laclau and Mouffe would argue, dislocation, all of which is accom-panied by the promise, the call of democracy to come.

What is crucial here is that an adequate post-structuralist account of democracy must be able, together with its working through of the moment of critical engagement, to articulate an ethos pertinent to democracy, and hence an account of subjectivity that thinks through what is presupposed in the assertion of our historical identifications. Thus, it has been necessary to flesh out an account of democratic subjectivity and community that goes beyond mere contextualism, if by the latter one understands the suggestion that any particular manner in which a relation between subjects is constituted is a matter (only) of historico-political articulation. While most post-structuralists are happy to outline the ontological characteristics of the subject as such, they tend to balk at developing a similar stance in terms of particular identifications for fear of falling into the sorts of idealization evident in deliberative accounts of democracy, or of getting entangled in the 'merely' ontical terrain. However, the pertinent distinction here is not that between abstraction and context (for such a distinction runs the risk of providing a problematic account of both) but between abstraction and idealization. Abstraction cannot be avoided while idealization should be. Seen from this vantage point, the demand is not for a substantive, thick account of what our democratic commitments ought to be, and of what substantive characteristics ideal democrats should have. Rather, it is for a more reflective attitude and thought about what it is that we do when we voice democratic claims, how we hold those claims, what it suggests about our own identities and that of others, and of the relations that hold between us; how we may voice dissent; how we may come to make claims in the first instance, and how new claims force the reconstitution of the symbolic terrain. To avoid teleology and the positing of substantive ideals, which must hold for everyone, we need to think of the democratic ethos as the starting-point, not a substantive ideal to be striven for. Hence the emphasis in Derrida and Cavell on both the call and thus futural dimension of democracy, and the nearness (next-to-us) and urgency of the call.

5   Conclusion: aversive democracy – exemplarity, imagination and passion

> The point is not to win an argument (that may come late in the day) but to manifest for the other another way.[1]

In this concluding chapter, I draw together the threads of the argument that constitute the grammar of what I have called aversive democracy. On the one hand, this grammar includes the vocabularies we use and the practices we engage in. But it also relates to the way these delimit the 'say-able' and the 'do-able' – that which is intelligible to us at any point in time. And finally, it concerns the possibility of challenges to existing grammars by new democratic claims, which may transform – or indeed, affirm – this grammar. Throughout I have foregrounded the importance of both the terms of argumentation and its structure. However, I have also sought to go beyond these more traditional concerns so as to consider both the rhetoricality of our practices and their bodily visceral character. In addition to this refocusing of democratic grammar, I have also sought to unpack the role of subjectivity in a democratic grammar by focusing on the importance of identification with a grammar as well as the logic of its embedding and challenges to existing grammars. I have argued that identification is important in accounting for the constitution of the democratic subject, and it is here that the emergence of new claims, as well as the different forms of relation constituted amongst democratic subjects, has received attention. Rancière and Laclau provided the starting-point here. I drew

---

[1] S. Cavell, *Conditions Handsome and Unhandsome. The Constitution of Emersonian Perfectionism*, The Carus Lectures, 1998 (Chicago: University of Chicago Press, 1990), p. 31.

on Rancière to think through the eruption of new demands and the consequent refashioning of 'common' spaces of argumentation, and on Laclau for an account of the mechanisms through which claims are universalized (through the constitution of equivalential chains). Wittgenstein's account of aspect dawning and change was introduced to analyse the interplay between tradition and innovation in this process. Finally, Cavell's insights into the commitments we make in the articulation of claims have been used to provide a more nuanced analysis of the relations obtaining between democratic subjects and the responsibilities we assume in making claims. An exposition of Derrida's 'democracy to come' and 'the call of exemplarity' in Cavell – in short, the idea of 'living in a promise' – provided an entry-point into fleshing out the perfectionist account of aversive democracy as taking seriously the role of imagination in constituting democratic subjectivity and the horizon of expectation of a democratic grammar. A further consideration of this horizon furnishes the material for drawing these arguments together, so as to delineate the distinctive features of an aversive account of democracy.

Our contemporary world is replete with examples of significant events and figures that contribute to our understanding of the character and staging of struggles in present-day politics. One only needs to think here of a Desmond Tutu, a Nelson Mandela and an Aung Sang Suu Kyi; of Sabra and Chatila; of the Tiananmen 'tank man' and, more recently, of Seattle and the 'Make Poverty History Campaign'; the Indonesian tsunami and Katrina. More prosaic local examples may be added to this list.[2] The exemplarity of the example, as I have argued in Chapter 4, is not given. Rather, it is constituted in a process of struggle and through political articulation. And in every case, it is interesting to inquire into how we account for the hold that these events and individuals have on our imagination, and for their status

---

[2] Linda Zerilli's insightful discussion of the Milan Collective's work demonstrates the work of such a local exemplar. See L. M. G. Zerilli, *Feminism and the Abyss of Freedom* (Chicago: University of Chicago Press, 2005), pp. 93–124.

as exemplars. What, if anything, do they tell us about the workings of
political imagination? Is it possible to learn something about aversive
democracy from these examples? To flesh out answers to some of
these questions in the light of the discussion of aversive democracy
thus far, requires, as I have pointed out earlier, a work of theorizing
both about the conditions under which a grammar may become
problematized and the place of such problematization within a
democratically oriented political grammar. Different dimensions of
this theme were addressed in Chapters 2, 3 and 4 respectively, with
regard to the interplay between tradition and innovation; the relation
between the police and politics in Rancière; the need to address both
the emergence of new claims and the effects such claims may have on
an existing political grammar (aspect dawning and aspect change);
and finally, on what, in a democracy, one may expect in terms of
responses to such newly voiced claims.

The dislocation of a given grammar, occurring for instance
through the articulation of novel demands – those demands that do
not find expression in available political vocabularies – or the reformulation of existing ones in new directions, is a precondition for
thinking about the transformation of a political grammar. Yet, as I
have argued, dislocation and change need not be thematized on the
model of either revolutionary upheaval, where everything changes, or
conservative change, where, allegedly, nothing changes. Rather, as
Cavell puts it, a shift in direction, 'as slight as a degree of the com-
pass' may make all the difference in the world somewhere down the
road.[3] Dislocation, in this sense, provides no substantive direction to
political identification. If one's subjectivity is put into question by
a dislocatory event, the very fact that the grammar of one's world
is shaken precludes any readily available responses. As Laclau puts
it, the freedom won in relation to a structure is initially a traumatic fact.[4] But this freedom won is freedom insofar as we are able to

[3] Cavell, *Conditions Handsome and Unhandsome*, p. 31.
[4] E. Laclau, *New Reflections on the Revolution of Our Time* (London: Verso, 1990), p. 44.

discern other possibilities, other ways of being in the world. Walker characterizes this sense in the following way:

> Having choices ... entails possessing sufficient imaginativeness and strength to light out from the common ways, and this in turn entails cultivating the dispositions and capacities that will allow us to exercise the Protean flexibility that unlocks the pleasures to be found in alternative pathways.[5]

To break out from the common way presupposes not only a sense of dislocation, however small, but also the availability of an alternative imaginary horizon, something transcending the here and now, disclosing at least the possibility of new worlds. It is here that the exemplars mentioned above come to play their role in contemporary democratic life.

These exemplars, 'manifesting another way', are always singular, yet in their singularity they facilitate the glimpsing of a universal, of another way of doing things. Think here again of both Nelson Mandela and Aung Sang Suu Kyi. The figure of Mandela, for instance, captures significant elements of aversive subjectivity. These include, for instance, the demand to be heard, even though under the political grammar of apartheid his claims to equality could not be registered; in his continued refusal, even after years of imprisonment, to succumb to a simplistic demonization of 'whites', preferring to denounce and stand at the head of a struggle against a *systematic* form of oppression; and in his rejection of every attempt to glorify him personally, always referring his power and presence back to the democratic struggle and organization which he represented. In this sense, it could be argued that such manifestations of other ways of doing things, transcending our present horizons, play something of the role books of advice to princes played in the past.[6] They help to

---

[5] B. Walker, 'Thoreau on democratic cultivation', *Political Theory* 29 (2001), 175. It should be noted that Cavell is quite clear that for Emerson, the necessary capacities are universally present. Cultivation is thus not a matter of capacity.

[6] See Walker, 'Thoreau on democratic cultivation'.

cultivate a certain comportment towards others as well as towards the self. It is helpful in this respect to look further into three particular aspects, all of which are important in the cultivation of a democratic ethos. The first, as I have already indicated, concerns the role of the exemplar in constituting alternative imaginary horizons, or in deepening existing ones; the second concerns, more specifically, the issue of the cultivation of a democratic ethos, and the third, that of democracy and passion. Resources to help us address these concerns are plentiful in the traditions of thinking that I have drawn upon in this book. Cavell's reading of Emerson, which I discussed in Chapter 4, and his account of Nietzsche's 'Schopenhauer as educator' are particularly important in this respect, and it is to a discussion of the latter that I now turn.

EXEMPLARS, EXEMPLARITY AND UNIVERSALIZATION

Cavell, as I have noted in Chapter 4, takes issue with Rawls's account of perfectionism, which suggests that perfectionism involves elitist presuppositions.[7] Rawls takes Nietzsche to be the best example of what he calls strict or extreme perfectionism, which he contrasts to the more moderate perfectionism of Aristotle. Perfectionism, on Rawls's reading, is defined as a 'teleological theory directing society to arrange institutions and to define the duties and obligations of individuals so as to maximize the achievement of human excellence in art, science, and culture'.[8] This principle can be either one amongst several, or the sole one that directs the organization of institutions and the definition of the duties and obligations of individuals. But, as Mulhall points out, everything depends upon how one understands the notion of maximization here. Should society 'ensure the maximal distribution of some species of achieved excellence', like 'high culture' or, rather, should it 'encourage the maximum number of

---

[7] See J. Rawls, *A Theory of Justice* (Oxford: Oxford University Press, 1973), section 50.
[8] Rawls, *A Theory of Justice*, p. 325.

individuals to attempt to excel themselves'?[9] As suggested in the previous chapter Cavell, following Emerson, argues for the latter:

> Emersonian Perfectionism – place it as the thought that 'the main enterprise of the world for splendour, for extent, is the upbuilding of a man' – is not an elitist call to subject oneself to great individuals (to the 'one or two men' 'in a century, in a millennium') but to the greatness, the thing Emerson calls by the ancient name of the genius, in each of us; it is the quest he calls 'becoming what one is', and I think, 'standing for humanity'.[10]

Emersonian perfectionism is committed to turn away from present society, not in order to maximize its distribution of qualities, but to encourage individuals or rather, to provoke them to go beyond their current selves and to strive towards an unattained self. On this reading, perfectionism does not entail the sort of elitism that Rawls fears is present – on his reading – in Nietzsche:

> The absolute weight that Nietzsche sometimes gives the lives of great men such as Socrates and Goethe is unusual. At places he says that mankind must continually strive to produce great individuals. We give value to our lives by working for the good of the highest specimens.[11]

On Rawls's account, Nietzsche's perfectionism has anti-democratic implications, since it supposes that we subordinate the design of our lives and of our political institutions to enable the 'highest specimens' to achieve their ends. Cavell's Emersonian perfectionism clearly wishes to put into question these claims, and he does so, *inter alia*, by teasing out what Nietzsche (here clearly following Emerson) means by exemplars, or 'specimens' as Rawls puts it. It should

---

[9] S. Mulhall, *Stanley Cavell. Philosophy's Recounting of the Ordinary* (Oxford: Clarendon Press, 1994), pp. 267–8.

[10] S. Cavell, 'What is the Emersonian event? A comment on Kateb's Emerson', *New Literary History* 25 (1994), 951–2.

[11] Rawls, *A Theory of Justice*, p. 325.

be noted there that Rawls follows in a long tradition translating Nietzsche's term *'Exemplar'* as 'specimen'. Both Cavell and Conant, who taught a course together at Harvard on moral perfectionism, focus upon the fact that the use of 'specimen' carries biologistic overtones and, hence, miss the genealogy and implications of the Nietzschean term *'Exemplar'*. This term is important in the history of German philosophical discussion of the concept of genius and also plays a key role in Kant's *The Critique of Judgement* where Kant argues that taste can be cultivated only 'through the contemplation of exemplary instances of aesthetic production' or 'works of genius'.[12] Conant notes that Nietzsche preserves certain important features of Kant's theory, namely, the fact that 'genius represents a kind of excellence which makes a demand on us'; that the kind of demand it makes on us cannot, however, 'be formulated in terms of an explicit rule and cannot be attained through following a rule-governed procedure'. Instead, this demand 'requires our assent' regardless of the fact that it is 'inarticulate', and finally assent here 'expresses itself in an effort to treat the source of the demand as an exemplar to be "followed" or "emulated"'.[13]

Conant's reading of Nietzsche's 'Schopenhauer as Educator'[14] offers an excellent starting-point in order to flesh out what is at stake in the question of exemplarity, investigating as it does not only the status and characteristics of the exemplar itself, but also the key question of our relation to such exemplars.[15] To start with, it is useful to list what Conant regards as the three central characteristics of an exemplar. The first is that an exemplar is to be compared and contrasted with members of its own genus; it is not something of an entirely

[12] J. Conant, 'Nietzsche's perfectionism: A reading of *Schopenhauer as Educator*', in R. Schacht (ed.), *Nietzsche's Postmoralism* (Cambridge: Cambridge University Press, 2001), p. 192.
[13] Conant, 'Nietzsche's perfectionism', p. 193.
[14] F. Nietzsche, 'Schopenhauer as educator', in *The Complete Works of Friedrich Nietzsche*, ed. O. Levy, vol. II, *Thoughts out of Season, Part Two* (London: T. N. Foulis, 1909).
[15] Conant, 'Nietzsche's perfectionism', pp. 181–257.

different nature. The second aspect concerns its exemplarity: an exemplar 'illustrates a feature(s) of interest which other members of the genus display in varying degrees'; and the third, its exemplariness, the fact that it is distinguished 'by the pronounced degree to which it displays the feature in question'. These conditions are important as they make it clear that for Nietzsche, the educative role of the exemplar – the fact that it discloses my concealed but higher self – can only be fulfilled if something or someone is both related, similar to us (exemplarity is a mark of this) and different from us (exemplariness is an indicator of inessential difference). This, as Conant and Cavell point out, clearly has anti-elitist connotations, since everyone has a higher self. However, this higher self only comes into view through a 'confrontation with what you trust and admire in an exemplary other. The *lineaments of such a self are not specifiable in advance of such a confrontation.*'[16] To emphasize a point made earlier, there is no pre-given self; no self with clearly specified characteristics acting as a model to be followed or, as in moral theories, a historical or evolutionary telos.[17] It is only in the moment of what Conant calls 'confrontation' and Laclau 'dislocation' that the provocation (an Emersonian term) to the self emerges. Hence, the role of the exemplar is 'to unsettle us'.[18] And, as we have noted, for Laclau, the freedom won in relation to a dislocated structure is initially a traumatic fact,[19] one that unsettles us and thus provokes us into thinking about other/further possibilities. There is, Cavell argues, no guarantee that we will realize those possibilities; rather, we need to work for it, continuously, since 'there is no single final state of the self upon accession to which our doubleness will vanish ... there is no guarantee that the self will achieve or maintain integrity; it may rather lapse into frozen passivity'.[20]

---

[16] Conant, 'Nietzsche's perfectionism', p. 203 (emphasis added).
[17] Conant, 'Nietzsche's perfectionism', p. 214.
[18] Conant, 'Nietzsche's perfectionism', p. 208.
[19] Laclau, *New Reflections*, p. 44.
[20] Mulhall, *Stanley Cavell*, p. 257.

This, of course, immediately raises the question as to what my relation to an exemplar should be. Nietzsche does not, as Rawls argues, suggest that we make ourselves subservient to great artists and great philosophers. Rather, his account furnishes a picture of a self that comes to question itself (by virtue of feeling ashamed) through its attachment to the exemplar. Conant highlights the fact that Nietzsche's phrase – 'only he who has attached his heart to some great human being is by that act consecrated to culture' – is followed by the specification that 'the sign of that consecration is that one is ashamed of oneself without any accompanying feeling of distress'. Hence, one cannot read the image of discipleship into Nietzsche. Nevertheless, attachment to the exemplar is crucial. Recall our earlier discussion of *identification-as*: this process is vital to our attachments and commitments. However, as Conant points out, it does not translate – at least not in Nietzsche – into an image of subservience and discipleship. Rather, it is an attachment that allows us to see other possibilities of being and acting, which then become *superfluous* once they become effective. We are thus not 'hailed', on this account, to become disciples. This discussion prepares the way for an answer to the question of who your exemplars are. Conant suggests that for Nietzsche, they are 'those individuals who are able to trigger this experience of impersonal shame in you'.[21] Hence, 'following' an exemplar is not, as for Kant, a matter of imitation, as such imitation involves faithlessness to oneself.[22] Neither is it, as for elitists, a matter of discipleship. Instead,

> 'Following' an exemplar is not a matter of following in someone's footsteps (*jemandem nachgehen*), but of regarding someone as an exemplary instance of ... 'faithfully following in one's *own* footsteps' (*sich selber treulich nachgehen*).[23]

This discussion of exemplarity in Nietzsche, who follows Emerson in this respect, is extremely helpful in fleshing out the way

---

[21] Conant, 'Nietzsche's perfectionism', p. 206.   [22] Ibid.   [23] Ibid.

in which exemplars may operate in a political imaginary in general, and in a democratic grammar specifically. A key aspect of it concerns the fact that the exemplar is to be constituted as an exemplar and in politics, as I have argued in Chapter 2, this process often takes an analogical and/or equivalential form. Hence, it could be understood as a form of hegemonic universalization in which, as Zerilli puts it, 'commonalities must be *articulated* through the interplay of diverse political struggles – rather than discovered and then merely followed, as one follows a rule'.[24] The operation of an exemplar within the context of a democratic grammar, moreover, takes an educative form, but one which is anti-elitist, unsettling and instituting relations of freedom as well as non-subservient attachment and identification.

EXEMPLARITY AND DEMOCRATIC POLITICS: 'AN AFRICAN GIFT'[25]

> Imagination of justice is essential to the aspiration of a democratic society.[26]

Let us look here at the case of the Truth and Reconciliation Commission (TRC) in South Africa, brought into being through an act of Parliament – the Promotion of National Unity and Reconciliation Bill of 1995 – in the wake of the first democratic elections in 1994.[27] The fact that 'truth commissions' have become somewhat commonplace in our contemporary world should not lead us to

---

[24] L. M. G. Zerilli, ' "This universalism which is not one": A review of Ernesto Laclau's *Emancipation(s)'*, *Diacritics* 28, no. 2 (1998), 3–20.

[25] Former US ambassador to South Africa, James Joseph, so described the TRC. Quoted in E. Kiss, 'Moral ambition within and beyond political constraints: Reflections on restorative justice', in R. I. Rotberg and D. Thompson (eds.), *Truth v. Justice. The Morality of Truth Commissions* (Princeton, N.J.: Princeton University Press, 2000), p. 92.

[26] S. Cavell, *Cities of Words* (Cambridge, Mass.: The Belknap Press of Harvard University Press, 2004), p. 14.

[27] The basis for the TRC was laid in 1993, with the adoption of the Interim Constitution. For a brief presentation of the events leading up to the establishment of the TRC and its specific features, see A. Boraine, 'Truth and reconciliation in South Africa', in Rotberg and Thompson (eds.), *Truth v. Justice*, pp. 141–57.

underestimate their profound impact, both within South African society and in our wider political landscape.[28] Indeed, the fact that such commissions are regularly invoked as 'solutions' to situations of conflict and societies in transition is evidence enough of the extent to which they have become exemplary of the idea that citizens may be called upon to account for themselves in the presence of fellow citizens.

The South African TRC was explicitly set up to confront the legacies of the past so that citizens could live together in a democratic society. In this sense, the TRC could be seen to function as a 'founding project', which aimed to address the moral and political needs 'arising from attempts to found a new democratic order in the aftermath of the political atrocities and/or social injustices of a prior regime'.[29] It is important in this respect, that unlike examples of tribunals elsewhere, the TRC was established as a parliamentary commission, and its mandate was drawn up after a series of parliamentary hearings and debates, as well as international conferences. This public and democratic character was sustained in its actual proceedings.[30]

The TRC set out to offer both survivors and perpetrators of gross abuses of human rights the opportunity to give voice, on the one hand, to their anguish, to unacknowledged wrongs, as well as denied aspirations and lives lived under dehumanizing conditions

[28] Du Bois notes that others have looked 'expectantly towards South Africa for a precedent on dealing with past injustice in the transition to democracy'. F. Du Bois, ' "Nothing but the truth": The South African alternative to corrective justice in transitions to democracy', in E. Christodoulidis and S. Veitch (eds.), *Lethe's Law. Justice, Law and Ethics in Reconciliation* (Oxford: Hart Publishing, 2001), p. 92. For a comparative perspective on truth commissions, see P. B. Hayner, 'Fifteen truth commissions – 1974 to 1994: A comparative study', *Human Rights Quarterly* 16 (1994), 597–655.

[29] A. du Toit, 'The moral foundations of the South African TRC: Truth as acknowledgment and justice as recognition', in Rotberg and Thompson (eds.), *Truth v. Justice*, pp. 124–5. Du Toit points out that truth commissions are both backward- and forward-looking, since they are designed to deal with the past with a view to inaugurate a democratic future.

[30] Du Toit, 'The moral foundations of the South African TRC', p. 129.

and, on the other hand, to provide information, express regret, and ask forgiveness.[31] The TRC literally sought to forge a space in which hitherto unheard voices could express themselves and articulate, often for the first time, their experiences.[32] Antjie Krog, who observed the process, summarizes one example of the staging of the 'victim hearings' as follows:

> The TRC ritual claimed official space – the city hall ... It demanded respect of everybody for the victims – usually female, usually illiterate, usually old. The victim was called to the stage. She was put at ease. The earphones were explained, the translation, she was addressed in her mother tongue, she was addressed in terms of respect. She was welcomed. All of this is extremely important within a society brutalised for so long ... Then the ritual claimed space and respect for the intimate – because the first question usually was: tell us about X, what kind of child he was? How do you remember him? ... it immediately personalised the tone – inviting the personal to become part of the narrative ... This was followed by asking the victim to interpret the incident ... How did she understand it? The last stage was when the chair ... transcended the story by linking it to the whole community and

---

[31] This is a much commented-upon characteristic of the TRC and much debate took place on the standing accorded to victims and perpetrators respectively. It should also be noted that the law did not require of participants to express remorse but only to make a full and complete disclosure of their wrongdoings. For amnesty to be granted, it had to be applied for on an individual basis; applicants had to detail information pertaining to specific human rights violations; and such acts had to be judged to form part of a wider political event or perpetrated in the name of a political organization.

[32] There were in excess of 70 public hearings focusing on the testimony of individual victims of gross human rights violations and over 22,000 statements of survivors were recorded. C. Villa-Vicencio and W. Verwoerd, 'Constructing a report: writing up the "truth" ', in Rotberg and Thompson (eds.), Truth v. Justice, pp. 281–2. It should be noted that despite the efforts of the TRC, it was criticized for not giving sufficient support, by way of counselling, for instance, to victims in the aftermath of their giving testimony. See A. Gutman and D. Thompson, 'The moral foundations of truth commissions', in Rotberg and Thompson (eds.), Truth v. Justice, p. 30.

the country ... explaining the importance of a particular incident in the broader scheme of the freedom of South Africa.[33]

Under these circumstances the opportunity was created to articulate past experiences, losses and traumas and, in the process, to work towards a transformation of the relations between the citizens of the new South Africa. For instance, one survivor of human rights violations, blinded as a result of an assault by a police officer suggested that after his testimony to the TRC, he felt that 'what has been making me sick all the time is the fact that I couldn't tell my story. But now ... it feels like I got my sight back by coming here'.[34]

One should not overestimate the possible reach and effects of the transformative power of the TRC. There were and are many who were highly critical of the process, who rejected and/or ridiculed its proceedings for widely diverging reasons. Its critics came both from within the ranks of those unwilling to acknowledge the wrongs of the past and from those who felt that the process subverted the search for justice.[35] Those who thought it too beholden to a religious paradigm also criticized it, and so did those who feared that it would create an opportunity simply to 'rewrite' the past and install a new national myth.[36]

---

[33] A. Krog, 'The TRC and national unity', in R. Dorsman, H. Hartman and L. Notenboom-Kronemeijer (eds.), *Truth and Reconciliation in South Africa and the Netherlands* (Utrecht: SMI Special No. 23, 1999), pp. 18–19.

[34] Quoted by Kiss, 'Moral ambition', in Rotberg and Thompson (eds.), *Truth v. Justice*, p. 72.

[35] Some critics of the TRC have argued that it sacrificed justice in the name of reconciliation. This captures something of the views expressed by the family of Biko, Mxenge and Ribeiro, who challenged the removal of their right to seek civil redress as a result of amnesty being granted. For a discussion of the amnesty process in the Amnesty Committee of the TRC and its relation to law and legal reasoning, see S. Veitch, 'The legal politics of amnesty', in Christodoulidis and Veitch (eds.), *Lethe's Law*, pp. 33–45.

[36] I discuss this issue in more depth in two separate articles. See A. J. Norval, 'Memory, identity and the (im)possibility of reconciliation: The work of the Truth and Reconciliation Commission in South Africa', *Constellations* 5 (1998), 250–61; and Norval, 'Reconstructing national identity and renegotiating memory: The work of the TRC', in T. Blom Hansen and F. Steppuput (eds.), *States of Imagination. Ethnographic Explorations of the Post-Colonial State* (Durham, N.C.: Duke University Press, 2001), pp. 182–202.

Nevertheless, one should not underestimate what it has achieved during the period of transition. While it is clear that the TRC only started what needs to be an ongoing process on many levels and in many areas of life,[37] it is possible to discern a number of areas in which it has made a lasting contribution. These included the fostering of democratic subjectivity through giving a space to new voices and demands; a provocation to open and democratic debate – about issues, processes and institutions – as well as reflection on the character of justice, truth and the role of memory and reconciliation in a fledgling democracy.

Some critical discussion of the very processes instituted by the TRC has been concerned with the assumption of a transparent relation between speaking and the restoration of dignity, between giving voice to past wrongs, and personal and public reconciliation to the past and to fellow citizens. Ross, for instance, argues that the Commission worked with a model of voice in which the 'transparency of communication and clarity in reception are presumed', while 'the unevenness of social fields and their saturation with power are not'.[38] While it is no doubt the case that this naïve vision of communication may have been in place it could not, however, be argued to have dominated the process and its consequences in any simplistic sense. Just as I have argued earlier, while the deliberative conception of dialogue remains trapped in a picture of voice as immediate and transparent, the actual practices of deliberation offer a much more complicated picture of the issues involved in and generated by processes of deliberative interaction themselves. However, this critique of the empirical limits of transparency, as I have argued, is

---

[37] In this respect Dyzenhaus notes that the TRC, far from completing a process, in fact is only the start of a process yet to be accomplished. In this sense the TRC should be seen as having established 'an archive which others must now investigate and supplement'. D. Dyzenhaus, 'Survey article: Justifying the Truth and Reconciliation Commission', *Journal of Political Philosophy* 8 (2000), 490, note 75. See also D. Dyzenhaus, *Judging the Judges, Judging Ourselves. Truth, Reconciliation and the Apartheid Legal Order* (Oxford: Hart Publishing, 1998), pp. 178–83.

[38] F. C. Ross, 'On having voice and being heard: Some after-effects of testifying before the South African Truth and Reconciliation Commission', *Anthropological Theory* 30 (2003), 327.

not sufficient. Throughout this text I have sought to draw on problematizations of this picture. These included, first, deconstructive readings of voice, in particular Derrida's reading of Husserl in *Speech and Phenomena*, which foregrounds the limits of an argument in empirical terms, and draws attention to the in-principle opacity of voice, even and particularly to the self. Secondly, I have discussed accounts that raised the question of the very possibility of the emergence of voice, in both Rancière and Cavell. And thirdly I have developed accounts questioning the possibility and transparency of rationality in their emphasis on rhetoricality as constitutive of the practices of reason-giving in the work of Grassi and Laclau.

Given these critiques, it could be asked: how is it still possible to offer a positive reading of the processes of the TRC? My argument is that these critiques do not erase the voice, do not direct us away from a concern with it, but rather attend to the plethora of difficulties constitutive of this terrain. Rather than rejecting the processes of the TRC for its simplicity and apparent transparency, its naïve assumption about the healing power in giving voice, and its confessional character, the TRC should be read as one site that exemplifies the question of voice in all its complexities: the difficulties associated with – and the struggles constitutive of – the opening of that very space to address the past; the difficult emergence of ordinary voices; the provocation of these voices; the attendant denials and questioning of the self, of the past, of community and of responsibility for each of them; and the founding of the contours of a new conception of democratic community in its wake, a founding which is incomplete and requires refounding in a variety of different sites.

As Tully has noted with respect to contemporary constitutionalism, it is characterized not by one national narrative, but by 'a diversity of criss-crossing and contested narratives through which citizens participate in and identify with their associations'.[39] So it is

---

[39] J. Tully, *Strange Multiplicity. Constitutionalism in an Age of Diversity* (Cambridge: Cambridge University Press, 1995), p. 183.

with the workings of the TRC.[40] This is particularly clear in the debate it fostered around truth, memory, reconciliation and justice. The movement from 'justice' *tout court*, to 'restorative' and 'transitional' justice is a case in point.[41] The latter terms emerged to capture complexities associated with conceptions of justice, not present in or not foregrounded in retributive conceptions of justice. Kiss puts it this way:

> truth commissions have struggled with basic questions about what justice requires in relation to survivors, perpetrators and entire nations scarred by a brutal past ... Out of these struggles new vocabularies of truth and justice emerged, as well as a new institutional repertoire for pursuing them.[42]

In addition to the new institutional forums created, it is frequently noted that the concept of 'transitional justice' aims to capture specific characteristics of the 'kind of justice distinctive to nations on the rocky road from authoritarian regimes', such as 'their turn towards truth commissions, practices of memorialization and their relations to law and constitutionality'.[43] I will discuss this movement to a different kind of justice shortly. But it is necessary to reflect, for a moment, on the emergence of new institutional forms. While the

---

[40] Contemporary literature often contrasts the workings of truth commissions to that of constitution-making, with the former being cast in an inferior role *vis-à-vis* the latter. Du Toit, for instance, notes the distance he takes from Ackerman, who treats truth commissions as essentially backward looking (Du Toit, 'The moral foundations of the South African TRC', p. 125). In contrast to those who view constitutions as fixed moments inaugurating unchallengeable agreements, Tully's analysis draws out the contingencies of these agreements and their character as politically negotiated accommodations. If viewed in this light, the differences with truth commissions are much less stark. Both are, as Du Toit points out, historical founding projects.

[41] There is considerable debate on the relation between these conceptions of justice. Some commentators, such as Dyzenhaus, argue that restorative justice does indeed retain traces of a retributive conception of justice. See Dyzenhaus, 'Survey article', p. 478.

[42] Kiss, 'Moral ambition', p. 70.

[43] D. Herwitz, 'The future of the past in South Africa: on the legacy of the TRC', *Social Research* 72 (2005), 539.

TRC did follow in the wake of other examples of truth commissions it nevertheless had to conceive of much of its own institutional forms and forums without reference to prior examples. As I have already noted, the initial conception of the TRC arose from within a series of discussions and debates, including international conferences, and while its conception was part of a larger negotiated settlement which took a particular view on the question of amnesty, its roots in a process of open discussion were crucial to the whole of its functioning. These new forums, the Amnesty, Human Rights Violations, and Reparation and Rehabilitation Committees, were all premised upon a different conception of justice articulated in the course of its conception and creation, and utilized new forms of publicity.[44]

The idea of 'restorative justice', which emerged out of the actual experiences of truth commissions, aims explicitly to restore the humanity and civil dignity of victims.[45] What is at stake when victims tell their own stories, as Du Toit points out, is the right to frame their accounts from their own perspectives, and for this to be recognized as 'legitimate sources of truth with claims to rights and justice'.[46] Allen's account captures a crucial aspect of this process:

> [G]iving victims an opportunity to tell their stories demonstrates that they are now admitted to [sic] the category of responsible agency from which the predecessor regime attempted to exclude them. It is a form of recognition that acknowledges the historical fact of exclusion from legal recognition and seeks to reverse the imposition of passive status, by encouraging victims to act in public by telling their stories.[47]

---

[44] Minow notes that the proceedings of the TRC were deliberately well publicized through daily radio and TV broadcasting, the development of partnerships with community organizations to communicate its work, an advertising campaign to publicize activities. See M. Minow, 'The hope for healing: What can truth commissions do?', in Rotberg and Thompson (eds.), *Truth v. Justice*, pp. 238–9.

[45] Kiss, 'Moral ambition', p. 71.

[46] Du Toit, 'The moral foundations of the South African TRC', p. 136

[47] Jonathan Allen, quoted in Dyzenhaus, 'Survey article', p. 484.

Though it should be noted that the language of 'recognition' and 'admission to' suggests a passive attitude on the part of the survivor, as well as a top-down process, neither of which is warranted in this case, Allen captures the sense in which the political grammar shifted as a result of the process. This process, as Kiss notes, required the invention of new practices and norms, including 'norms of respectful listening, which allow people to tell their stories without interruption; rituals of acknowledgement and respect (such as the practice, in stark contrast to that prevalent in courtrooms, of commissioners rising when witnesses enter to give evidence); and the provision of support services by psychologists and social workers'.[48]

Indeed, one of its most serious contributions could be argued to be exactly the extent to which the TRC's practices provoked discussion, debate, contestation, soul-searching, anger and challenge. The testimony of a former South African spy at a commission hearing makes this point:

> It is therefore not only the task of the members of the security forces to examine themselves and their deeds. It is for every member of society to do so. Our weapons, ammunition, uniforms, vehicles, radios and other equipment were all developed and provided by industry ... Our chaplains prayed for our victory and our universities educated us in war.[49]

The claims and allegations made did indeed provoke a sense of 'shame', in the Nietzschean sense, a distance from a (former) self, and the need to work towards a further self. As we have noted above, this entails many different aspects: work on the self, which in turn affects and inspires a different relation to others. These embrace, among other things, work on history and one's account of one's own place in it;[50]

---

[48] Kiss, 'Moral ambition', p. 73.

[49] Craig Williamson quoted in Villa-Vicencio and Verwoerd, 'Writing up the "truth" ', p. 288.

[50] In the period leading up to and in the aftermath of the first democratic elections in 1994, there was much public debate on the nature of history and the difficult task of reworking the history of apartheid. The TRC itself contributed greatly to this process.

work on society and the forging of open and democratic institutions. And, as Cavell alerts us, there is always the risk that we do not take up this work, refuse to attend to the work on the self and on society, which is demanded and required, and thus fall into conformism or lapse into cynicism.

Indeed, the truth commission fulfilled, if imperfectly, many of these functions and it opened up opportunities to take up these issues in other contexts. Institutionally, for instance, it called to task professions such as the medical and juridical establishments.[51] Moreover, there are many moving personal accounts of survivors of both individual and systematic abuse, which not only led to a deep questioning of the 'morality' of each of the participants in the apartheid order, but also created a focus on unacknowledged, but systematic harms.[52] Importantly, the whole process, including the debates around it, inaugurated, embodied and inspired a particular view of the future: a democratic openness to contestation in which history is understood as something 'writerly'.[53] The TRC clearly

As one commentator notes, the stories told during its hearings 'may very well be some of the first steps in the rewriting of South African history on the basis of validated mass experience'. (See N. Ndebele, 'Memory, metaphor, and the triumph of narrative', in S. Nuttall and C. Coetzee (eds.), *Negotiating the Past. The Making of Memory in South Africa* (Cape Town: Oxford University Press, 1998), p. 20.) Many publications focus on different aspects of this process. A very interesting account of 'public history' is provided in Coombes' study of visual culture in South Africa after 1994. Coombes sets out to investigate 'how one might embody new national histories in the public sphere that engaged larger structural narratives and material conditions *and* individualized experiences without reducing their public expression to either some monolithic representation of "the struggle" or some unlocated and ahistorical notion of individualized experience and that might adequately signal ... the compromised, complicated texture of living under and fighting against apartheid'. A. E. Coombes, *History after Apartheid. Visual Culture and Public Memory in a Democratic South Africa* (Durham, N.C.: Duke University Press, 2003), p. 10.

[51] See, for instance, Dyzenhaus, *Judging the Judges*.

[52] See, for instance, the discussion of gender and political violence in S. Meintjies and B. Goldblatt, 'Gender and the Truth and Reconciliation Commission: A submission to the Truth and Reconciliation Commission', May 1996 (www.truth.org.za/submit/gender.htm).

[53] I use the term in Barthes' sense, for whom the reader is no longer a consumer but a producer of the text. See R. Barthes, *S/Z*, trans. R. Millar (Oxford: Basil Blackwell, 1974).

does not have a monopoly on these processes. As some commentators observe, it is:

> only one of the structures through which we should hope to dismantle the old regime of truth to replace it with new and multiple narratives. We must remain aware of the dangers of replacing apartheid's false utopian historicism with our own new orthodoxies. As we construct new historical narratives, it will be in the currency of *heterotopias*, multiple idealisms, rather than the single-mindedness of utopia ... Our state-sponsored Commission has no monopoly on processes of historical rectification.[54]

Insofar as the TRC opened up areas of contestation around the character of nationhood, national identity, history, truth and justice, which were previously deeply sedimented and resistant to interrogation, it did so in the name of a democratic future, that is, a different future which both acts as a measure against which past and present actions may be judged and as a continual inspiration 'to do better'. It is in precisely this sense that the TRC is a very contemporary exemplar. The TRC cannot be imitated in any simplistic sense; any re-enactment and reiteration of a process such as this in a different context cannot but be singular if it is going to succeed. Its functioning has had a continuing capacity to unsettle us, both through a reminder of what has been and what we could be, but without the comfort of a simplistic and uniform model of democracy and nationhood. But the TRC also enjoins us to take responsibility for our societal arrangements; as it is one of the processes through which I come to recognize 'society and its government' to be constituted as mine, as Cavell puts it. In other words, I am not only answerable to it, but for it. It is precisely in this sense that the TRC, more so than the actual process of drawing up the new South African constitution, played a central role in the founding of a new, democratic community.

---

[54] Asmal, Asmal and Roberts, quoted in Norval, 'Reconstructing national identity', 193.

And in this process of founding, 'manifesting for the other' of another way was and remains crucial. This was embodied significantly in the much remarked-upon attitude of generosity of the victims, which was sometimes expressed in the spirit of *ubuntu*, the African concept of humanness. The 'Postamble' to the interim constitution, which set the tone for the work of the TRC, proclaimed 'a need for understanding but not for vengeance, a need for reparation but not for retaliation, a need for *ubuntu* but not for victimization'.[55] Its call to community both constitutes claims in the name of others and opens up a space for individual differences – it fosters community at the same time as provoking debate and contestation. Hence, it inaugurates a constitutively incomplete process, one in which the role of imagination is central. As Njabulo Ndebele remarks, the real challenge is 'to stimulate the imaginations of its peoples through voices that can go beyond the giving of testimony toward creating new thoughts and new worlds'.[56]

CULTIVATION AS/AND DEMOCRATIC RENEWAL

Imagining the perfected democratic city does not exempt us from acting in the present scene of imperfection ... On the contrary, this imagining is what enables us to act, that is, to exist in freedom from a despair of democracy.[57]

The first step in attending to our education is to observe the strangeness of our lives, our estrangement from ourselves, the lack of necessity in what we perceive to be necessary.[58]

[55] Kiss, 'Moral ambition', p. 81.

[56] Ndebele, 'Memory, metaphor, and the triumph of narrative', p. 28.

[57] Cavell, 'What is the Emersonian event?', 957.

[58] This remark by Cavell (quoted in A. Norris, 'Political revisions: Stanley Cavell and political philosophy', in A. Norris (ed.), *The Claim to Community. Essays on Stanley Cavell and Political Philosophy* (Stanford, Calif.: Stanford University Press, 2006), p. 91) clearly resonates with Foucault's conception of genealogy. For an insightful consideration of Cavell's moral perfectionism and Foucault's ethics, see D. Owen, 'Perfectionism, parrhesia, and the care of the self: Foucault and Cavell on ethics and politics', in *The Claim to Community*, pp. 128–55.

The exemplar, conceived in the Nietzschean–Emersonian sense, in fostering an identification that does not end in discipleship, acts as a key mechanism in the cultivation of democratic renewal. Nietzsche's understanding of the relation between the exemplar and the self is significant here. For Nietzsche, as I have stressed, this relation is not one of imitation but of being provoked to challenge the current self in the name of further possibilities. His characterization and enactment of his relation to his own readers is a case in point; once understood, it becomes superfluous (not unlike Wittgenstein's ladder). Hence, living up to the demands of a democratic exemplar should be understood, not as a model to be imitated but as a particular practice and attitude to be iterated, in the sense in which Derrida uses this term. And crucially, as I have argued with respect to Cavell's reading of Nora, this ethos is a provocative one.

Cavell's reading here not only foregrounds the important challenges faced by and inaugurated by those whose demands cannot be heard in the dominant political discourse, but it also emphasizes the specificity of a democratic response to such demands.[59] As he argues, it is not sufficient to say ' "This is simply what I do," and wait'. Instead, the alternative is to find oneself dissatisfied with what one does and with the order for which one has responsibility. *This* is where the core of the democratic response is to be found: in the responsibility to respond to claims, to acknowledge 'society's distance from perfect justice' and to cultivate an aversive disposition.[60] Such a disposition is not one that can be thought of in terms of

---

[59] In the fact of non-agreement, Cavell argues that we learn that 'there is no us (yet, maybe never)'. Cavell, *The Claim of Reason*, pp. 19–20.

[60] Owen notes a similar point: 'Cavell's contribution to, and intervention in, democratic culture consists in both his efforts to provide us with examples of such responsiveness to others, to draw to our attention this overlooked dimension of modern culture, and to exemplify such responsiveness in his encounters with the works of modern culture (I note the democratic impulse in Cavell's *choice* – perhaps as a necessity for him – to focus on Hollywood films rather than confine his attention to avant-garde art).' See Owen, 'Perfectionism, parrhesia, and the care of the self', pp. 153–4.

accomplishment, completion and achievement. Rather, it is one of constitutive incompletion, one that needs to be recurrently (re)-discovered, so that democratic hope is kept alive 'in the face of disappointment with it'.[61] Furthermore, this emphasis on the inevitable ways in which our societies must fall short of 'perfect justice', is one of the most distinctive and thought-provoking aspects of Cavell's writing on democratic politics. For the emphasis in Cavell is not simply on incompletion *tout court*, but on the fact that this incompletion – and with it, imperfection – demands of us a response and responsibility for the ways in which our societies fall short. We can, no longer, if we ever could, simply turn away from any particular injustice perpetrated. Given that society is ours, we are always already implicated and compromised by the actions perpetrated in our names. As Cavell puts it:

> we are, or at any hour may become, aware of the reality of what it means to say that our consent is demanded, and that it is given, what it means that my society is mine, that I am the judge of the case whether our partial justice is good enough to participate in whole-heartedly.[62]

In attempting to live up to this responsibility, through living aversively, there are no rules that can simply be followed, no ready recipes of political engagement, no set political institutions in and through which this may occur. Nevertheless, democratic exemplars may, as I have argued, provide us with some guidance as to our conduct, guidance that, nevertheless, has to be taken in a certain way.[63]

---

[61] Cavell, *Conditions Handsome and Unhandsome*, p. 56.

[62] S. Cavell, 'The incessance and the absence of the political', in *The Claim to Community*, p. 297.

[63] Guidance, or education here is not about new information, but is concerned with learning that 'finding and forming of my knowledge of myself' simultaneously requires finding and forming of my knowledge of membership of a community. See, Cavell, *The Claim of Reason*, p. 25.

PASSIONATE SUBJECTIVITY

A performative utterance is an offer of participation in the order of the law. And perhaps we can say: A passionate utterance is an invitation to improvisation in the disorders of desire.[64]

In Chapter 2, I noted Bohman's suggestion that we need to give more attention to perlocutionary (as opposed to illocutionary) utterances. There the argument was advanced in terms of the inescapable rhetoricality of our language. I also noted, in my discussion of aspect dawning and change in Wittgenstein, the importance of 'identification-as', taking up Laclau and Mouffe's work on the role of passion in politics.[65] What is needed, however, is a connection between the domain of language and the passions – a terrain of long-standing concern in psychoanalysis – that would allow us to think systematically about passionate expression. (Though this is not to ignore the space for and pertinence of silence and other non-linguistic modes of expression. Cavell notes, for instance, the many senses in which silence could be understood, and I have noted throughout the importance of the visceral in politics.)[66] These connections are forged

---

[64] S. Cavell, *Philosophy the Day after Tomorrow* (Cambridge Mass.: The Belknap Press of Harvard University Press, 2005), p. 19.

[65] There has been a recent spate of interest in the role of passion in and its exclusion from (liberal) politics. See, for instance, A. Abizadeh, 'Banishing the particular: Rousseau on rhetoric, *patrie*, and the passions', *Political Theory* 29, no. 4 (2001), 556–82; C. Hall, ' "Passions and constraint": The marginalization of passion in liberal political theory', *Philosophy and Social Criticism* 28, no. 6 (2002), 727–48; G. Marcus, *The Sentimental Citizen: Emotion in Democratic Politics* (University Park: Pennsylvania State University Press, 2002); S. Mendus, *Feminism and Emotion: Readings in Moral and Political Philosophy* (New York: St Martin's Press, 2000); P. W. Kahn, *Putting Liberalism in its Place* (Princeton, N.J.: Princeton University Press, 2005); M. Walzer, *Politics and Passion. Towards a More Egalitarian Liberalism* (New Haven, Conn.: Yale University Press, 2004).

[66] Silence, as it is with voice, has many modalities, each of which must be investigated. Silence may come as a result of 'being silenced, from not wanting to say something or not sensing the right to say something ... That speech is not everything is true; that speechlessness may be forced, and that speech is sometimes difficult, is something else.' (Cavell, *Philosophy the Day after Tomorrow*, p. 179.) See also my discussion of the role of monuments in Norval, 'Memory, identity and the (im)possibility of reconciliation'; and discussion of other forms of artistic

in an acute fashion in Cavell's most recent writings on Austin, in which he sets out to develop a characterization of what he calls 'passionate utterances' along similar lines to those conditions Austin specifies for illocutionary actions.[67]

As the opening quote (of this closing section of the text) suggests, the perlocutionary domain is contrasted with that of the illocutionary domain because of the absence of convention, given institutions and rules of behaviour. The illocutionary is the terrain of the law – akin to Rancière's police and to the domain of the social in Laclau and Mouffe's terminology – while the perlocutionary is that of desire, and thus makes room for imagination, virtuosity and 'unequally distributed capacities'.[68] In discussing what he calls passionate utterances, Cavell deploys examples from ordinary, civilian life, rather than 'judgments directed by one person to another', such as occur in courts of law where we find verdicts accompanied by assignments of penalty.[69] To return for a moment to the earlier discussion of the TRC, there, as well, the domain with which we are concerned is not that of a given and fixed institutional terrain, or a class of actions for which there already exist clearly delineated and accepted procedures. This parallel is even clearer when we look further at the examples Cavell adduces: 'You know he took what you said as a promise', which invokes moral encounters, but 'without mediation or arbitration'.[70] More generally, Cavell notes that the kind of verbs used in perlocutionary speech does not allow 'unprotected' use of the first person pronoun. They include, for instance, verbs such as 'hearten, inspire, rouse, embolden', eminently the sort of vocabulary associated with passionate politics and the domain of

commemoration in M. Godby, 'Memory and history in William Kentridge's *History of the Main Complaint*', in Nuttall and Coetzee, *Negotiating the Past*, pp. 100–11.

[67] The conditions for the felicity of illocutionary acts are stipulated in J. L. Austin, *How to Do Things with Words*, ed. J. O. Urmson and M. Sbisà (Oxford: Oxford University Press, 1962), pp. 15–16.

[68] Cavell, *Philosophy the Day after Tomorrow*, p. 173.

[69] Cavell, *Philosophy the Day after Tomorrow*, p. 177.   [70] Ibid.

value. This resonates, as I have suggested, in important respects with the domain of practices in which the TRC engaged and was constituted: not the terrain of the law, of courts and of conventionalized judgements, but a terrain in which an other is addressed and is being constituted in the act of so addressing. As Cavell succinctly puts it: 'In perlocutionary acts, the "you" comes essentially into the picture.'[71]

But, as we have seen from our earlier discussion, there is no pregiven subject of address, as it is precisely in the articulation of a claim that the other is constituted as the subject of the address, and the self is posited as standing in relation to that other. I must, says Cavell, '*declare* myself (explicitly or implicitly) *to have standing* with you ... in the given case'.[72] Moreover, the moment of the political consists precisely in 'singling you out' and attempting 'to recognise or create a group to whom I speak, in its difference from another group'.[73] Returning, once again, to the example of the TRC, the statements by victims and perpetrators, quite apart from their factual content, had the function of provocation of an other, of attempting to bring a community into being by the act of declaration, statement and confession. My declaration to have standing with you seeks, in turn, to provoke a response. This response may take many forms and could take issue with any of the foregoing conditions specified by Cavell. For instance, you may

> deny that I have that standing with you, or question my
> consciousness of my passion, or dismiss the demand for the kind of
> response I seek, or ask to postpone it, or worse. I may or may not
> have further means of response. (We may understand such
> exchanges as instances of, or attempts at, moral education.)[74]

---

[71] Cavell, *Philosophy the Day after Tomorrow*, p. 180.
[72] Cavell, *Philosophy the Day after Tomorrow*, p. 185.
[73] Cavell, *Philosophy the Day after Tomorrow*, p. 182. This formulation is analogous to Laclau and Mouffe's characterization of the political.
[74] Cavell, *Philosophy the Day after Tomorrow*, p. 182.

Refusal to engage, or to respond, as I have argued in the discussion of Nora in Chapter 4, may have various consequences. As Cavell argues, you may deny that I have standing with you. For example, in the case of the TRC, this sort of refusal took many forms and came from different quarters, including those who questioned its very existence as a legitimate and proper organization to deal with the matters at hand, as well as those who questioned the 'even handedness' of the TRC in its dealing with perpetrators and survivors respectively. These responses are part and parcel of the process of instituting a democratic ethos of contestation, and it should be noted that if rejection was sufficiently widely present, it would have made the very operation of the process itself well near impossible. Similarly, questions were often raised about the sincerity – or lack of sincerity – among participants, and in particular of perpetrators. The questioning of De Klerk's sincerity, who after all won the Nobel Peace prize with Mandela, is a case in point, and is echoed in the more recent cases where the sincerity of politicians has been questioned. One only needs to think in this regard of the widespread distrust of Blair on the reasons for the invasion of Iraq and the popular suspicion of the Spanish government's response to the Madrid bombings. The kinds of response demanded were equally questioned in the case of the TRC: is reconciliation the right register in which to deal with past human rights abuses in the context of a country attempting to establish a new democracy? Can an apology be demanded? Is an apology offered in response to a demand a (real) apology? In this case, once again, while one may hold that the grammar of apologizing suggests that it must be offered freely, an apology offered, even unwillingly, has public consequences and political effects, which may be far-reaching. Each and every one of these possibilities and web of available and even unthought, unprecedented responses have consequences for the future of the community envisaged. As Austin suggests, our word is our bond. It is in and through our

ordinary engagements that bonds are created and dissolved; that pro-
vocations are offered and rejected, taken up, contested. It is here, in this
responsiveness that our democratic freedoms and responsibilities are
to be found and constituted.

Bibliography

Abizadeh, A., 'Banishing the particular. Rousseau on rhetoric, *patrie*, and the passions', *Political Theory* 29, no. 4 (2001), 556–82.

Ackerman, B. and J. S. Fishkin, 'Deliberation day', *The Journal of Political Philosophy* 10, no. 2 (2002), 129–52.

Akkerman, T., 'Urban debates and deliberative democracy', *Acta Politika* 1 (2001), 71–87.

Aronovitch, H., 'The political importance of analogical argument', *Political Studies* 45 (1997), 78–92.

Austin, J. L., *How to Do Things with Words*, ed. J. O. Urmson, and M. Sbisà (Oxford: Oxford University Press, 1962).

Badiou, A., *Ethics. An Essay on the Understanding of Evil*, trans. Peter Hallward (London: Verso, 2001).

Baker, G. P. and P. M. S. Hacker, *Wittgenstein. Meaning and Understanding, Essays on the Philosophical Investigations*, vol. I (Oxford: Basil Blackwell, 1983).

Balibar, E., 'Ambiguous universality', *Differences: A Journal of Feminist Cultural Studies* 7, no. 1 (1995), 48–74.

Barber, B. R., *Strong Democracy* (Berkeley: University of California Press, 1984).

Barber, B. R., 'Foundationalism and democracy', in S. Benhabib (ed.), *Democracy and Difference. Contesting the Boundaries of the Political* (Princeton: Princeton University Press, 1996), pp. 348–59.

Basu, A., 'Dialogic ethics and the virtue of humor', *The Journal of Political Philosophy* 7, no. 4 (1999), 378–403.

Barthes, R., *S/Z*, trans. R. Millar (Oxford: Basil Blackwell, 1974).

Baz, A., 'What's the point of seeing aspects?', *Philosophical Investigations* 23, no. 2 (2000), 97–121.

Bender, J. and D. E. Wellbery, 'Rhetoricality: On the modernist return of rhetoric', in J. Bender and D. E. Wellbery (eds.), *The Ends of Rhetoric. History, Theory, Practice* (Stanford, Calif.: Stanford University Press, 1990), pp. 3–39.

Benhabib, S., 'The democratic moment and the problem of difference', in S. Benhabib (ed.), *Democracy and Difference. Contesting the Boundaries of the Political* (Princeton, N. J.: Princeton University Press, 1996), pp. 3–18.

Benhabib, S., 'Toward a deliberative model of democratic legitimacy', in S. Benhabib (ed.), *Democracy and Difference. Contesting the Boundaries of the Political* (Princeton, N.J.: Princeton University Press, 1996), pp. 67–94.

Benhabib, S., 'Liberal dialogue versus a critical theory of discursive legitimation', in N. L. Rosenblum (ed.), *Liberalism and the Moral Life* (Cambridge, Mass.: Harvard University Press, 1998), pp. 143–56.

Bernstein, R. J., *The New Constellation. The Ethical–Political Horizons of Modernity/Postmodernity* (Cambridge, Mass.: MIT Press, 1992).

Bernstein, R. J., '"Laws, morals, and ethics": The retrieval of the democratic ethos', *Cardozo Law Review* 17 (1996), 1127–46.

Blaug, R., 'New theories of discursive democracy', *Philosophy and Social Criticism* 22, no. 1 (1996), 49–80.

Bohman, J., 'Emancipation and rhetoric: The perlocutions and illocutions of the social critic', *Philosophy and Rhetoric* 21, no. 3 (1988), 185–204.

Bohman, J., 'Critical theory and democracy', in D. M. Rasmussen (ed.), *Handbook of Critical Theory* (Oxford: Blackwell, 1996), pp. 190–215.

Bohman, J., *Public Deliberation. Pluralism, Complexity, and Democracy* (Cambridge, Mass.: The MIT Press, 1996).

Bohman, J., 'Two versions of the linguistic turn: Habermas and poststructuralism', in M. Passerin D'Entrèves and S. Benhabib (eds.), *Habermas and the Unfinished Project of Modernity* (Cambridge: Polity Press, 1996), pp. 197–220.

Bohman, J., '"When water chokes": Ideology, communication, and practical rationality', *Constellations* 7, no. 3 (2000), 382–92.

Borradori, G., *Philosophy in a Time of Terror. Dialogues with Jürgen Habermas and Jacques Derrida* (Chicago: University of Chicago Press, 2003).

Boraine, A., 'Truth and reconciliation in South Africa', in R. I. Rotberg and D. Thompson (eds.), *Truth v. Justice. The Morality of Truth Commissions* (Princeton, N.J.: Princeton University Press, 2000), pp. 141–57.

Bouveresse, J., *Wittgenstein Reads Freud*, trans. C. Cosman (Princeton, N.J.: Princeton University Press, 1995).

Brennan, W. J., 'Reason, passion and "the progress of the law"', *Cardozo Law Review* 10 (1988), 3–23.

Brockelman, T., 'The failure of the radical democratic imaginary: Žižek versus Laclau and Mouffe on vestigial utopia', *Philosophy and Social Criticism* 29 (2003), 183–208.

Butler, J., 'Critically queer', in J. Butler, *Bodies that Matter* (London: Routledge, 1993).

Butler, J. and E. Laclau, 'The uses of equality', *diacritics* 27, no. 1 (1995), 3–19.

Butler, J., E. Laclau and S. Žižek, *Contingency, Hegemony, Universality. Contemporary Dialogues on the Left,* Phronesis (London: Verso, 2000).

Caputo, J. D., 'Without sovereignty, without being: Unconditionality, the coming God and Derrida's democracy to come', *Journal for Cultural and Religious Theory* 4 (2003), 9–26.

Cavell, S., *Must We Mean What We Say?* (New York: Charles Scribner's Sons, 1976).

Cavell, S., *The Claim of Reason. Wittgenstein, Skepticism, Morality, and Tragedy* (Oxford: Oxford University Press, 1982).

Cavell, S., *This New Yet Unapproachable America* (Alburquerque, N. Mex.: Living Batch Press, 1989).

Cavell, S., *Conditions Handsome and Unhandsome. The Constitution of Emersonian Perfectionism,* The Carus Lectures, 1988 (Chicago: University of Chicago Press, 1990).

Cavell, S., 'What is the Emersonian event? A comment on Kateb's Emerson', *New Literary History,* 25 (1994), 951–8.

Cavell, S., *Cities of Words. Pedagogical Letters on a Register of the Moral Life* (Cambridge, Mass.: The Belknap Press of Harvard University Press, 2004).

Cavell, S., *Philosophy the Day after Tomorrow* (Cambridge, Mass.: The Belknap Press of Harvard University Press, 2005).

Cavell, S. 'The incessance and absence of the political', in A. Norris (ed.), *The Claim to Community. Essays on Stanley Cavell and Political Philosophy* (Stanford, Calif.: Stanford University Press, 2006), pp. 263–317.

Chambers, S. A., 'The language of disagreement'. Paper delivered to the Poststructuralism and Radical Politics Conferece: 'Fidelity to the Disagreement: Jacques Rancière and the Political', Goldsmiths College, London, 16–17 September 2003. See (www.homepages.gold.ac.uk/psrpsg/ranciere.doc).

Chambers, S. A., 'The politics of literality' (http://muse.jhu.edu/journals/theory_and_event/toc/archive.html#8.3).

Chambers, S., *Reasonable Democracy. Jürgen Habermas and the Politics of Discourse* (London: Cornell University Press, 1996).

Churchill, J., 'Rat and mole's epiphany of Pan: Wittgenstein on seeing aspects and religious belief', *Philosophical Investigations* 21, no. 4 (1998), 152–72.

Cohen, J., 'Democracy and liberty', in J. Elster (ed.), *Deliberative Democracy* (Cambridge: Cambridge University Press, 1998), pp. 185–231.

Coles, R., 'Of democracy, discourse, and dirt virtue', *Political Theory* 28 (2000), 540–64.

Conant, J., 'Nietzsche's perfectionism: A reading of *Schopenhauer as Educator*', in R. Schacht (ed.), *Nietzsche's Postmoralism* (Cambridge: Cambridge University Press, 2001), pp. 181–257.

Connolly, W. E., *Identity\Difference. Democratic Negotiations of Political Paradox* (Ithaca, N.Y.: Cornell University Press, 1991).

Connolly, W. E., 'Democracy and contingency', in J. H. Carens (ed.), *Democracy and Possessive Individualism. The Intellectual Legacy of C. B. Macpherson* (Albany: State University of New York Press, 1993), pp. 193–219.

Connolly, W. E., *The Ethos of Pluralization* (Minneapolis: University of Minnesota Press, 1995).

Connolly, W. E., 'Twilight of the idols', *Philosophy and Social Criticism* 21 (1995), 127–37.

Connolly, W. E., 'Speed, concentric cultures, and cosmopolitanism', *Political Theory* 28, no. 5 (2000), 596–618.

Coombes, A. E., *History after Apartheid. Visual Culture and Public Memory in a Democratic South Africa* (Durham, N.C.: Duke University Press, 2003).

Copi, I. M. and C. Cohen, *Introduction to Logic*, 9th edn (New York: Macmillan, 1994).

Cornell, D., '"Convention" and critique', *Cardozo Law Review* 7 (1986), 679–91.

Critchley, S., *The Ethics of Deconstruction. Derrida and Levinas* (Oxford: Blackwell, 1992).

Critchley, S. and O. Marchart (eds.), *Laclau. A Critical Reader* (Abingdon, Oxon.: Routledge, 2004).

Crusius, T. W., 'Foreword', in E. Grassi, *Rhetoric as Philosophy*, trans. J. M. Krois and A. Azodi (Carbondale and Edwardsville: Southern Illinois University Press, 2001), pp. xi–xviii.

Dallmayer, F. R., 'Critical theory criticized', *Philosophy of the Social Sciences* 2, no. 3 (1972), 211–29.

Dallmayr, F., 'Laclau and hegemony: Some (post) Hegelian caveats', in S. Critchley and O. Marchart (eds.), *Laclau. A Critical Reader* (Abingdon, Oxon.: Routledge, 2004), pp. 35–53.

Deranty, J.-P, 'Jacques Rancière's contribution to the ethics of recognition', *Political Theory*, 31, no. 1 (2003), 136–56.

Derrida, J., *Speech and Phenomena*, trans. D. B. Allison (Evanston, Ill.: Northwestern University Press, 1973).

Derrida, J., *Of Grammatology*, trans. G. Spivak (Baltimore, Md.: The Johns Hopkins University Press, 1974).

Derrida, J., *Limited Inc.* (Evanston, Ill.: Northwestern University Press, 1988).

Derrida, J., 'Politics and friendship. A discussion with Jacques Derrida', Centre for Modern French Thought, University of Sussex, 1 December 1997. At (www.hydra.umn.edu/derrida/pol+fr.html).

Derrida, J., *Politics of Friendship*, trans. George Collins (London: Verso, 1997).

Derrida, J., *Rogues. Two Essays on Reason*, trans. P.-A. Brault and M. Naas (Stanford, Calif.: Stanford University Press, 2005).

Dodds, E. R., *Plato, Gorgias. A Revised Text with Introduction and Commentary* (Oxford: Oxford University Press, 1959).

Dronsfield, J. and N. Midgley (eds.), *Responsibilities of Deconstruction* (PLI, *Warwick Journal of Philosophy* 6, University of Warwick, 1997).

Dryzek, J. S., 'Political and ecological communication', *Environmental Politics* 4 (1995), 10–30.

Dryzek, J. S., *Deliberative Democracy and Beyond*, Oxford Political Theory (Oxford: Oxford University Press, 2000).

Du Bois, F., ' "Nothing but the truth": The South African alternative to corrective justice in transitions to democracy', in E. Christodoulidis and S. Veitch (eds.), *Lethe's Law. Justice, Law and Ethics in Reconciliation* (Oxford: Hart Publishing, 2001), pp. 91–114.

Du Toit, A., 'The moral foundations of the South African TRC: Truth as acknowledgment and justice as recognition', in R. I. Rotberg and D. Thompson (eds.), *Truth v. Justice. The Morality of Truth Commissions* (Princeton, N.J.: Princeton University Press, 2000), pp. 122–40.

Dyzenhaus, D., *Judging the Judges, Judging Ourselves. Truth, Reconciliation and the Apartheid Legal Order* (Oxford: Hart Publishing, 1998).

Dyzenhaus, D., 'Survey article: Justifying the Truth and Reconciliation Commission', *Journal of Political Philosophy* 8 (2000), 470–96.

Edwards, J. C., *Ethics without Philosophy. Wittgenstein and the Moral Life* (Tampa: University Presses of South Florida, 1985).

Elster, J., 'Introduction', in J. Elster (ed.), *Deliberative Democracy* (Cambridge: Cambridge University Press, 1998), pp. 1–18.

Fann, K. T., *Wittgenstein's Conception of Philosophy* (Berkeley: University of California Press, 1969).

Fearon, J., 'Deliberation as discussion', in John Elster (ed.), *Deliberative Democracy* (Cambridge: Cambridge University Press, 1998), pp. 44–68.

Ferrara, A., 'The communicative paradigm in moral theory', in D. M. Rasmussen (ed.), *Handbook of Critical Theory* (Oxford: Blackwell, 1996), pp. 119–37.

Fishkin, J. S., and P. Laslett (eds.), *Debating Deliberative Democracy* (Oxford: Basil Blackwell, 2003).

Flyvberg, B., 'Ideal theory, real rationality: Habermas versus Foucault and Nietzsche', Paper presented to the Political Studies Association's 50th Annual Conference, 'The Challenges for Democracy in the 21st Century', London School of Economics and Political Science, 10–13 April 2000, 6–7.

Fontana, B., C. J. Nederman, and G. Remer, 'Introduction: Deliberative democracy and the rhetorical turn', in B. Fontana, C. J. Nederman and G. Remer (eds.), *Talking Democracy. Historical Perspectives on Rhetoric and Democracy* (Pennsylvania: Pennsylvania State University Press, 2004), pp. 1–25.

Forester, J., *The Deliberative Practitioner* (Cambridge, Mass.: The MIT Press, 1999).

Fraser, N., 'Rethinking the public sphere: A contribution to a critique of actually existing democracy', in C. Calhoun (ed.), *Habermas and the Public Sphere* (Cambridge, Mass.: MIT Press, 1992), pp. 109–42.

Fraser, N., and A. Honneth, *Redistribution or Recognition?* (London: Verso, 2003).

Freeden, M., *Ideologies and Political Theory. A Conceptual Approach* (Oxford: Clarendon Press, 1996).

Gasché, R., *The Tain of the Mirror. Derrida and the Philosophy of Reflection* (Cambridge, Mass.: Harvard University Press, 1986).

Gasché, R., '"In the name of reason": The deconstruction of sovereignty', *Research in Phenomenology* 34, no. 1 (2004), 289–303.

Glock, H.-J., *A Wittgenstein Dictionary* (Oxford: Blackwell, 1996).

Glynos, J., 'Theory and evidence in the Freudian field: from observation to structure', in L. J. Glynos and Y. Stavrakakis (eds.), *Lacan and Science* (London: Karnac Press, 2002), pp. 13–50.

Glynos, J. and D. Howarth, *Logics of Critical Explanation in Social and Political Theory* (London: Routledge, 2007).

Godby, M., 'Memory and history in William Kentridge's *History of the Main Complaint*', in S. Nuttall and C. Coetzee (eds.), *Negotiating the Past. The Making of Memory in South Africa* (Cape Town: Oxford University Press, 1998), pp. 100–11.

Goodin, R. E., *Reflective Democracy*, Oxford Political Theory (Oxford: Oxford University Press, 2003).

Grassi, E., *Rhetoric as Philosophy*, trans. J. M. Krois and A. Azodi (Carbondale and Edwardsville: Southern Illinois University Press, 2001).

Griggs, S. and D. Howarth, 'Populism, localism and environmental politics: The logic and rhetoric of the Stop Stansted Expansion Campaign in the United Kingdom' (www.essex.ac.uk/centres/TheoStud/onlinepapers.asp).

Gutman A. and D. Thompson, 'The moral foundations of truth commissions', in R. I. Rotberg and D. Thompson (eds.), *Truth v. Justice. The Morality of Truth Commissions* (Princeton, N.J.: Princeton University Press, 2000), pp. 22–44.

Habermas, J., 'A reply to my critics', in J. B. Thompson and D. Held (eds.), *Habermas: Critical Debates* (Cambridge, Mass.: MIT Press, 1982), pp. 219–83.

Habermas, J., *Legitimation Crisis*, trans. T. McCarthy (London: Heinemann, 1976).

Habermas, J. *Between Facts and Norms. Contributions to a Discourse Theory of Law and Democracy*, trans. W. Rehg (Cambridge: Polity Press, 1997).

Hacker, P. M. S., *Insight and Illusion* (Oxford: Clarendon Press, 1972).

Hacker, P. M. S., *Wittgenstein: Meaning and Mind. Part 1: Essays* (Oxford: Blackwell, 1990).

Hacker, P. M. S., *Wittgenstein on Human Nature* (London: Phoenix Paperback, 1997).

Hacking, I., 'Language, truth, reason', in M. Hollis and S. Lukes (eds.), *Rationality and Relativism* (Oxford: Basil Blackwell, 1983), pp. 48–66.

Hacking, I., 'Styles of scientific reasoning', in J. Rajchman and C. West (eds.), *Post-Analytic Philosophy* (New York: Columbia University Press: 1985), pp. 145–65.

Hadad, S., 'Derrida and democracy at risk', *Contretemps* 4 (2004), 29–44.

Hall, C., ' "Passion and constraint": The marginalization of passion in liberal political theory', *Philosophy and Social Criticism* 28, no. 6 (2002), 727–48.

Hammer, E., *Stanley Cavell. Skepticism, Subjectivity and the Ordinary* (Cambridge: Polity, 2002).

Hampshire, S., *Justice is Conflict* (Princeton, N.J.: Princeton University Press, 2000).

Harrison, B., 'White mythology revisited: Derrida and his critics on reason and rhetoric', *Critical Inquiry* 25 (1999), 505–34.

Hayner, P. B., 'Fifteen truth commissions – 1974 to 1994: A comparative study', *Human Rights Quarterly* 16 (1994), 597–655.

Helsloot, N., 'Linguists of all countries ... !', *Journal of Pragmatics* 13 (1989), 547–66.

Herwitz, D., 'The future of the past in South Africa: On the legacy of the TRC', *Social Research* 72 (2005), 531–48.

Hesse, M., 'Habermas and the force of dialectical argument', *History of European Ideas* 21, no. 3 (1995), 367–78.

Heyes, C. J. (ed.), *The Grammar of Politics. Wittgenstein and Political Philosophy* (Ithaca, N.J.: Cornell University Press, 2003).

Honig, B., *Democracy and the Foreigner* (Princeton, N.J.: Princeton University Press, 2001).

Honig, B., 'The time of rights', keynote address, Sixth Essex Graduate Conference in Political Theory, 13–14th May 2005.

Houghton, D., *The Role of Analogical Reasoning in Novel Foreign Policy Situations*, Cambridge Studies in International Relations (Cambridge: Cambridge University Press, 2001).

Howarth, D., 'Ideology, hegemony and political subjectivity', in I. Hampsher-Monk and J. Stanyer (eds.), *Contemporary Political Studies 1996*, vol. II (Oxford: Political Studies Association of the UK, 1996), pp. 944–56.

Howarth, D., 'Complexities of identity/difference: the ideology of black consciousness in South Africa', *Journal of Political Ideologies* 2, no. 1 (1997), 51–78.

Howarth, D., 'Paradigms gained? A critique of theories and explanations of democratic transition in South Africa', in D. R. Howarth and A. J. Norval, *South Africa in Transition* (London: Macmillan, 1998), pp. 182–214.

Howarth, D., *Discourse* (Buckingham: Open University Press, 2000).

Jonsen, A. R. and S. Toulmin, *The Abuse of Casuistry* (Berkeley: University of California Press, 1988).

Kahn, P. W., *Putting Liberalism in its Place* (Princeton, N.J.: Princeton University Press, 2005).

Keenan, A., *Democracy in Question. Democratic Openness in a Time of Political Closure* (Stanford, Calif.: Stanford University Press, 2003).

Kiss, E., 'Moral ambition within and beyond political constraints: Reflections on restorative justice', in R. I. Rotberg and D. Thompson (eds.), *Truth v. Justice. The Morality of Truth Commissions* (Princeton, N.J.: Princeton University Press, 2000), pp. 68–98.

Knight, J. and J. Johnson, 'What sort of political equality does deliberative democracy require?', in J. Bohman and W. Rehg (eds.), *Deliberative Democracy. Essays on Reason and Politics* (Cambridge, Mass.: The MIT Press, 1997), pp. 279–320.

Kohn, M., 'Language, power, and persuasion: Towards a critique of deliberative democracy', *Constellations* 7, no. 3 (2000), 408–29.

Krog, K., 'The TRC and national unity', in R. Dorsman, H. Hartman and L. Notenboom-Kronemeijer (eds.), *Truth and Reconciliation in South Africa and the Netherlands* (Utrecht: SMI Special No. 23, 1999), pp. 14–31.

Kuhn, T. S., *The Structure of Scientific Revolutions* (Chicago: University of Chicago Press, 1970).

Laclau, E. and C. Mouffe, *Hegemony and Socialist Strategy. Towards a Radical Democratic Politics* (London: Verso, 1985).

Laclau, E., *New Reflections on the Revolution of Our Time* (London: Verso, 1990).

Laclau, E., 'Universalism, particularism and the question of identity', in E. Laclau, *Emancipation(s)* (London: Verso, 1996), pp. 20–35.

Laclau, E., 'Deconstruction, Pragmatism, Hegemony', in S. Critchley, J. Derrida, E. Laclau and R. Rorty, *Deconstruction and Pragmatism*, ed. C. Mouffe (London: Routledge, 1996), pp. 47–68.

Laclau, E., 'Paul de Man and the politics of rhetoric', *Pretexts* 7, no. 2 (1998), 153–70.

Laclau, E., 'Identity and hegemony: The role of universality in the constitution of political logics', in J. Butler, E. Laclau and S. Žižek, *Contingency, Hegemony, Universality. Contemporary Dialogues on the Left*, Phronesis (London: Verso, 2000).

Laclau, E., 'Structure, history and the political', in J. Butler, E. Laclau and S. Žižek, *Contingency, Hegemony, Universality. Contemporary Dialogues on the Left*, Phronesis (London: Verso, 2000), pp. 182–212.

Laclau, E., 'Glimpsing the future: A reply', in Simon Critchley and Oliver Marchart (eds.), *Laclau. A Critical Reader* (London: Routledge, 2004), pp. 279–328.

Laclau, E., *On Populist Reason* (London: Verso, 2005).

Laden, A. S., *Reasonably Radical. Deliberative Liberalism and the Politics of Identity* (Ithaca, N.Y.: Cornell University Press, 2001).

Lefort, C., *The Political Forms of Modern Society* (Oxford: Polity Press, 1986).

Lefort, C., *Democracy and Political Theory* (Minneapolis: University of Minnesota Press, 1988).

Lloyd, G. E. R., *Polarity and Analogy* (Cambridge: Cambridge University Press, 1966).

Lueken, G.-L., 'On showing in argumentation', *Philosophical Investigations* 20, no. 3 (1997), 205–23.

Lukes, S., 'Of gods and demons: Habermas and practical reason', in J. B. Thompson and D. Held (eds.), *Habermas. Critical Debates* (Cambridge, Mass.: MIT Press, 1982), pp. 134–48.

Luntley, M., *Wittgenstein* (Oxford: Blackwell Publishing, 2003).

Macedo, S. (ed.), *Deliberative Politics* (Oxford: Oxford University Press, 1999).

Majone, G., *Evidence, Argument, and Persuasion in the Policy Process* (New Haven, Conn.: Yale University Press, 1989).

Marcus, G., *The Sentimental Citizen: Emotion in Democratic Politics* (University Park: Pennsylvania State University Press, 2002).

McCarthy, T. and S. C. Studd (eds.), *Wittgenstein in America* (Oxford: Clarendon Press, 2001).

McFee, G., 'Wittgenstein on art and aspects', *Philosophical Investigations* 22, no. 3 (1999), 262–84.

Meehan, J., 'Feminism and Habermas' discourse ethics', *Philosophy and Social Criticism* 26, no. 3 (2000), 39–52.

Meintjies, S. and B. Goldblatt, 'Gender and the Truth and Reconciliation Commission: A submission to the Truth and Reconciliation Commission', May 1996 (www.truth.org.za/submit/gender.htm).

Mendus, S., *Feminism and Emotion. Readings in Moral and Political Philosophy* (New York: St Martin's Press, 2000).

Miller, D., 'Deliberative democracy and social choice', in D. Held (ed.), *Prospects for Democracy. North, South, East, West* (Cambridge: Polity Press, 1993), pp. 74–92.

Miller, D., 'Is deliberative democracy unfair to disadvantaged groups', in M. Passerin D'Entrèves (ed.), *Democracy as Public Deliberation* (Manchester: Manchester University Press, 2002), pp. 201–25.

Minow, M., 'The hope for healing: What can truth commissions do?', in R. I. Rotberg and D. Thompson (eds.), *Truth v. Justice. The Morality of Truth Commissions* (Princeton, N.J.: Princeton University Press, 2000), pp. 235–60.

Mouffe, C. (ed.), *Gramsci and Marxist Theory* (London: Routledge and Kegan Paul, 1979).

Mouffe, C. (ed.), *Dimensions of Radical Democracy* (London: Verso, 1992).

Mouffe, C., *The Return of the Political* (London: Verso, 1993).

Mouffe, C., 'Democratic politics and the question of identity', in J. Rajchman (ed.), *The Identity in Question* (London: Routledge, 1995), pp. 33–45.

Mouffe, C., 'Politics, democratic action, and solidarity', *Inquiry* 39 (1995), 99–108.

Mouffe, C., *The Democratic Paradox* (London: Verso, 2000).

Mouffe, C., 'Politics and Passion: The stakes of democracy', Centre for the Study of Democracy Perspectives, 2002.

Mulhall, S., *On Being in the World. Wittgenstein and Heidegger on Seeing Aspects* (London: Routledge, 1990).

Mulhall, S., *Stanley Cavell. Philosophy's Recounting of the Ordinary* (Oxford: Clarendon Press, 1994).

Mulhall, S., 'Promising, consent, and citizenship: Rawls and Cavell on morality and politics', *Political Theory* 25 (1997), 171–92.

Mulhall, S., *Inheritance and Originality. Wittgenstein, Heidegger, Kierkegaard* (Oxford: Clarendon Press, 2001).

Ndebele, N., 'Memory, metaphor, and the triumph of narrative', in S. Nuttall and C. Coetzee (eds.), *Negotiating the Past. The Making of Memory in South Africa* (Cape Town: Oxford University Press, 1998), pp. 19–28.

Nietzsche, F., 'Schopenhauer as Educator', in O. Levy (ed.), *The Complete Works of Friedrich Nietzsche*, vol. II, *Thoughts Out of Season, Part Two* (London: T.N. Foulis, 1909).

Nietzsche, F., 'On truth and lies in a nonmoral sense (1873)', in K. Ansell Pearson and D. Large (eds.), *The Nietzsche Reader* (Oxford: Blackwell Publishing, 2006), pp. 114–23.

Norris, A., 'Political revisions: Stanley Cavell and political philosophy', *Political Theory* 30 (2002), 828–32.

Norris, A., 'Political revisions: Stanley Cavell and political philosophy', in A. Norris (ed.), *The Claim to Community. Essays on Stanley Cavell and Political Philosophy* (Stanford, Calif.: Stanford University Press, 2006), pp. 80–97.

Norval, A. J., 'Frontiers in question', *Acta Philosophica* 2 (1997), 51–76.

Norval, A. J., 'Memory, identity and the (im)possibility of reconciliation: The work of the Truth and Reconciliation Commission in South Africa', *Constellations* 5 (1998), 250–61.

Norval, A. J., 'Future trajectories of research in discourse theory', in D. Howarth, A. J. Norval and Y. Stavrakakis (eds.), *Discourse Theory and Political Analysis* (Manchester: Manchester University Press, 2000), pp. 219–36.

Norval, A. J., 'Radical democracy', in J. Foweraker and B. Clarke (eds.), *Dictionary of Democratic Thought* (London: Routledge, 2001).

Norval, A. J., 'Reconstructing national identity and renegotiating memory: the work of the TRC', in T. Blom Hansen and F. Stepputat (eds.), *States of Imagination. Ethnographic Explorations of the Post-Colonial State* (Durham, N.C.: Duke University Press, 2001), pp. 182–202.

Norval, A. J., 'Hegemony after deconstruction: The consequences of undecidability', *Journal of Political Ideologies* 9, no. 2 (2004), 139–57.

Norval, A. J., 'Democratic identification: A Wittgensteinian approach', *Political Theory* 34 (2006), 229–55.

O'Neill, M., 'Explaining "the hardness of the logical must": Wittgenstein on grammar, arbitrariness and logical necessity', *Philosophical Investigations* 24, no. 1 (2001), 1–29.

O'Neill, O., *Towards Virtue and Justice* (Cambridge: Cambridge University Press, 1996).

O'Neill, O., 'Political liberalism and public reason: A critical notice of John Rawls, *Political Liberalism*', *The Philosophical Review* 106, no. 3 (1997), 417.

O'Neill, O., *Bounds of Justice* (Cambridge: Cambridge University Press, 2000).

Outhwaite, W., *Habermas. A Critical Introduction* (Cambridge: Polity Press, 1994).

Owen, D., 'Cultural diversity and the conversation of justice', *Political Theory* 27, no. 5 (1999), 579–96.

Owen, D., 'Democracy, perfectionism and "undetermined messianic hope"', in C. Mouffe and L. Nagl (eds.), *The Legacy of Wittgenstein: Pragmatism and Deconstruction* (Frankfurt am Main: Peter Lang, 2001), pp. 139–56.

Owen, D., 'Genealogy as perspicuous representation', in C. J. Heyes (ed.), *The Grammar of Politics. Wittgenstein and Political Philosophy* (London: Cornell University Press, 2003), pp. 82–96.

Owen, D., 'Perfectionism, parrhesia and the care of the self: Foucault and Cavell on ethics and politics', in A. Norris (ed.), *The Claim to Community. Essays on Stanley Cavell and Political Philosophy* (Stanford, Calif.: Stanford University Press, 2006), pp. 128–55.

Panagia, D., 'The predicative function in ideology: On the political uses of analogical reasoning in contemporary political thought', *Journal of Political Ideologies* 6, no. 1 (2001), 55–74.

Panagia, D., 'The force of political argument', *Political Theory* 32, no. 6 (2004), 825–48.

Passerin D'Entrèves, M. (ed.), *Democracy as Public Deliberation* (Manchester: Manchester University Press, 2002).

Pelletier, D., V. Kraak, C. McCullum, U. Uusitalo and R. Rich, 'The shaping of collective values through deliberative democracy: An empirical case study from New York's North County', *Policy Sciences* 32 (1999), 103–31.

Pohlhaus, G. and J.R. Wright, 'Using Wittgenstein critically', *Political Theory* 30, no. 6 (2002), 800–27.

Putnam, R. D., *Bowling Alone. The Collapse and Revival of American Community* (New York: Simon and Schuster, 2000).

Rancière, J., *The Names of History*, trans. H. Melehy (Minneapolis: University of Minnesota Press, 1994).

Rancière, J., 'Post-democracy, politics and philosophy', interview with J. Sumič and R. Riha, in D. Howarth and A. J. Norval (eds.), *Reconsidering the Political*, special issue of *Angelaki* (1994), 171–8.

Rancière, J., *On the Shores of Politics*, trans. Liz Heron (London: Verso, 1995).

Rancière, J., *Disagreement. Politics and Philosophy*, trans. J. Rose (Minneapolis: University of Minnesota Press, 1999).

Rancière, J., 'Ten theses on politics', *Theory and Event*, trans. Davide Panagia, 5, no. 3 (2001) (http://muse.jhu.edu/journals/theory_and_event/v005/5.3ranciere.html).

Rancière, J., *The Politics of Aesthetics. The Distribution of the Sensible*, trans. Gabriel Rockhill (London: Continuum, 2004).

Rawls, J., *A Theory of Justice* (Oxford: Oxford University Press, 1973).

Rehg, W., 'Translator's introduction', in J. Habermas, *Between Facts and Norms. Contributions to a Discourse Theory of Law and Democracy*, trans. W. Rehg (Cambridge: Polity Press, 1997), pp. ix–xxxvii.

Renn, O., T. Webler and P. Wiedemann (eds.), *Fairness and Competence in Citizen Participation. Evaluating Models for Environmental Discourse* (Dordrecht: Kluwer Academic Publishers, 1995).

Ross, F. C., 'On having voice and being heard: Some after–effects of testifying before the South African Truth and Reconciliation Commission', *Anthropological Theory* 30 (2003), 325–41.

Rousseau, J. J., *The Social Contract* (London: Penguin Classics, 1968).

Sanders, L. M., 'Against deliberation', *Political Theory* 25, no. 3 (1997), 347–76.

Scheuerman, W. E., 'Between radicalism and resignation: Democratic theory in Habermas in *Between Facts and Norms*', in P. Dews (ed.), *Habermas. A Critical Reader* (Oxford: Blackwell, 1999), pp. 153–77.

Shapiro, M. J., 'Radicalizing democratic theory: Social space in Connolly, Deleuze and Rancière', Paper delivered to the Poststructuralism and Radical Politics Conferece: 'Fidelity to the disagreement: Jacques Rancière and the political',

Goldsmiths College, London, 16–17 September 2003. See (www.homepages. gold.ac.uk/psrpsg/ranciere.doc).

Shusterman, R., 'Putnam and Cavell on the ethics of democracy', *Political Theory* 25 (1997), 193–214.

Skinner, Q., *Reason and Rhetoric in the Philosophy of Hobbes* (Cambridge: Cambridge University Press, 1996).

Sparti, D., 'Responsiveness as responsibility: Cavell's reading of Wittgenstein and King Lear as a source for an ethics of interpersonal relationships', *Philosophy and Social Criticism* 26 (2000), 81–107.

Stoker, G. *Why Politics Matters. Making Democracy Work* (Basingstoke: Palgrave Macmillan, 2006).

Sumič, J., 'Anachronism of emancipation or fidelity to politics', in S. Critchley and O. Marchart (eds.), *Laclau. A Critical Reader* (Abingdon, Oxon.: Routledge, 2004), pp. 182–98.

Sunstein, C., 'The law of group polarization', *The Journal of Political Philosophy* 10, no. 2 (2002), 175–95.

Thomson, A. J. P., *Deconstruction and Democracy*, Continuum Studies in Continental Philosophy (London: Continuum, 2005).

Thomson, A. J. P., 'What's to become of "democracy to come"?', *Postmodern Culture* 15 (2005) (http://muse.jhu.edu/demo/postmodern_culture/v015/15.3thomson. html).

Todorov, T., *Theories of the Symbol*, trans. Catherine Porter (Ithaca, N.Y.: Cornell University Press, 1984).

Toulmin, S., *Return to Reason* (Cambridge, Mass.: Harvard University Press, 2001).

Tully, J., 'Wittgenstein and political philosophy: understanding practices of critical reflection', *Political Theory* 17, no. 2 (1989), 172–204.

Tully, J., *Strange Multiplicity. Constitutionalism in an Age of Diversity* (Cambridge: Cambridge University Press, 1995).

Tully, J., 'Political philosophy as a critical activity', *Political Theory* 30, no. 4 (2002), 533–55.

Tully, J., 'Wittgenstein and political philosophy: Understanding practices of critical reflection', in C. J. Heyes (ed.), *The Grammar of Politics. Wittgenstein and Political Philosophy* (Ithaca, N.Y.: Cornell University Press, 2003), pp. 17–42.

Veitch, S., 'The legal politics of amnesty', in E. Christodoulidis and S. Veitch (eds.), *Lethe's Law. Justice, Law and Ethics in Reconciliation* (Oxford: Hart Publishing, 2001), pp. 32–45.

Vickers, B., *In Defence of Rhetoric* (Oxford: Clarendon Press, 1998).

Villa-Vicencio C. and W. Verwoerd, 'Constructing a report: Writing up the "truth"', in R. I. Rotberg and D. Thompson (eds.), *Truth v. Justice. The Morality of Truth Commissions* (Princeton, N.J.: Princeton University Press, 2000), pp. 279–94.

Waldron, J., *The Dignity of Legislation* (Cambridge: Cambridge University Press, 1999).

Walker, B., 'Thoreau on democratic cultivation', *Political Theory* 29 (2001), 155–89.

Walzer, M., 'A critique of philosophical conversation', *The Philosophical Forum* 21, no. 1–2 (1989–90), 182–96.

Walzer, M., *Thick and Thin. Moral Argument at Home and Abroad* (Notre Dame, Ind.: University of Notre Dame Press, 1994).

Walzer, M., *Politics and Passion. Towards a More Egalitarian Liberalism* (New Haven, Conn.: Yale University Press, 2004).

Ward, H., A. J. Norval, T. Landman and J. Pretty, 'Open citizens' juries and the politics of sustainability', *Political Studies*, 51 (2003), 282–99.

Warren, M., 'Democratic theory and self-transformation', *American Political Science Review* 86, no. 1 (1992), 8–23.

Warren, M., 'The self in discursive democracy', in Stephen White (ed.), *The Cambridge Companion to Habermas* (Cambridge: Cambridge University Press, 1995), pp. 167–200.

Warren, M. 'What can democratic participation mean today?', *Political Theory* 30, no. 5 (2002), 677–701.

Warren, M. E., 'What should and should not be said: Deliberating sensitive issues', *Journal of Social Philosophy* 37, no. 2 (2006), 163–81.

Weeks, E. C., 'The practice of deliberative democracy: Results from four large-scale trials', *Public Administration Review* 60, no. 4 (2000), 360–72.

White, S. K., *The Recent Work of Jürgen Habermas. Reason, Justice and Modernity* (Cambridge: Cambridge University Press, 1989).

White, S., *Political Theory and Postmodernism* (Cambridge: Cambridge University Press, 1991).

White, S., 'After Critique: Affirming subjectivity in contemporary political theory', *European Journal of Political Theory* 2, no. 2 (2003), 209–26.

Widder, N., *Genealogies of Difference* (Urbana, Ill.: University of Illinois Press, 2002).

Wiley, J., 'Review essay: The impasse of radical democracy', *Philosophy and Social Criticism* 28 (2002), 483–8.

Wittgenstein, L., *On Certainty*, ed. G. E. M Anscombe and G. H. von Wright, trans. D. Paul and G. E. M. Anscombe (Oxford: Basil Blackwell, 1979).

Wittgenstein, L., *Wittgenstein's Lectures, Cambridge 1932–35*, ed. A. Ambrose (Oxford: Basil Blackwell, 1979).

Wittgenstein, L., *Philosophical Investigations*, ed. G. E. M. Anscombe and R. Rhees, trans. G. E. M. Anscombe (1958; Oxford: Basil Blackwell, 1984).

Wittgenstein, L., *Lectures and Conversations on Aesthetics, Psychology and Religious Belief*, ed. Cyril Barrett (Oxford: Basil Blackwell, 1989).

Wollstonecraft, M., *Vindication of the Rights of Woman*, ed. with introduction M. Brody (London: Penguin Books, 1983).

Wood, D., 'The experience of the ethical', in R. Kearney and M. Dooley (eds.), *Questioning Ethics. Contemporary Debates in Philosophy* (London: Routledge, 1999), pp. 105–19.

Young, I. M., 'Difference as resource for democratic communication', in J. Bohman and W. Rehg (eds.), *Deliberative Democracy. Essays on Reason and Politics* (Cambridge, Mass.: MIT Press, 1997), pp. 383–406.

Zerilli, L. M. G., '"This universalism which is not one": A review of Ernesto Laclau's *Emancipation(s)*', *Diacritics* 28, no. 2 (1998), 3–20.

Zerilli, L. M. G., 'Doing without knowing: Feminisms' politics of the ordinary', *Political Theory* 26, no. 4 (1998), 434–58.

Zerilli, L. M. G., *Feminism and the Abyss of Freedom* (Chicago: University of Chicago Press, 2005).

Zerilli, L. M. G., '"We feel our freedom": Imagination and judgment in the thought of Hannah Arendt', *Political Theory* 33, no. 2 (2005), 158–88.

Žižek, S., *The Sublime Object of Ideology* (London: Verso, 1989).

Žižek, S., *For They Know Not What They Do. Enjoyment as a Political Factor* (London: Verso, 1991).

Žižek, S., *The Ticklish Subject* (London: Verso, 1999).

Žižek, S., 'Melancholy and the act', *Critical Inquiry* 26 (2000), 657–81.

Index

deliberative tradition (cont.)
  universalization and 20–6
  'voice' and 141
  see also Habermas, J.
demands 18–19
  articulation of 157
  emergence of new 65, 74, 76
  equivalential 156
  eruption of 96
  extension of 153
  post-structuralists and 74, 78, 80–1,
    83–4
  universalization and 49–50, 52
  see also claims
democracy
  cultivating renewal 207–9
  democracy to come 145–52
  moment of 79, 105–6
  process model of 28, 33
  radical/plural 152–4
  rethought 53–5
  theory reoriented 9–13
  see also deliberative tradition;
    perfectionism; post-structuralist
    tradition
depoliticization 41
Deranty, J.-P. 78n
derivatives of action 27, 35
Derrida, J. 9–10, 32, 95, 201, 208
  democracy to come 145–51, 179–88
  hospitality 149–50
  identity and 154, 166, 183, 184–6
  iterability 166
  promise of democracy and 145–52, 188
dialogical model 98
difference 26, 34–5, 41, 103
  logic of 85, 155
  similarities and 94–6, 166
disagreement 78, 175
  see also universalization and
    disagreement
disappointment 4–5, 7
discipleship 195, 208
disclosure 99–100, 102–3
  community and 174
discourse 178
  of application 99
  ethics 34
  practical 36
  theory 30–2
  types of 28–9, 178
  see also argumentation
disidentification 142

dislocation 39, 52, 82, 101, 142, 194
  political grammar and 108, 123, 127,
    130–3, 189–90
disorientation 108, 127
disputieren 103, 103n
disruption 96, 122
dissent 41, 96, 174, 179
distortion 68
diversity 34–5
  awareness 167
  cultural 164, 166
Doll's House (Ibsen) 180–2
Dryzek, J. S. 24, 67–8, 70–1
Du Bois, F. 197n
Du Toit, A. 203

economic–corporate struggles 49
elections 151
  moment of 45
elements
  rearrangement of 109–11, 117
  rearticulating 128
Elster, J. 37–8
emancipation 69, 154
emergence of demands 65, 74, 76
Emerson, R. W. 12, 175–7, 191, 192,
  195, 208
emotions 68
emptiness 97
empty signifiers 3, 47, 81, 155
engagement 138, 168
  critical 55, 175
  passionate 124–5
  Wittgenstein's 107–11
enigma of metaphor 94–5
epistemic authority 25, 37, 43, 141
epistemic equality 67
equality 25, 43, 96, 101, 179
  deliberative tradition 65–74
  epistemic 67
  post-structuralist tradition 74–87
    equivalence 79–87
    eruption 74–9
  reason and rhetoric 64–74
equivalence 179, 179n
  chains of 80–1, 83–4, 155
  demands and 156
  equality as 79–87
  logic of 155
eruption, moments of 95–6, 187–9
ethical–political discourses 29
ethics 168, 168n, 171
  discourse 34

connections establishment 128–9
of democracy 79, 105–6
disruptive 122
elections 45
of eruption 95–6, 187–9
of grip 122
inscribed 78n
of institution 135
interruptive 84
of metaphor 94
of naming 143
of newness 115
of politics 75, 158
of reactivation 138
of response 171
of subjectivity 105–6, 116, 116n, 124, 132
of totalization 83
morality 205
discourse 29, 178
ideals 27
leadership and 46
perfectionism 181
motivation 26–7n, 56
Mouffe, C. 5, 11, 97
equivalence and 79–81, 84
identity and 154–5, 156, 157–9, 184
negativity 160–3
radical democracy and 152–4, 175
subjectivity and 144, 210–11
universalization and 19–20, 41, 44, 45–6, 52
Mulhall, S. 106, 112, 128
identity and 169, 173, 177, 191
multiplicity 166, 177
awareness of 127

naming, moment of 143
narration 72–3
nation-state 163
naturalization 104
Ndebele, N. 207
negativity, identity as 154–63
negotiation 60, 104, 167
new evidence, Wittgenstein and 109–10
New Reflections on the Revolution of Our Time (Laclau) 51
newness, moment of 115
Nietzsche, F. 73, 122, 175, 179, 191–5, 204, 208
Nobel Peace prize 213
norms 28
dimensions 96

general 99
guidelines 64
preconditions 39
noticing connections 110
novelty 117
number 149n

obedience 172
On Certainty (Wittgenstein) 125
On Populist Reason (Laclau) 156
O'Neill, O. 2n, 3n
ongoing processes 32–8
ontology
claims 39
contingency and 51–2
emphasis on 54
openness 166, 182, 183
oppression 153
ordinary, the 88, 168
activities 9–10, 108–9
other, the 34, 149–50
overlapping interests 27
Owen, D. 122, 129–30, 144, 147n

pain behaviour 168–9
Panagia, D. 90, 93–5
paradox of aspect dawning 106
participation 120
common 136
particularism 46–8, 49–50, 93
passion 68, 210n
engagement with 124–5
subjectivity and 210–14
perfect justice 182, 209
perfectionism 5–8, 147n, 152
aversive identity and 173, 175–8, 181, 183
Cavell 4–7, 12, 16, 141, 144, 147, 173–83, 187, 191–5, 207
exemplars and 191–3
processual perfectionism 144, 152
perlocutionary domain 69–70, 211–12, 214n
perspective 78
perspicuous representation of reasoning 44
persuasion 38, 49, 53–4, 103, 111, 125
rhetoric and 69, 72, 91
philosophical conversation, key characteristics of 60
pictures
analogy as 89, 91
aspect perception and 111–12, 117